LITTLE LINDY
IS KIDNAPPED

LITTLE LINDY IS KIDNAPPED

How the Media Covered
the Crime of the Century

THOMAS DOHERTY

COLUMBIA UNIVERSITY PRESS   NEW YORK

Columbia University Press
Publishers Since 1893
New York   Chichester, West Sussex
cup.columbia.edu

Library of Congress Cataloging-in-Publication Data

Names: Doherty, Thomas, author.
Title: Little Lindy is kidnapped : how the media covered the crime of the century / Thomas Doherty.
Description: New York City : Columbia University Press, 2020. |
Includes bibliographical references and index.
Identifiers: LCCN 2020009654 | ISBN 9780231198486 (cloth) |
ISBN 9780231552653 (ebook)
Subjects: LCSH: Lindbergh, Charles Augustus, 1930-1932,—Kidnapping—
Press coverage.
Classification: LCC HV6603.L5 D64 2020 | DDC 070.4/49364154—dc23
LC record available at https://lccn.loc.gov/2020009654

∞

Columbia University Press books are printed on permanent and
durable acid-free paper.

Printed in the United States of America

Front cover photo: Outside the Hunterdon County Courthouse in Flemington, New Jersey, the expectant crowd and the media await the jury's verdict in the Trial of the Century, February 13, 1935.

Back cover photo: Charles Lindbergh leaves the back entrance of the Hunterdon County Courthouse, Flemington, New Jersey, January 10, 1935.

CONTENTS

For Sandra

A PREFATORY NOTE

This is a true media book not a true crime book. The detective work examines the ways the newspapers, radio, and newsreels covered what they rightly figured was the Crime of the Century, though they were still only one-third into it.

The guilt of the man executed for the crime remains, in some circles, a matter of controversy, but the justice of the verdict is the topic for a different book. To lay my cards on the table, I accept the conventional wisdom—that Bruno Richard Hauptmann planned the kidnapping of, and killed, either maliciously or through misadventure, the twenty-month-old son of Charles and Anne Lindbergh on the night of March 1, 1932. Yet anyone looking at the strange circumstances surrounding the case must admit that the kidnap-murder of the Lindbergh baby is a story that defies neat resolution, that to open the case files and sift through the evidence boxes is to get emmeshed in a web of loose ends and unlikely occurrences. Many of the smartest armchair detectives of the day, including criminal attorney Samul S. Leibowitz and journalist Adela Rogers St. Johns, believed that Hauptmann must have had at least one accomplice. I demur, but concede the possibility.

Experts on the Lindbergh case will notice that I have not mentioned some signature incidents or followed up on some tantalizing clues. The metal thumb guard Betty Gow found while strolling down the gravel road at Highfield on April 1, 1932—was it overlooked by the New Jersey state troopers, who overlooked so much, or was it planted for her to find on the day before

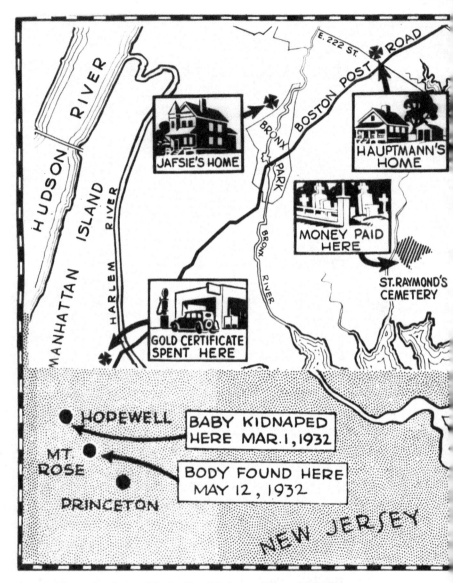

A map of the principal sites of the Lindbergh kidnap-murder published on
September 20, 1934, after the capture of Bruno Richard Hauptmann.

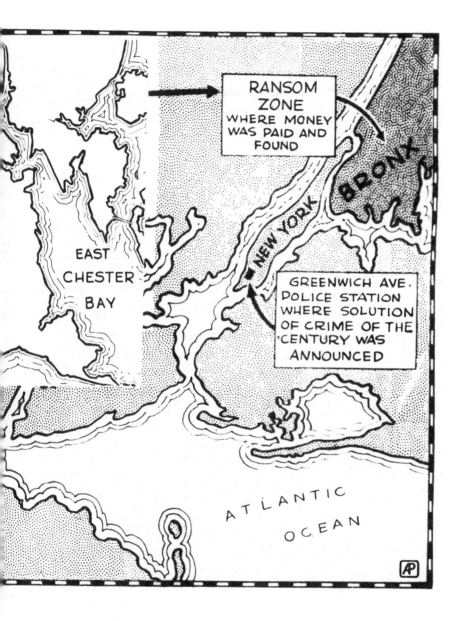

Dr. John F. Condon exchanged the ransom money with Cemetery John? The address and phone number that belonged to Dr. Condon, written on a closet door in Hauptmann's Bronx home—did Hauptmann write it or was it planted by a malicious cop or newspaperman? I have not attempted to give a comprehensive, no-stone-unturned account of the Lindbergh case—to examine every piece of evidence found at the crime scene, every witness questioned, and every legal maneuver in the trial. I have streamlined the crime story to give the reader the background necessary to appreciate what I have foregrounded, the media story.

I hope readers who dissent from my approach—and verdict—will nonetheless find the media story illuminating. For each of the three news lanes on the information highway, the Lindbergh case marked a transformative passage. Surprisingly, despite the many works chronicling the case, little has been written about the media angle of this most media-saturated of stories. The cultural historical synchronicity alone offers fertile terrain: the crime coincided with the tipping-point moment of penetration for radio and sound newsreels.

In tracing the media trail, I have also tried to evoke the emotions that Americans felt when following the news of the tragedy that had befallen the most beloved couple of the time. It would be naïve not to acknowledge the tawdry voyeurism in the curiosity and the competitive exhilaration in the coverage, but it would be too cynical not to appreciate the sympathetic bond the story engendered on all sides—in investigators, journalists, and ordinary Americans who grabbed a newspaper extra, reached for the dial, or watched the newsreels in pity and horror. The news was taken to heart; it concerned the loss of a baby everyone knew by his nickname.

LITTLE LINDY
IS KIDNAPPED

PROLOGUE

The Sky God

"In the spring of '27," recalled a wistful F. Scott Fitzgerald, still dazzled by the natural phenomenon from four years earlier, "something bright and alien flashed across the sky," a meteor in the form of a young man "who seemed to have nothing to do with his generation."[1]

Fitzgerald meant that Charles Augustus Lindbergh was everything the Jazz Age was not: serious, traditional, and quiet—quietly professional, quietly determined, and quietly heroic, a self-made man who earned his wealth and fame not by investing on margin or coining advertising slogans or playacting on the silent screen, but with an awe-inspiring feat of individual initiative and dauntless courage. In an age of crass ballyhoo and false gods, Lindbergh was the real McCoy.

A Thirty-Three-and-a-Half-Hour Vigil

At 7:22 A.M., on the drizzly morning of May 20, 1927, Lindbergh—twenty-five years old, lean as a rail, movie-star handsome—took off in a balsa wood monoplane from Roosevelt Field on Long Island destined for Le Bourget Field outside of Paris, a distance of 3,640 miles. He flew alone, and he flew nonstop. The "blind" plane had no direct field of vision ahead; the pilot depended on a periscope for forward orientation and looked out the side windows to get his bearings and make landings. Built just weeks before under Lindbergh's supervision by Ryan Airways, Inc. of San Diego, California, the aircraft was named the *Spirit of St. Louis*, in honor of the consortium of pubic-spirited citizens from Missouri who bankrolled the enterprise. In the previous century, when humanity was still tethered to the ground, St. Louis had been the gateway to the American West, the starting point for pioneers embarking on a dangerous pilgrimage through Indian country. Lindbergh's journey also broke a trail into a new frontier—and history.

Born on February 4, 1902, in Detroit, Michigan, descended from flinty Swedish stock, Lindbergh was reared in Minnesota, the son of a prominent attorney, businessman, and Republican congressman and a schoolteacher. Too young to have served in and been disillusioned by the Great War, he fell in love with its terrifying new combat weapon and by age nineteen had earned his pilot's license. Abandoning the study of mechanical engineering at the University of Wisconsin, he barnstormed across the Middle and Far West, thrilling crowds at county fairs and air shows with stunt flying and parachute jumps.

In 1924, seeking experience with higher-performance aircraft, Lindbergh enrolled as a cadet in the Army Service training school at Brook Field, San Antonio, Texas. After graduating, he declined a regular commission, opting instead to join the Missouri National Guard to become an airmail carrier, the modern-day version of a Pony Express rider. Already he was a legend in aviation ranks for his preternatural skill in the cockpit and death-defying good luck. By 1925, he had survived disintegrating wings, stalled engines, and four emergency parachute jumps.

Despite his at-one-ness with flying machines, Lindbergh was no cock of the air. As Fitzgerald understood, he was the embodiment of the anti-zeitgeist, a bottled-up man beating against the main currents of his time—cool and reserved where the Jazz Age was hot and brassy.

Unlike the man, however, the flight to Paris was very much of its time, another in the series of get-rich-quick schemes that stoked the engine of the Roaring Twenties. In 1919, Raymond Orteig, a wealthy New York hotelier, had put up a prize of $25,000 to be awarded to the first man or men to fly across the Atlantic, New York to Paris or vice versa, nonstop. Like so much else in the 1920s, it was a publicity stunt, about speed, machines, and grabbing the main chance. It might be deemed a pseudo-event were not the stakes so high and the risks so real. Less than two weeks prior to Lindbergh's flight, two French flyers, Capt. Charles Nungesser and Capt. François Coli, had taken off in the opposite direction, carrying with them the hopes of their countrymen. Somewhere over the Atlantic, the pair vanished, never to be heard from again.

That morning at Roosevelt Field, Lindbergh was not the only contestant vying for the grand prize. Better known and more experienced flyers also watched the skies, waiting for a break in the weather, going through checklists. Commodore Richard E. Byrd, famed for his polar explorations, was backed by big money and an expert crew. Pilot Lloyd W. Bertaud and navigator Charles A. Levine were also in the running with a Bellanca monoplane, but the two men were squabbling and Levine had filed a court injunction to replace his pilot.[2] Lindbergh was young and handsome, he was underfinanced, he was flying alone, and he loved his mother. Little wonder he became the sentimental favorite.

As soon as Lindbergh hit the ignition—the plane seemed to take forever taxiing down the muddy runway before sluggishly gaining altitude, barely clearing a line of telegraph wires—a thirty-three-and-a-half-hour vigil was kept by every American within arm's reach of a newspaper or earshot of a radio. Never before had so many people been so passionately caught up in the same unfolding story at exactly the same time. The rush of shared feeling was a wholly new sensation and, because it was new, all the more exhilarating.

Stories abound about the unity of emotion and intensity of engagement Americans felt while Lindbergh was aloft. At Yankee Stadium that Friday night, the main event was a heavyweight bout between two hardscrabble boxers, both from Boston: the Lithuanian Jack Sharkey, the odds-on favorite, and the Irishman Jimmy Maloney, the crowd darling. Yet except for the high rollers with serious money on the line, the outcome of the fight was a secondary consideration. From ringside to the last row, the talk was only about Lindbergh. Darting though the aisles, newsboys sold extras bannering the latest Lindbergh news. Fans lunged for papers, tossing out coins, heedless of the change.

Before the fight commenced, announcer Joe Humphries strode to the center of the ring and bellowed out the news that Lindbergh had been spotted three hundred miles out to sea and all was well. The crowd roared, giddy with relief and excitement. Humphries had to wave his hands for silence before he could continue. When the crowd finally hushed, a voice from the stands shouted, "He's the greatest fighter of them all!" Pandemonium—more shouting, more hurrahs. Amid the **din**, Humphries again begged for silence. When the ovation subsided, he asked that everyone stand to observe a silent moment of prayer for Lindbergh's safe landing in France. From ringside, a grizzled sports writer looked back "as 40,000 people rose as one and stood with heads bared. . . . On the upturned faces at this moment, there was none which did not show anxiety in his or her face."[3] Sharkey knocked out Maloney in the fifth round, but the emotion in the stadium had already been spent.

Throughout the nation, families sitting down to supper also murmured prayers for Lindbergh's safety. In Indiana, Pennsylvania, a teenager named Jimmy Stewart requisitioned the window of his father's hardware store to install a model of the *Spirit of St. Louis* and a makeshift map with the Woolworth Building on one side and the Eiffel Tower on the other. "Every time I got a flash that a fishing boat or a steamer had sighted Lindbergh's plane, I rushed to the store window and moved my model plane closer to France," Stewart recalled.[4]

The last sightings of Lindbergh's plane came at 7:45 P.M. EST, Friday night, from off the coast of Newfoundland, transmitted by shortwave radio from spotter ships at sea. After that, throughout the long night, as the plane flew over the icy North Atlantic to the British Isles—nothing, no word for hours, an ominous radio silence.

On Saturday morning, Americans awoke hungry for news—perhaps from the morning paper at the doorstep or from an extra edition purchased at the corner newsstand or—a new option on the media menu—from a radio, in 1927 still something of a luxury item for upwardly mobile families.

The hours ticked by, an anguish of waiting, until at 10:30 A.M., shortwave wire reports, passed on by teletype to radio and the newspapers, confirmed sightings of the *Spirit of St. Louis* off the coast of Ireland. The most perilous part of the trip—across the Atlantic—had been traversed. But would the exhausted pilot make it all the way to Paris?

Meanwhile, the citizens of France were tracking Lindbergh as if he were a native son. As darkness fell outside Paris, half a million Frenchmen, tense with expectation, congregated at the airfield at Le Bourget. At 10:52 P.M. Lindbergh touched down, safe and sound—at the far end of the field, fortunately, where he was quickly spirited away, else he might have been torn apart by the adoring mob.[5]

Back home, the news of Lindbergh's landing passed like an electric current via radio bulletins, teletype, screaming newsboys, and word of mouth.

Charles Lindbergh and U.S. ambassador to France Myron T. Herrick appear at the window of the U.S. Embassy in Paris, May 22, 1927.

The surge of relief gave way to an orgy of jubilation, an outburst of such force and magnitude that journalists at the time and historians ever since have resorted to the language of psychosis to conjure the extremes of exultation: mass hysteria, wild rapture, a nation gone mad. Looking back, eyewitnesses who felt the purblind bliss in the spring of '27 struggled to describe—and explain—the waves of adulation that swept across America.

In Europe, meanwhile, the French, the Belgians, and the British proved no less susceptible to Lindbergh fever than the Americans. A model of dignified comportment and natural grace, he was the most popular emissary from the New World since—Buffalo Bill? Ben Franklin? In Paris, the morning after his arrival, in a gesture that endeared him to the French, he paid a respectful visit to the mother of the lost French flyer Nungesser. In Brussels, he placed a wreath on the tomb of Belgium's Unknown Solider. In London, he attended a Memorial Day service at St. Margaret's Church, visited King George and Queen Mary at Buckingham Palace, and received a standing ovation from the

House of Commons. Everywhere, the crowds were delirious. Presuming intimacy, the press called him "Lindy," a moniker that stuck. He was also called "Lucky Lindy," though the ratio of luck to skill tilted heavily toward the latter.

Back home, civic dignitaries competed to show fealty by showering honors upon Lindbergh. Streets and babies were named after him, as were dances— most memorably, the Lindy Hop—and, far less memorably, a sheaf of disposable Tin Pan Alley tunes with titles like "Lucky Lindy," "The Eagle of the U.S.A.," and "Like an Eagle He Flew Into Our Hearts."[6] He was the first living person to have his exploit commemorated on a U.S. postage stamp.

The newly anointed national treasure wanted to fly back to America over Siberia, but President Calvin Coolidge refused to risk so valuable a citizen to Soviet airspace. He ordered the *U.S.S. Memphis* to transport Lindbergh, now promoted to the rank of colonel, to Washington, D.C.

On June 11, 1927, accompanied by a fleet of warships that sailed down the Chesapeake to the Potomac, the *Memphis* arrived bearing its precious cargo. All of official Washington and most of the population turned out to hail the hero. Every politician in town angled to get a photograph of himself standing next to the abashed Lindbergh. At Monument Grounds, a startlingly effusive President Coolidge praised the "genuine exemplar of fine and noble virtues" and awarded him the Distinguished Flying Cross.

Miffed that Washington, D.C., had pulled rank to be the first city to celebrate Lindbergh's homecoming, New York prepared a massive blowout that would put the dowdy capital to shame. A flotilla of what seemed like every seaworthy vessel anchored in New York Harbor sailed as honor guard to Lindbergh as he landed by amphibious plane and coasted into Pier A. A blizzard of ticker tape rained down as he rode through midtown, waving and looking chagrined. It was a reception never surpassed for sheer over-the-moon joy and ticker tape tonnage.

When a nation takes leave of its senses, the condition demands a cultural diagnosis. Looking back from the vantage of 1931, when the glow from the rapture was still warm, the cultural historian Frederick Lewis Allen speculated that for an age that overturned old laws and burned its candle at both ends, that raced headlong into the revolution of morals and manners wrought by the amplified Jazz Age, Lindbergh harkened back to an older, traditional American archetype—a frontiersman of few words and true grit.[7] He was also—and this was not incidental—a Nordic Protestant in an age thick with swarthy Catholics from the villages of the Southern Mediterranean and exotic Jews from the shtetls of Eastern Europe. "He is a lanky, six-foot blond Viking type," was how an early hagiography described the perfect specimen of American manhood.[8] In race no less than temperament, Lindbergh was a throwback to a less mixed and mixed-up time.

For anyone who was there, the memory of the magic moments never faded. In 1956, the humorist Fred Allen, something of an avatar of the Jazz Age himself, narrated a landmark archival documentary on NBC called *The Jazz Age*. When rewinding the bathtub-gin-soaked hoopla and addled ballyhoo of the 1920s, Allen's commentary drips sarcasm, his nasal voiceover laced with the rueful knowledge that the crazed binge was running smack into the stock market crash and the long hangover of the Great Depression. Yet when Allen relates the story of Lindbergh's flight across the Atlantic, his tone becomes hushed and reverent. Nearly thirty years after the fact, even a diehard cynic gets a lump in his throat when he remembers the dappled glory that was Lindbergh's solo flight to Paris.

Nearly twenty years later, the memory was still fresh to another connoisseur of irony, the literary critic Northrop Frye. In 1975, lecturing to an undergraduate class at Harvard University, Frye strained to evoke the hero worship that was more than hero worship, the besotted devotion to the man who had flown so close to the sun and not crashed to earth. This was not the transient notoriety of the Girl of the Year or the other blips on the cultural radar fluttering around the first famous-for-fifteen-minutes decade. "When I was a young man," Frye told his students, "we worshiped a Sky God and his name was Charles Lindbergh."[9]

The Star-Making Machinery of 1927

For the media of the day, the Sky God was a godsend: a retinue of eager tribunes heralded his ascent and threw garlands. Indeed, without the networks of mass communication feeding off and fueling the adoration—the saturation coverage from syndicated wire reports, radio bulletins, and the newsreels—the intimate identification of so many Americans with Lindbergh would never have been so close or felt so keenly. No less than the *Spirit of St. Louis*, the star-making machinery of 1927 was a marvel of modern technology that bore the flyer aloft.

The first inkling of how the modern media might forge a vicarious kinship had occurred two years earlier. In 1925, a luckless spelunker named Floyd Collins became trapped in a crevice in Sand Cave, Kentucky. Wire service reporters typed out minute-by-minute updates on his plight. Much of the nation hung on every word, absorbed in the life-and-death struggle of a man none had heard of hours before and, upon getting the awful news that Collins had lost his fight for survival, grieved along with his family. (This being the 1920s, while Collins's body still lay in its dank tomb, his father and brother went into show business, telling their story at state fairs and vaudeville theaters.[10])

Lindbergh's spectacular flight and serene charisma ratcheted up the emotional investment exponentially, but it was the connective tissue woven by electronic communication that bound Americans—and much of the wired world—to his person. The media-made universality of the experience generated a kind of hive mind, with all antennae tingling at the same instant, tuned to the same wavelength. First, he is off, airborne, then he is spotted off the coast of Newfoundland, followed by—nothing, an information blackout, until, fifteen hours later, he emerges from the clouds off the coast of Ireland, followed by the escalating rush of anticipation as he glides into the home stretch. "It is claimed that over 350,000,000 people glued their eyes on Lindbergh from Friday morning to Saturday night and thereafter," reported *Variety*, the show-business weekly. "Through his unparalleled feat he has become the best exploited person of a century."[11]

The newspapers were the established clarions, each major metropolis served by morning, afternoon, and evening editions, and, when momentous news broke, a special "extra" edition hyping the can't-wait story. Newsboys hawked the issues on street corners, shouting out the headlines. At night, before retiring, the man of the house might stroll to the corner newsstand to purchase the "bulldog"—the last late evening edition—of his local paper.

But just as the printed page had overtaken the hear-ye, hear-ye declamations of the town crier, the newspaper was being chased by a pair of high-tech rivals on the information highway. Also tracking Lindbergh's passage were two new voices in the media chorus: broadcast radio and the sound newsreel. One was still in embryo and the other was introduced especially for the occasion, but both were already revolutionizing the delivery and reception of news. By 1927, the new electronic media had penetrated just deep enough to send a shared rush of adrenaline through the American bloodstream.

Radio was the decisive addition. Even more than the telegraph, its nineteenth-century progenitor, radio made news instantaneous and close to home. "America as a whole first learned of the success of young Charles Lindbergh's New York to Paris non-stop flight from radio receiving sets," *Variety* stated flatly. "Just ten minutes after the boy landed, the news was being broadcast to listeners-in."[12]

Upon Lindbergh's return, radio solidified its promotion up the media hierarchy. In an unprecedented demonstration of broadcast technology, virtually every second of Lindbergh's reception in Washington was aired nationwide over a fifty-two-station hookup. Announcer Graham McNamee, who cheekily called his subject "the famous boy-and-colonel," escorted listeners from the Navy Yard to the grandstand where President Coolidge pinned the DFC on Lindbergh's coat. From a booth atop the Washington Monument, WRC announcer Philips Carlin provided color commentary while colleague John B. Daniel tracked the parade up Pennsylvania Avenue from a position on the steps of the Treasury building.[13] Also broadcast was the extravagant reception hosted that night by Washington's National Press Club with Lindbergh as guest speaker. Financed by Hollywood mogul William Fox and produced by theatrical impresario Samuel L. "Roxy" Rothafel, the show featured a thirty-six-piece orchestra assembled on twenty-four hours' notice. Every American in range of a radio was invited to listen in.

New York also cleared the airwaves to fete Lindbergh—tracking his progress from New York Harbor and along Fifth Avenue and broadcasting his speeches at the luncheons and dinners given in his honor. "After hearing announcers describe the pushing and milling thousands along the march route, it seemed to many that the best place to view the parade was at home near the receiving end of a radio set," concluded the *New York Times*.[14] On Flag Day, June 14, Lindbergh and Old Glory were saluted together at a grand dinner presided over by New York's rascally Mayor Jimmy Walker, a soirée broadcast "to the ears of the listening audience" by NBC's Blue Network.[15]

Even as radio spread out to pervade the atmosphere, a rival medium was challenging its monopoly on the sounds of the Lindbergh story. The year Lindbergh flew across the Atlantic was also the year that the motion-picture medium found its voice with the technology of synchronous sound. The screen could not compete with radio bulletins or newspaper extras for speed of delivery—film had to be shot, developed, edited, and distributed to theaters, a process that usually took days—but it could offer vivid moving pictures of the hero—and, for the first time, the accompanying soundtrack.

Fox News, soon to be renamed Fox Movietone News, had recently perfected an optical sound-on-film process, as opposed to the sound-on-disk Vitaphone process that Warner Bros. touted later that year with the epochal release of *The Jazz Singer* (1927), the feature film that shattered the mute solemnity of the silent screen. With the photogenic Lindbergh scheduled to take off from Roosevelt Field, the newsreel company decided to put the technology to the test. A crew was waiting by the side of the runway, camera mounted on a tripod, sound microphone raised and ready.

Fox editors rushed the sound pictures through the production process—developing, printing, and distributing the footage with breakneck speed. That same afternoon, the sound-on-film footage of Lindbergh's takeoff unspooled at the Roxy Theatre in New York. Moviegoers were mesmerized. "The roar of the propellers is heard, and when the gallant aviator leaves the earth, the cheers of the throng on the field come to the ears of the spectators in the audience," reported an awestruck Mordaunt Hall, the film critic for the *New York Times*. "Yesterday afternoon [May 20] this short feature not only stirred up enthusiastic applause, but in all sections of the theater many persons shouted and hurrahed." At the packed evening shows, the standing-room-only crowds of six thousand rose as one, cheering and applauding, drowning out the soundtrack.[16] The Roxy's featured attraction that evening was a madcap boxing comedy entitled *Is Zat So?* (1927), not that it mattered.

Across the ocean, newsreel crews waited at Le Bourget to record the images (though not the sounds) of the plane landing and the pilot stepping from the cockpit. Unfortunately, the cameramen had set up their equipment and lights near the main terminal. The *Spirit of St. Louis* landed at the far end of the field, out of sight of the cameras. Searchlights swept the crowd, catching night-for-night images of the mob rushing toward the plane, but no pictures as it taxied to a stop, the propeller blades miraculously missing the first wild spectators racing to meet the pilot. Two uniformed French aviators hustled Lindbergh away, again out of camera range. Not until the next afternoon, outside the U.S. Embassy in Paris, where Lindbergh had spent the night, did the newsreels obtain shots of the refreshed but dazed pilot, smiling warily, in a borrowed ill-fitting suit, first on the balcony, where he unfurled a French flag with U.S. Ambassador Myron Herrick, and then on the steps below, where the cameramen finally got a close-up of the American idol. He looked magnificent.[17]

The Lindbergh-in-Paris footage was shipped back to America aboard the fast liner *U.S.S. Majestic*, which anchored in New York Harbor on the morning of May 30. The liner was met by a special revenue ship which, while still on the water, rushed the film through the red tape of customs and thence to shore, whereupon the newsreel companies grabbed the prints and sped the film to the first-run Broadway houses. By late morning, shots of ecstatic Frenchmen racing across Le Bourget field to greet Lindbergh were playing in New York and prints were being shipped to theaters across the country.[18] "The greatest newsreel story in history!" screamed ads. "Lindbergh's arrival in Paris!"

On June 11, 1927, when the conquering hero returned to native shores, Fox News scored another first for the motion-picture medium as President Coolidge's comments—and Lindbergh's—were recorded by the sound cameras. At the Roxy and other theaters, an eighteen-minute newsreel short of the event became the main attraction. "Some of the picture houses early in the Lindbergh day neglected to grasp the strength of the Lindbergh newsreel," noted *Variety*. Not for long. "It's all Lindy and stands as a special insert on the program" was the policy by afternoon.[19] Exhibitors played the newsreels for weeks.

On June 15, 1927, two days after the eruption of Lindymania down Fifth Avenue, New Yorkers could watch themselves in the newsreels as a whirlwind of ticker tape filled the screen. "With each new day the newsreel is playing a more important part not only with theaters but in the daily lives of all," wrote Jack Alicoate, editor-publisher of the New York–based trade paper the *Film Daily*, bragging about the unique impact of the newsreels when set against the newspapers and radio. "There is more of a genuine thrill in one hundred feet of Lindy on the screen than in one hundred pages of cold type."* His colleague Red Kann agreed, praising the newsreels with an astute prophecy: "The pictures are history making. The best shots, no matter who takes them, will find their way into government archives in Washington."[20]

Of course, Hollywood tried to lure the star whose name was already in lights. The money dangled before him was mind-boggling: $2,000,000 for appearances on stage and in state fairs, promised one promoter, with $1,000,000 more in the movies. MGM cabled Lindbergh with an offer to

---

* Ninety feet of 35mm film equals about one minute of running time.

appear in its forthcoming aviation adventure *War Birds*. Paramount Pictures bid $1,000,000 for a single movie. Roxy Rothafel said Lindbergh only had to work two weeks to pocket $50,000.[21] True to type, however, Lindbergh refused to cash in on his fame, at least in the more vulgar manner. He did not mount a vaudeville act and go on tour; he did not go Hollywood and reenact his exploits for a biopic; and he did not lend his face to advertisements for shirts or cigarettes (though he did endorse the "faithful Waterman" pen he took with him on the *Spirit of St. Louis* "to mark the route on my maps").

Over the next years, moviegoers who wished to swoon over Lindbergh had to be satisfied with seeing him in the newsreels. Newsreel editors gladly obliged, featuring him incessantly, tracking his every move. For years after, on the anniversary of the Lindbergh flight, Fox Movietone released special reviews of the halcyon days, with a voiceover reminding viewers that it was Fox Movietone and Fox Movietone alone that had secured the only sound pictures of the *Spirit of St. Louis* taking off from Roosevelt Field. "Still thrilling despite the years," marveled Roy Chartier, *Variety*'s man on the newsreel beat, watching a recap in 1930.[22] Whenever a close-up of Lindbergh appeared on the newsreel screen, audiences burst into applause.

Meanwhile, the man in the spotlight was attempting to have a personal life, his attitude to the throngs of reporters and photographers who traveled in his wake ranging from shy to stoic to—in time—surly.

In December 1927, while in Mexico City preparing for a goodwill tour of Central and South America, America's "uncrowned prince" met his princess, the bookish Anne Spencer Morrow, the twenty-one-year-old daughter of Dwight W. Morrow, ambassador to Mexico and former partner with J. P. Morgan and Company. Pretty, smart, well-born, and, as it turned out, a game life partner who developed into a skilled copilot and gifted memoirist, she was deemed a worthy match, an all-American girl "as clean as a waterfall and as fine as a pine tree."[23] On May 27, 1929, as thousands of other all-American girls sighed in envy, Lindbergh was married at the Morrow estate in Englewood, New Jersey. Front pages—but no newsreel shots—printed the nuptials.

The wait for an heir to the Lindbergh line began immediately. The suspense ended on June 22, 1930, when a healthy baby boy, Charles Augustus Lindbergh Jr., was born at the Morrow estate. Inevitably, the tabloids christened him Little Lindy.

The duties of parenthood did not tie down either Lindbergh. In May 1931, Anne won her pilot's license, perfectly executing the required landings and

Charles and Anne Lindbergh on the waters of Hudson Bay at a stopover in Churchill, Manitoba, on their way to Japan, August 3, 1931.

figure eights in a secret exam session.[24] Two months later, "the Flying Lindberghs" undertook a historic flight to the Far East to chart air routes and demonstrate the safety of air travel, with Anne serving as copilot, navigator, and radio operator. Prior to embarking, the couple, along with Ambassador Morrow and his wife, agreed to a photo op at the Morrow vacation home in North Haven, Maine. Universal Newsreel cameraman Earl Moffet snuck into the backyard and poked his camera through a hedge to get "the first sitting of the Lindbergh eaglet" in the issue released on August 5, 1931. "Paramount News also snuck some pictures of the baby and his nurse," noted *Variety*. "Both claimed first pictures of the kid."[25]

One of Lindbergh's most ardent admirers did not need to sneak behind hedges to gain entry into the family circle. He was perhaps the only man in America who rivaled the flyer as a figure of popular esteem, a man who, unlike Lindbergh, had the common touch, who genuinely liked people, and who wore his fame easily.

The coveted first newsreel pictures of fourteen-month-old Charles Augustus Lindbergh Jr., with his Scotch terrier, being wheeled by nurse Betty Gow at the Morrow estate in New Haven, Maine, August 3, 1931.

The cowboy-philosopher Will Rogers was in a class by himself. A star of stage, screen, and radio, the beloved humorist dispensed horse sense in a drowsy Oklahoma drawl that belied his whiplash wit. Rogers wrote a syndicated column printed on the front page of subscribing newspapers—less than a hundred words usually, comprised of folksy aphorisms, wry observations, and good-natured zingers. Rogers boasted that he never met a man he didn't like, and it was a rare man who did not return the compliment.

On February 14, 1932, Rogers, who had visited the Lindbergh home earlier that week, shared a vignette that he knew would warm the hearts of his readers. "The Lindbergh baby is the cutest thing you ever saw, walking, talking," he enthused, joshing that little Charlie "disgraced the Lindbergh name by crying to come with Mrs. Rogers and I in the car."

Less than three weeks later, a stricken Rogers would write, "I wish we had taken him home with us and kept him."[26]

Chapter 1

THE CRIME OF THE CENTURY

O n March 1, 1932, at 10:46 P.M., a blunt teletype from the New Jersey State Police transmitted the word:

Colonel Lindbergh's baby kidnapped from Lindbergh home in Hopewell, New Jersey, some time between 7:30 P.M and 10:00 P.M. this date. Baby is nineteen months old, and a boy. Is drest in a sleeping suit. Request that all cars be investigated by police patrols. Authority State Police, Trenton, New Jersey, 10:46 P.M.[1]

Within minutes, in newsrooms across America, the urgent bells on wire service machines were clanging madly, the signal that five-alarm news was breaking. Within the hour, the information was being flashed on radio. Before midnight, newsboys were hawking extras emblazoned with seventy-two-point Bodini bold headlines. "Lindbergh Baby Kidnapped!" they yelled, stopping pedestrians in their tracks. "Little Lindy Kidnapped!" A day later, the final pillar of the media triumvirate weighed in with an all-points bulletin. "Nation Aroused at Revolting Kidnapping of Lindbergh Baby!" exclaimed the title cards in the newsreels.

The news that the son of the most beloved couple in America had been stolen from his crib sent the police of New Jersey and New York, state and local, into frenetic action. Shocked, outraged, and determined, the authorities in both states mobilized virtually every uniformed cop and plainclothes detective on the payroll. "You must work on your time off and sacrifice your sleep," New York police commissioner Edward P. Mulrooney told his 17,183-man force. "Devote all of your attention to this case."[2] The New York auxiliaries would be needed: the enormity of the case overwhelmed the resources and outpaced the skills of New Jersey's finest.

Also hoping to ride into the breech, and grab the media spotlight, was a contingent from J. Edgar Hoover's Bureau of Information, not yet elevated to acronym fame as the FBI. In 1932, Hoover was already beginning to make the investigation of crime a matter of scientific method, data collection, and bureaucratic procedure, but the instinctive reliance on Washington, D.C., when confronted by crisis was not yet a national reflex. Crime fell under the jurisdiction of local law enforcement—the county sheriff, the state troopers, the cop on the beat. Hoover arrived in Hopewell to share his expertise, but the New Jersey police told him to take a hike. Jealous of their turf, the local cops neither sought help nor shared information.[3] The Lindbergh case would change all that forever.

On the day after the kidnapping of the Lindbergh baby, the police attempt a reconstruction of the crime, March 2, 1932.

Equally energized by the crime—maybe even more energized—were the legions of journalists working in print, over the air, and behind the newsreel cameras. For the three branches of the American media, the Lindbergh kidnapping presented unique challenges and new opportunities. Each played to its strengths: the print press for comprehensiveness of coverage, offering column inch after column inch of detailed reporting and lavishing full-page spreads on maps, diagrams, and photographs for a readership whose appetite for Lindbergh news was insatiable; the radio for immediacy and speed; and the newsreels for the visual allure of motion pictures on a big screen. The Lindbergh story was a transformative moment for each lane on the information highway. The responses set the patterns for the media coverage of every shock wave that would rock American culture for the rest of the century, and beyond.

Who Would Do Such a Thing?

What happened in the second-floor nursery of the Lindbergh home in Hopewell during the mid-evening hours of Tuesday, March 1, 1932, would be forever disputed—every piece of evidence, every notation on the timeline, and every eyewitness account dissected, turned over, second-guessed, and gainsaid. As in any criminal case, agreed-upon facts vie with contested evidence, plausible speculation with bizarre theories. The Lindbergh baby kidnapping generated more than its share of stranger-than-fiction plot twists that might be coincidental—the loose ends that will never be tied up because that is the way life is—or that, when added up and weighed together, are too suspiciously odd to be mere happenstance, hinting at darker possibilities and conspiratorial hands. Surely, most thought at the time and many have thought since, what transpired was so uncanny and awful that the tentacles of sinister forces must have been at work, that so foul a deed could not have been the act of a lone perpetrator.[4] Some of the mysterious blanks would never be filled in, but the questions all circled back to the same heart-stopping absence: the baby was gone.

As if to heighten the murky tonalities, the scene of the crime came shrouded in the trappings of a Gothic novel: a vista gray, gloomy, dank, and foggy. Situated in the dreary Sourland Mountain region of New Jersey, eight miles from Princeton, fourteen miles from the state capital in Trenton, and three miles from the hamlet of Hopewell, the nearest town, the Lindbergh residence, grandly christened Highfield, was isolated by design, chosen for the seclusion not the scenery. The remote location would ensure a measure of privacy for a man who had enjoyed precious little since May 20, 1927.

Highfield was staffed by a husband-and-wife pair of servant-caretakers: the English butler, Oliver Whately, and his spunky wife Elsie, housekeeper and cook. Twenty-five-year-old Betty Gow, a pretty nurse-nanny from Scotland, helped Anne care for the baby. All the servants, and many more peripheral players, would become household names far beyond New Jersey.

The Hopewell residence was still under construction, so during the weekdays the Lindberghs typically stayed with Anne's mother at the regal Morrow estate on the outskirts of Englewood, "an enormous Georgian mansion set in wooded slopes," as Anne remembered it, known as Next Day Hill. Presided over by Mrs. Dwight Morrow—her husband had died the previous October, less than a year after being elected to the U.S. Senate—the Englewood manor was a monument to extravagance that most Americans glimpsed only in MGM movies. Twenty servants were employed to keep the grande dame and her family in the style to which they were accustomed.[5]

The Lindberghs reserved the Hopewell site for settling-in stays on the weekends, allowing the family to get a feel for the house while supervising the final stages of construction. That weekend, however, Charles Jr. had contracted a cold and, not wanting to expose him to the chilly winds, the couple decided to extend their stay in Hopewell and not return to Englewood as per custom. On Monday, Anne summoned Betty Gow from the Morrow estate to come to Hopewell to help with the baby.

Another departure from the usual pattern was that Lindbergh, though scheduled to attend a banquet in his honor that night at New York University, had forgotten about the commitment—something that had never happened before to the man who always charted his movements with precision. On the fateful night, the baby and his father were both in a place neither would normally have been.

Charles Jr.'s nursery was on the southeast corner of the second floor of the house; his father's study was directly below. At 7:00 P.M. Betty and Anne put the child to sleep. He was dressed in a woolen sleeping suit and tucked under a blanket, fastened to the mattress with safety pins. A thumb guard, to prevent the child from sucking his thumb, was put on each thumb.

At 7:30 P.M., Betty peeked in to the nursery to check on the child. He was sleeping peacefully. Sometime later, reading in the study below, Lindbergh heard a sharp crack, as if a tree branch had broken, but, on such a windy night, he thought nothing of it.

At 10:00 P.M., before retiring, Betty returned to the nursery for a final check on the baby. He was not in his crib. She assumed Anne or the colonel must have picked him up for comfort or play.

Betty checked first with Anne and then with the colonel. Neither had seen the child.

Dreading the worst, panic escalating, the three rousted the household and swept the rooms. Lindbergh grabbed a rifle and checked the grounds. A frantic search turned up nothing.

At 10:25 P.M., Lindbergh called the New Jersey State Police. "This is Charles Lindbergh," he told a disbelieving Lt. Daniel J. Dunn. "My son has been kidnapped." Suspecting a crank, Dunn called back to confirm the identity of the caller. When he heard the same voice, he assured Lindbergh, "Men are on their way."[6]

Only then, going back to the nursery, did Lindbergh spot, overlooked in the first panic, a note lying on the radiator case by the window.

By midnight, dozens of uniformed police and plainclothes detectives were swarming around the house and trampling about the grounds. They were joined by squadrons of reporters working the story and curiosity seekers drawn by the lights.

Col. H. Norman Schwarzkopf, commander of the New Jersey State Police, a man who looked as formidable as his name, arrived and took command. Colonel Schwarzkopf would be the face of law enforcement during the Lindbergh case, the man who issued statements on the Lindberghs' behalf and answered questions from the press. Yet he was not truly in charge of the investigation. No ordinary crime victim, the father of the kidnapped child called the shots. Afraid of making a decision that might jeopardize the safety of the baby, and overawed by America's national hero, Colonel Schwarzkopf and the law enforcement authorities in both New Jersey and New York deferred to Lindbergh throughout the ordeal.

For generations raised on the *CSI* and *Law and Order* franchises, when every junior G-man knows the crucial importance of securing a crime scene and observing the protocols of gathering and preserving evidence, the staggering level of investigative incompetence by the local constabulary will seem

Newspaper- and cameramen inspect photographs of the Lindbergh baby, displayed against a shutter of the Lindbergh home, March 2, 1932.

like professional malpractice or intentional sabotage. No crack forensics team wearing latex gloves scoured the grounds, carefully putting evidence into ziplock bags with tweezers; no yellow police tape cordoned off the area. Even by the sleuthing standards of 1932, it was amateur hour. The New Jersey police did not even have a crime lab. J. Edgar Hoover suspected that Colonel Schwarzkopf had spent the funds allocated by the state legislature on fancy new police uniforms.

Three pieces of evidence on the lawn beneath the nursey window were too conspicuous to be missed by the state troopers: a jerry-built wooden ladder, in three pieces, rigged to come apart, presumably to fit into an automobile; a chisel, presumably to jimmy open the shutters and window of the nursery; and a footprint, with the imprint of a sock around it, presumably to soften the footfall of the wearer, visible in the mud.

The person or persons who left behind the implements and made the impression had vanished into the blustery New Jersey night.

The Snatch Racket

For all the shock of the Lindbergh baby kidnapping, the crime was but the highest-profile instance of a criminal enterprise that had become all too common by the early 1930s, a shameful consequence of Prohibition, the ignoble experiment that spawned a nation of scofflaws and seeded the ground for organized crime. "The kidnapping is only the climax of a wave of such cases," lamented the *New York Daily News*. "Chicago civic leaders estimate that 2,000 persons have paid ransom to kidnappers in this country in the last two years." The plague of kidnappings was reminiscent of "feudal days when barons kidnapped one another for ransom" and a sign that "we are headed back toward the Dark Ages."[7]

To crime reporter Edward Dean Sullivan, the Dark Ages had already returned. "For the last five years in America, kidnapping has been an accepted and important factor in the 'big money rackets' of this crime-ridden country," warned Sullivan in 1932. "Although in itself the Lindbergh kidnapping was the most spectacular smirk yet registered by the underworld at law and police power, it was a crime of the old school in its details." Sullivan estimated that since 1929 some 2,500 kidnapping cases had been reported, almost all committed by "regularly organized and gang-supported" hoods seeking to expand their empire from bootlegging to another profit center. The name on the street—and in the tabloids—for the system of exchange was "the snatch racket."[8]

In context, then, the familiarity of the crime in Hopewell was almost reassuring. The course of events would follow a series of predictable act breaks: the victim is snatched, the ransom is demanded, a clandestine meeting is arranged, the money and the victim are exchanged, and the kidnapper is caught and brought to justice. That is, if all went well.

Yet little about the Lindbergh case played out according to script. Cruel hoaxes, oddball characters, bungling investigators, red herrings and blind alleys, suspects and leeches, crime bosses and low-level thugs, and innocents caught in the backwash would sidetrack the linear trajectory before the final stop shattered all hopes for a happy ending.

In the weeks that followed the bolt from Hopewell, as the press screamed and speculated, the real news was going on behind the scenes, only bits and pieces of which leaked out through the media. When the full tale was told, it beggared belief.

The first bizarre turn came with the entry into the case of Dr. John F. Condon, a Mr. Micawber–like character who would bask in the glow of Lindbergh-fueled celebrity for the rest of his life.[9] A vigorous seventy-one years old, six feet tall and powerfully built, he was a retired Bronx high school principal and professor of education at Fordham University. An immaculate dresser and a bit of a dandy, known on sight throughout his home turf of the Bronx, Condon had a Teddy Roosevelt–like faith in the spiritual benefits of physical fitness and enough peculiar quirks and rough edges to lend color and whimsy to a case deficient in both. He was a raging blowhard and an insufferable egotist, but he was also, almost certainly, just what he appeared to be: a man incensed that the baby of the American hero had been snatched from his crib in the dead of night. He stood ready to do all he could to get back the child—to spend his fortune, to risk his life.

Dr. Condon had an opinion on everything and the firm belief that everyone wanted to hear it. For years, he had written letters, articles, and poetry for his local paper, the *Bronx Home News*, to share his wisdom and vent his gripes. On March 8, 1932, the paper published a letter from Condon in which he made a proposal with slim chance of ever being accepted. He personally offered a $1,000 reward for the safe return of the Lindbergh baby—and volunteered himself as the intermediary for the ransom exchange.

Unbelievably (and many would never believe it), Condon got a quick response. The next day, a letter arrived at his address. Written in second-language English and strewn with misspellings (was the sender an ill-educated foreigner? a sly native speaker trying to misdirect the police?), the letter designated Condon as the go-between in the ransom negotiations for the Lindbergh baby. The *Bronx Home News* was a hometown paper with a circulation of around 150,000. Condon's correspondent had to be part of a limited readership.

Condon contacted Highfield and got through to Col. Henry Breckinridge, the high-powered lawyer and family friend who was acting as all-purpose handler and first-line buffer between crank callers and the Lindberghs. The parents had a sure way to tell if a caller really had possession of their child: Charles Jr. had two overlapping toes on his right foot, a piece of information never revealed to the public.

The kidnapper's note did not mention the toes, but it contained solid proof that the writer was no crank: an envelope within the letter to Condon contained a letter addressed to Lindbergh and the letter printed an exact

Dr. John F. Condon, the eponymous Jafsie, with his friend, former boxer Al Reich (right), leaving the Bronx Courthouse on May 14, 1932.

reproduction of a telltale symbol the kidnapper had left at the bottom of the original ransom note to verify his identity—a peculiar design made up of three overlapping circles with holes in the center of each. Neither the existence of the three-circled sign nor its description had been made public. Only the kidnapper or an accomplice could have duplicated the image. The letter to Lindbergh also upped the ransom from the $50,000 demanded in the original note to $70,000. It included instructions, with a drawing and dimensions, for the construction of a wooden box to hold the ransom money.

Condon was driven out to Highfield that very night. He persuaded Lindbergh that he was on the level and, despite the evident danger, not out for personal gain. That night, he slept on the floor in the baby's nursery, the only vacant room in the house. Upon waking, Condon poked about the crime scene, heedless of the still-extant evidence—footprints on the floor, a palm print on the windowsill, and the placement of items in the baby's crib, from which he took two safety pins. Cowed by Lindbergh, the New Jersey police had not taken even the most elementary precautions to secure the premises.

With the entrance of the erratic and eccentric Dr. Condon, a sequence of novelistic turns and spins took the case into weird terrain, the details of which were kept under wraps by a press corps respectful of Lindbergh's request for discretion and terrified that their zeal for a scoop might endanger the child. Henceforth, a narration of the pivotal events of the crime—the first meeting with the kidnapper to discuss the terms of the ransom payment and a second meeting to exchange the money—is based solely on Condon's uncorroborated account of what he did, heard, and witnessed.

Following instructions, and in constant consultation with Colonel Breckinridge and Lindbergh, Condon put an advertisement in the *New York American* to alert the kidnapper that negotiations should proceed. On a self-aggrandizing whim, he took the phonetic pronunciation of his initials—JFC—and signed himself "Jafsie," a moniker that came to outshine his surname. The *Bronx Home News* and the *New York American* were the most important newspapers in the Lindbergh case, not because of any news they broke but because they served as secure hotlines between Condon and the kidnapper of the Lindbergh baby.

On March 11, the *New York American* published Condon's cryptic message:

Money is ready. Jafsie.

In truth, the message was only semi-cryptic. The Lindbergh case was on the mind of every reader, professional journalist or not. Anyone who read the fine print suspected a connection.

That same day at noon—the *New York American* was a morning paper—Condon received a phone call. He was out of the house, and his wife took the message from a man she described as having "a rather guttural voice, with a quite strong accent; I would say it was a German voice."

That night the man called again—same voice, same accent. "I saw your ad in the *New York American*," he said. Contact had been established. The caller told Condon to stay home at night and "you will hear from us." Then he clicked off.

The man was as good as his word. The next night, March 12, at around 8:30 P.M., a taxicab driver, Joseph Perrone, rang the doorbell at Condon's home and delivered an envelope addressed with the now-familiar penmanship of printed block letters and numerals. Perrone said a man had hailed him just south of the spacious greenery of Van Cortlandt Park in the Bronx, told him to deliver the letter, and handed him a dollar. Perrone took careful note of the man's appearance and thought he acted funny.

The letter contained instructions for a clandestine meeting that very night. Condon's good friend and business partner, Al Reich, a former professional boxer, chauffeured Condon, a nondriver, to the meeting place. They were first led to a hot dog stand, where further instructions were left under a rock. The pair were then guided to a street bordering the Woodlawn Cemetery in the Bronx. "When they shoot you tonight, they won't have to carry you far," cracked Reich.

Condon got out of the car and made himself conspicuous, walking about, fiddling with the kidnapper's letter. Between the bars of the cemetery gate, a man suddenly appeared waving a white handkerchief. Condon approached. "Have you *gottit* the money with you?" he rasped in the same German-accented voice Condon had heard over the telephone.

Before too much conversation had ensued, the man heard a sound and panicked. He agilely vaulted over the cemetery fence and ran off down the street. A cemetery guard had approached. Condon covered for the runner. "He's with me," he told the guard. The fit septuagenarian ran after the man and caught up with him in a clump of trees near a little shack in Van Cortlandt Park, the wooded area adjacent to the cemetery.

Condon grabbed the man by his left arm. In full schoolteacher mode, he berated him for fleeing. "You should be ashamed of yourself!" The two then sat down on a bench facing 233rd Street. Condon asked the man his name and the man told him "John," so Condon dubbed the stranger "Cemetery John," a perfect alias for a shadowy bogeyman. But was the contact man the mastermind? A coconspirator? A paid intermediary?

Cemetery John demanded the ransom, but Condon said that no money would be handed over without proof that he had possession of "the package."

"Vat if the baby is dead?" Cemetery John blurted out. "Vould I burn if the baby is dead?"

The question rattled Condon, but the man insisted that the baby was safe and well. Reassured, Condon now needed to be convinced that Cemetery John was the actual kidnapper and not just a middleman. He showed him the two safety pins he had taken from the baby's crib. Cemetery John identified them ("Those pins fastened the blankets to the *maddress* in the baby's *grib*.") and told where they had been placed ("Near the top. Near the pillow.") Only someone who had been in the nursery on the night of the crime could have known that.

For an hour and fifteen minutes, Condon and Cemetery John sat together on the bench talking. In the semidarkness, Condon studied the man's face: he was smooth shaven, with a small mouth and deep-set eyes above high cheekbones, about thirty-five years of age, five feet nine inches in height, and of medium build. The accent was obviously German, and Condon tried to trip him up by suddenly asking, "Bist du Deutsch?" but Cemetery John did not take the bait. The two agreed on more messages via the newspapers, and the man promised to send Condon "a token" of possession—the baby's sleeping suit. He then slipped into the darkness of the woods.

On Wednesday, March 16, after three tense days of waiting, Condon received in the mail an oblong package wrapped in brown paper. He did not open the package, but notified Colonel Breckinridge. Lindbergh would come to Condon's house as soon as he could dodge the press staked out around Hopewell.

It was not until 1:30 A.M. that Lindbergh, disguised in amber-colored glasses and wearing a cap, entered Condon's home. He opened the package and tenderly examined the contents—a gray, woolen sleeping suit, size two, his son's outfit. "I wonder why they went to the trouble of having it cleaned?" he puzzled.

The package also contained a letter, with the symbol of the three overlapping circles with three holes in the center of each. The letter told Condon to put an ad in the *New York American* and the *Bronx Home News* saying the money was ready. The kidnapper also complained about the three dollars in postage he had to pay to mail the sleeping suit.

Condon confirmed receipt in an ad the next morning:

I accept. Money is ready. John, your package is delivered and is O.K. Direct me. Jafsie.

Later that day, Colonel Breckinridge arrived at Condon's house with a package containing $50,000 in ransom money. Condon took the package to his local bank for safekeeping where, unbeknownst to him, agents from the U.S. Treasury recorded the serial numbers of the banknotes. The serial numbers from an additional $20,000 that J. P. Morgan and Company had added to the sum to make up the balance of the $70,000 were also recorded. Most of the bills, in five-, ten-, and twenty-dollar denominations, were "gold certificate" notes issued in 1928. It was to be the smartest and most crucial intervention by law enforcement in the entire case, done with Lindbergh's reluctant acquiescence at the insistence of the Treasury men.

At this point, the prolific letter-writing kidnapper went suddenly, maddeningly silent. To roust him, Condon ran a series of increasingly desperate ads in the *Bronx Home News*. On March 26, in all caps, Condon pleaded:

MONEY IS READY. FURNISH SIMPLE CODE FOR US TO USE IN PAPER. JAFSIE.

"Our nerves were near the breaking point by this time," recalled Condon. Finally, the kidnapper relieved the tension by mail. "There is absolutely no fear about the child," the letter assured him. "All is well."

Condon still wanted proof of life, but he was overruled by Breckinridge and Lindbergh. On March 31, Condon placed an ad agreeing to the kidnapper's terms: $70,000 up front.

I ACCEPT. MONEY IS READY. JAFSIE

Condon received a letter the next day saying that instructions for a meeting would be forthcoming. He was told to place a final ad reading "Yes everything OK." In incorrect grammar but with a good understanding of when the local papers went to press, the kidnapper said: "If it is too late we put it in the *New York American* for Saturday morning. Put it in *New York Journal*." Condon complied.

On April 2, 1932, Condon and Colonel Breckinridge prepared the money in two bundles: $50,000 in a wooden box as per instructions and an additional $20,000 in a separate bundle. Lindbergh later arrived at Condon's house and helped cram the money into the wooden box. Then the three men waited.

At 7:45 P.M. the doorbell rang and a taxi driver (this second driver was never heard from again) delivered a letter from the kidnapper. It gave instructions to drive to a greenhouse on Tremont Avenue in the Bronx where further directions would be found. Lindbergh insisted on driving Condon to the rendezvous. Condon noticed a revolver under Lindbergh's jacket.

For the second time, Condon would be led to a graveyard, St. Raymond's Cemetery in the Bronx. The scene chosen for the ransom exchange might have been lifted from the first reel of a Universal horror film: a meeting with a body snatcher in a cemetery at night.

Lindbergh waited in the car, within earshot. From behind one of the monuments, Condon was beckoned by a familiar Teutonic voice.

"Hey Doktor! Over here! Over here!"

Still hoping to see the baby before handing over the money, Condon had left the box with the ransom money in the car with Lindbergh. However, Cemetery John refused to show Condon the baby. In turn, Condon refused to turn over the money without, of all things, a receipt. The kidnapper left to write out a receipt and Condon returned to the car for the ransom money. Condon had bargained him down from $70,000 to the original $50,000 demanded in the first ransom note, a well-intentioned gesture that infuriated Treasury agents who wanted as much ransom money as possible in circulation.

Condon returned with the $50,000 and waited for Cemetery John to come back with the receipt. Cemetery John showed up precisely thirteen minutes after the pair had parted. Condon turned over the money and pocketed the receipt; the kidnapper gave him a note with information about the whereabouts of the baby. "Don't open that note for six hours," he ordered. Then he sped away.

Back in the car, Condon directed Lindbergh to a small house and told him to stop. They sat on the stoop and opened the note. It said the boy was on a boat—written "boad"—called the *Nelly*, being cared for by two people who knew nothing about the kidnapping. The boat was docked between Horseneck Beach and Gay Head near Elizabeth Island, north of Martha's Vineyard off the coast of Massachusetts.

To Condon's consternation, Lindbergh did not go immediately to Elizabeth Island but to a residence off Central Park owned by the Morrow family. Two Treasury agents were waiting. The men debriefed Condon. Following his description, they produced a drawing of a man who, said Condon, "bore an amazing resemblance to the John of Woodlawn and St. Raymond's Cemeteries."

The T-men told Condon they already had a profile of the likely perpetrator: "When we find our man, we expect to find a German carpenter who lives in the Bronx."

Chapter 2

A STORY THAT PENETRATED THE THICKEST SKIN

Shortly after 11:00 P.M. on March 1, 1932, Laura Vitray, a reporter for the *New York Evening Journal*, was at her typewriter in the city room racing to meet a deadline. A gruff rewrite man sidled up to her and growled, "The Lindbergh kid has been kidnapped."

"Like fun it has," Vitray snapped, though she probably used a less printable expletive. Thinking it a bad joke, she continued typing.[1]

"Five minutes later," recalled Vitray, "still not completely recovered from the daze of it, I was in an auto, with two others, racing out of New York, hitting the high roads of New Jersey at sixty-five miles an hour, burning up space between the metropolis and sleepy Hopewell." To the hyperkinetic journalists from New York, hayseed Hopewell would always be a sleepy backwater.

Vitray was a self-described ink-stained wretch working for one of the twelve daily newspapers that blanketed the five boroughs—broadsheets and tabloids, respectable and sensationalistic, sober and garish. Despite her gender, she was no Miss Lonelyhearts and emphatically not among the ranks of the "sob sisters"—female journalists relegated to drawing tears from housewives with lachrymose human-interest stories, heavy on long-suffering mothers and noble wives. Vitray was a hardened beat reporter who learned the trade as the first female copyeditor and headline writer for the *New York Evening Graphic*, the most lurid of the tabloids in a city with no shortage of same. In 1930, she was appointed to the city editor's desk of the *Graphic*, another first for her gender. As the sole "city editress" in town, she made good copy herself. "A tall slender woman in her early thirties, with dark bobbed hair, a rather gentle manner, pleasant voice and very feminine clothes, she has a bit of the aloof student look as she bends over her desk working," ran a gushing profile in the ladies' section—naturally—of a rival newspaper.[2] In 1931, media mogul William Randolph Hearst, who always had a keen eye for female talent, poached her for the *Journal*.

At 1:00 A.M. Vitray and her colleagues rolled into Hopewell. The town was wide awake and bustling with activity.

Gebhart's Hotel and Lunch Room, soon to be the preferred crash pad and watering hole for the invaders, was doing a brisk business. Already local merchants were eyeing the reporters as cash cows to be milked and price-gouged. Arriving in shifts from Trenton, Newark, New York, and Philadelphia, the influx meant a financial windfall for the town. The single taxi driver in Hopewell was soon augmenting his income with a fleet of drivers who charged a flat rate of $2 to be taken anywhere in town. Farmers rented out rooms and installed extra telephones; barns served as headquarters for teletype machines and office desks. Journalists shared scarce hotel rooms and slept in beds in rotating shifts. "The little town of Hopewell, 12 miles from Trenton, is the only community in the country that has gotten over the Depression," quipped *Variety*.[3]

Vitray reveled in the adrenaline rush, lacing her prose with hyperbole that, under the circumstances, was only mildly excessive. "The terrible disaster that had befallen [the Lindberghs] was about to metamorphose the world," she declared.

If not the world, then certainly the reporters in the cutthroat business of urban crime journalism, tabloid style. In the 1830s, New York had given birth to the genre when William Gordon Bennett, the pioneering editor-publisher of the *New York Daily News*, discovered that the denizens of the metropolis were more interested in ax murders, gang wars, homicidal love triangles, salacious divorce trials, and grisly executions than civic improvement and world affairs. For a penny a paper, uptown patricians and fresh-off-the-boat immigrants alike could partake of the pity and terror of the macabre tragedies besetting their neighbors. The buckets of blood spilling onto the sidewalks of New York—and Chicago, the second city moving up fast in the body count—fueled an explosion in newspaper production and taught a generation of journalists how to squeeze every ounce of profit from a suitably gory homicide. A sensational crime meant booming circulation and, for the reporter on the scene, a front-page byline.

The full-court-press coverage of the Lindbergh case outpaced anything ever logged in American police blotters—the unsolved murder of "the beautiful cigar girl" Mary Rogers in 1841, the jealous-rage shooting of architect Stanford White by millionaire Henry K. Thaw in 1906, and, in Chicago, the thrill killing of fourteen-year-old Bobby Franks by the Nietzschean lovers Nathan Leopold and Richard Loeb in 1924. "Never before in the history of journalism have 430 newspaper representatives been assigned to the same story as were gathered for the Lindbergh Baby saga," marveled Walter Winchell, the renowned radio personality and syndicated columnist for the morning tabloid the *New York Daily Mirror*. "There weren't that many covering the War Front. And for the first time too the local editorial rooms resembled those you see exaggerated in the magic lanterns [Winchellese for 'the movies']."[4] For once, the screaming headlines and the breathless superlatives seemed on the mark. *Editor & Publisher* called the kidnapping "the biggest human-interest story of the decade," but another instant tagline would stand the test of time: the Crime of the Century.

William Randolph Hearst was determined to own every angle of the story. Even before Orson Welles's *Citizen Kane* (1941) had imprinted the image of Hearst as an obsessive-compulsive antique collector and narcissistic editor-publisher who morphed from reformist muckraker to right-wing tycoon, he was a brand name often "more newsworthy than the names in his own headlines." In 1887, the fortunate son and heir to a gold-mine bonanza took over the struggling *San Francisco Examiner* and made it a launching pad for one for the great media empires of the twentieth century. He may not have founded all the newsprint innovations he was credited with (comic strips, gossip columnists, and full-page photos) or personally instigated the Spanish-American War, but he painted some of the boldest swaths of color onto the florid age of yellow journalism. At its height, in the flush days of the 1920s and before the Great Depression depleted even Hearst's seemingly bottomless pockets, his synergistic conglomerate included twenty-eight magazines, eight radio stations, a newsreel, a motion picture production company, a press service, and twenty-five major newspapers.[5] Feared and beloved by his editors and reporters, he was the hands-on paterfamilias and editor-in-chief from on high who still mocked up headlines and blue-penciled copy.

As soon as word of the kidnapping crossed the wires, Hearst moved to flood the zone. He assigned his entire staff of New York–based photographers

Media mogul William Randolph Hearst; his longtime love, the actress Marion Davies; and comedian Charles Chaplin at the Motion Picture Electrical Parade and Sports Pageant held at Olympic Stadium, Los Angeles, September 24, 1932.

to the Lindbergh case and dispatched two ambulances fitted with developing equipment to speed out to Hopewell. As sirens blared, pictures from the crime scene were developed during the ride back to New York to be ready for publication upon arrival. Hearst sent out the aces in his deck, including Winsor McCay, the animator and illustrator whose *Little Nemo* series had pioneered the art of the Sunday comic strip. Hearst himself appeared on the scene to inspire his troops by example.[6]

In the vanguard of the Hearst army, Laura Vitray drove the three miles out of Hopewell down a long black road to the Lindbergh home. In the nighttime sky, she watched as flare bombs from airplanes circling overhead lit up the darkness. New Jersey police zoomed past in squad cars.

The Highfield grounds were still open and accessible. Blithely contaminating the crime scene, the reporters—and police and lookie-loos—trampled the wet lawns and surrounding woods. "Up at the Lindbergh estate that night, with the indiscretion of reporters, we peered through the windows of the Lindbergh home," Vitray remembered, spying Anne Lindbergh in the living room, walking up and down, "nervous but dry-eyed, consulting with her servants." That Anne was not hysterical struck Vitray as curious, maybe suspicious.

Eventually, as the scrum of journalists grew, the police moved the reporters back from the main house. At 3:00 A.M., Vitray spotted another vehicle approaching the estate on "a steep and muddy lane"—Lindbergh's.

Lindbergh approached the reporters. "Boys," he said, ignoring the girl, "I rely on you to stay off the estate and not annoy me. For my part, I promise I'll give you a good break."

The pledge was an olive branch from an embittered adversary. In 1927, Lindbergh had tolerated the press with tight-lipped forbearance. By 1932, he was snippy and jealous of his privacy; he was particularly sensitive about press coverage of his newborn son. The hostility began from the moment of the boy's birth. To thwart New York tabloids hungry for the first pictures of the baby, Lindbergh took a photograph to the New York office of the Associated Press, stipulating that AP deny the picture to the *American, Journal, Mirror, Graphic,* and *News,* the worst of the tabloid lot in Lindbergh's mind. Later, when the papers erroneously reported that the child would be named Charles *Morrow* Lindbergh, an agitated Lindbergh showed up at the AP offices and berated the editors for their false scoop. "Lindy, for some reason or other, doesn't get along very well with New York newspapermen," *Variety* understated in 1930, though the reason—the relentless invasion of his privacy—was clear enough.[7]

Lindbergh spent the first full day after the kidnapping searching the Sourland Mountains on foot. Bedraggled and exhausted, he returned home, slept fitfully, and then met with a small delegation of newspapermen. The discussion was off the record, but later reports said he revealed nothing and would not confirm AP reports, already circulating due to loose-lipped state troopers, that a ransom note left in the baby's nursery contained a demand for $50,000.

Lindbergh then requested that the journalists depart the estate and informed them that henceforth all information would originate from the office of New Jersey governor A. Harry Moore in Trenton. From Lindbergh the request had the force of law—literally, as the state police began rousting the reporters from the grounds. They would not be called back until ten weeks later.

Cameramen huddle in the cold outside the gate of the Lindbergh home, March 7, 1932.

Star Bylines and Syndicated Prose

Laura Vitray was not a high-profile journalist whose byline drew readers. She was a beat reporter whose name might not even be typeset at the top of the stories she phoned in. However, the boom times for newspapers in the 1920s had thrown up a constellation of star reporters whose names, almost as much as the news of the day, sold papers. They were not going to sit on the sidelines—and on their laurels—back in the city room as the crime story of the century unfolded.

The columnist-editor Arthur Brisbane was the most prominent of the venerable old guard. Based at the *New York Evening Journal*, the sixty-eight-year-old pontificator held down the prestigious space column left ("portside" in city room lingo) on the front page of twenty-four newspapers nationwide.

His nominal boss, William Randolph Hearst, trusted Brisbane not only with the front pages of his newspapers but with his stock portfolio: on Brisbane's advice, and to his later regret, Hearst bought up sizable chunks of midtown Manhattan. Brisbane was the only journalist sweating out a deadline who doubled as a real estate magnate.

On March 10, Brisbane proved his worth by nabbing an interview with a uniquely credentialed criminal profiler: mob kingpin Al Capone, currently behind bars in Chicago while awaiting transfer to the federal penitentiary in Atlanta. A *Time* magazine cover boy in 1930, the cigar-chomping, plug-ugly thug lent a mugshot kisser to the brazen gangsterism of the Prohibition age. Scarface Al, as he was called in the tabloids but not to his face, was the celebrity boss of the Chicago mob and the brains behind the St. Valentine's Day Massacre of 1929. In 1931, Capone had finally been brought to something like justice when he was convicted of income tax evasion and sentenced to eleven years in federal prison. His plush suite in the Lexington Hotel on Michigan Avenue was exchanged for a spartan cell in the Cook County jail, though he still got room service courtesy of the bribable guards.

When Brisbane walked into Capone's cell, the mobster greeted him with the question on everyone's mind: Is there any news of the Lindbergh baby? For the next hour the newspaperman and the mobster spoke of little else except the fate of Little Lindy.

"I don't want any favors if I am able to do anything for that baby," Capone claimed. "If they will let me out of here, I will give any bond they require if they are interested in the child." Scarface Al was more than willing to post the necessary bond for his release and place himself in the custody of Thomas Callaghan, head of the United States Secret Service Guard. "And I will send my young brother to stay here in jail until I come back. You don't suppose anybody would suggest that I would double cross my own brother and leave him here, if I could get away from Callaghan?"[8]

Capone's altruistic gesture was rebuffed. Some suspected that the mobster himself had masterminded the kidnapping as part of a scheme to secure his release, but Walter Winchell scoffed at the notion, pointing out that police surveillance had put so much heat on the underworld that its profit stream was shut off. "No beer truck can safely crash the New Jersey passages or any State Road now," Winchell pointed out.[9]

The most famous byline of all belonged to Will Rogers, who just a few weeks earlier had spent a happy day with the Lindbergh family at the

Englewood estate. "What a shock it is to everybody," he wrote the morning after the news broke. "But how much more of a one it is when you have seen the baby and seen the affection of the mother and father and the whole Morrow family for the cute little fellow." Rogers recalled how Anne had sat for an hour on the floor in the sun parlor playing blocks with the child and how Lindbergh had playfully tossed a pillow at him. For the kidnapper of Little Lindy, the genial cowboy-philosopher was prepared to make an exception to his rule about never meeting a man he didn't like. "Why don't lynching parties widen their scope and take in kidnapping?"[10]

Brisbane, Winchell, Rogers, and other big names personalized the news for readers who read mostly unbylined copy written by hirelings and pasted together by anonymous editors. By the early 1930s, three press syndicates accounted for most of the prose typeset in American newspapers, providing more column inches than the reporters listed on the masthead: Associated Press (AP), United Press (UP), and International News Service (INS). The three press services held a hegemony over print news akin to that of the evening news programs telecast each night by NBC, CBS, and ABC during the glory days of broadcast television. Whether in New York or Los Angeles or thousands of small towns in between, the Big Three selling their mainly uncredited prose to subscribers standardized the consumption of news.

Associated Press was the oldest and most respected of the triad. Founded in 1846, a mere two years after the telegraph electrified the delivery of news, AP began as a classic cartel: rather than compete for time at the telegraph key, the big New York newspapers arranged to share and bundle news. By the turn of the century, the two-letter, all-caps imprint was better known than the name of any reporter, especially since AP was stingy about giving its scriveners credit.[11] By 1932, AP supplied copy to more than 1,300 newspapers and rightly billed itself as "the greatest clearing house for news in the world."[12]

AP's hustle on the night of the Lindbergh kidnapping showed why it was the team to beat—while confirming the journalistic axiom that it is better to be lucky than smart. In Newark, AP reporter W. A. Kinney was speaking on the phone with a New Jersey state trooper, checking out an inconsequential Lindbergh rumor, when the officer told him to hold the line, a message had just come in over the state police teletype.

"My God! Listen, AP!" yelled the officer. "Here's the State Police alarm. The Lindberghs' baby has been kidnapped!"

Kinney called Lindbergh's unlisted telephone number at Hopewell for confirmation and comment. "I have no statement to make at this time," said Lindbergh, in a tense voice that told Kinney the story was true.

Kinney had the AP bulletin on the wire at 11:03 P.M., simply copying the text of the state police alarm that went out at 10:46 P.M. under the AP logo and sending out a flash, all caps. The teletype machines in city rooms all over the nation rang with the news.

11:03 A. P. FLASH. LINDBERGH BABY KIDNAPPED. DETAILS FOLLOW.

Kinney then alerted AP's Trenton office, manned by twenty-eight-year-old Francis A. Jamieson, who in turn corralled his colleague Samuel G. Blackman from a nearby movie theater. The pair sped out to the Lindbergh home. They were the first journalists on the scene.

Butler Oliver Whately answered the knock on the door. "All we know is the baby isn't here," was his curt response.

After requisitioning a telephone from the closest house—that of a baker, who was not happy about being rousted from a sound sleep—and calling in the report, Blackman hustled back to Highfield. In the dark, he encountered four men, flashlights in hand, climbing into the window of an abandoned farmhouse looking for clues.

"Are you state troopers?" Blackman asked.

"Yes," said one of the men. Blackman knew the voice and, even in the darkness, recognized the profile, "and I am Charles Lindbergh."

Blackman and Lindbergh shook hands but the aviator was in no mood for an interview. "I'm sorry, Blackman, but I can't say anything now," Lindbergh said before returning to the house with two of the troopers.

The third trooper remained near the gate. Blackman pumped the officer for information; perhaps a palm was greased.

Returning to the home of the now wide-awake baker, Blackman phoned in his report to the AP desk in New York. He scooped the world on important details that Lindbergh wanted kept secret: the $50,000 ransom demand, the imprint of a single footprint below the window, and the discovery of a homemade ladder.

As the "leg men" on the scene, and as was now AP custom on a case of national significance, Jamieson or Blackman got byline credit on the stories they filed, but the actual writing was a collaborative effort, with rewrite men in both the Newark and New York bureaus honing the prose that was sent out over the AP wire and typeset in subscribing newspapers.[13] Over the next few days, careful not to push his luck and overstep boundaries, Jamieson got the first reports of a second ransom note sent to the Lindbergh home and a detailed account from Mrs. Lindbergh of the night's events.[14]

AP general manager Kent Cooper savored the margin of victory run up by his boys. "Outside of a man from a local Trenton newspaper, Blackman and Jamieson were the first newspapermen on the scene by several hours, and Associated Press coverage was so complete, comprehensive, accurate, and fast that for hours it was way ahead of all our wire service competitors, and has held that advantage," he beamed. "On the first bulletin, AP was ahead of one wire service by 32 minutes, and of the other wire service, 40 minutes."[15]

United Press meanwhile had secured an inside track on the story that it felt duty bound not to exploit. Officially incorporated in 1907, UP was the brainchild of E. W. Scripps, a visionary editor-publisher who wanted to crush AP's dominance over news gathering almost as much as he wanted to turn a profit. He did both. Being in second place, UP tried harder, and its reporters relished beating AP across the wires—if only by seconds—on an important beat. Yet as its archrival ran away with the Lindbergh story, UP ceded the field at the request of a deep source it could not refuse.

In the early morning hours of March 2, UP chief Karl Bickel was awakened by the telephone. He bolted upright when the caller identified himself and stated his purpose. "This is Colonel Lindbergh," he told Bickel. "We are in serious trouble. My son has been kidnapped."

Lindbergh wanted Bickel's advice on how best to handle the reporters swarming around the grounds at Highfield and likely scaring off the kidnapper from making contact. From New York, Bickel drove out to Hopewell and consulted with Lindbergh and Colonel Breckinridge. Forsaking the duties of his day job, he agreed to serve as Lindbergh's off-the-record media adviser for the duration of the crisis.

Bickel knew that Lindbergh's stature and the dread of causing harm to the baby would compel the press to cooperate. As long as newsmen were informed of important developments, Colonel Schwarzkopf could keep the media beast fed with daily news conferences. Also, the reporters pledged not to follow Lindbergh if he needed to slip away to meet the kidnapper. At no time in the history of journalism, boasted Bickel, "have newspapers gone so far as they have in this case to subordinate their competitive news interest to [the] end that the child be restored."[16]

Bickel was proud that his special access to the Lindberghs was never used to give UP the upper hand. The best token of Lindbergh's trust and confidence was that Bickel was given a copy of the symbol with which the kidnap letter was signed, a document kept locked in his safe at UP headquarters in New York.[17] It was a serious breach of the custody of evidence that would give rise to numerous conspiracy theories.

International News Service was the weak sister in the press syndicate troika. Founded in 1909 by William Randolph Hearst to service his newspaper chain, INS reflected the conservative outlook of "the Chief" and fancied itself a megaphone for the vox populi. Very much a dwarf beside the two giants, the underfunded outfit was derided as a "make-do wire service," but despite its lowly status, or because of it, INS inspired a fierce loyalty within its ranks.[18] AP and UP regularly accused INS of nicking their work product.

The press services, the beat reporters, the celebrity journalists—all knew that what was for the parents a waking nightmare was for them a once-in-a-lifetime career opportunity. Within weeks, two instantly outdated monographs, *True Story of the Lindbergh Kidnapping* by John Brandt and Edith Renaud, and *The Great Lindbergh Hullabaloo* by none other than Laura Vitray, were in bookstores.[19] Sensing a seller's market, other fast-buck artists—in Hollywood, on Broadway—sought to cash in on the tragedy. On the vaudeville stage, performers stopped the show for a moment of prayer and sang songs dedicated to the Lindberghs, but mind-reading acts went on hiatus, fearing questions about the whereabouts of the baby.[20]

Of course, politicians also elbowed in on the action to remind voters of their indispensability. Taking advantage of proximity, New Jersey governor Moore led the pack, shooting his mouth off before radio microphones and newsreel cameras. "I have absolute confidence that the baby will come back, alive and well," he declared early on. "I don't know when, but whenever it is, I am sure the child will be alive and well"—to which Laura Vitray responded, "How the governor got these constant health bulletins on the Lindbergh baby is a subject for conjecture."[21]

Conjecture in fact was the fallback pastime of the day, and not just for politicians. With few facts to report or hot leads to chase down, the press engaged in endless speculation, wishful thinking, and flights of pure fancy. "Return of the kidnapped Charles Lindbergh Jr. was expected hourly last evening," reported the *New York Daily News* on the second day out. A month later, hope was still springing. "Baby Charles Augustus Lindbergh is alive and well" was the soothing word from the *New York Daily Mirror*. The paper was "able to make this statement authoritatively, definitively, and reveal that incontrovertible evidence has come to hand that the child is prospering and will be in the pink of health when returned to his parents."[22] AP reporter Lorena Hickok explained but did not defend the reliance on fantasy. "Day after day, there would be nothing to write except what you could draw out of your imagination, and, after three or four days, imaginations began to wear pretty thin."[23]

Two assumptions informed almost all the press coverage. The first was that the kidnapping was the work of gangsters. The joint was cased, the getaway car was in place, escape routes were mapped out, and dragnets were eluded. Only seasoned, cold-blooded criminals could have successfully brought off such a daring and difficult snatch and held steady in the ensuing hysteria. "Back of the kidnapping of Charles A. Lindbergh Jr. is a story unprecedented in American crime annals—the rise of the gangs since Prohibition and the development of kidnapping for ransom as a major industry," asserted Fred Pasley in the *New York Daily News*. Pasley, the author of the not-ironically-titled *Al Capone: The Biography of a Self-Made Man* (1930), left open the possibility that the crime was the work of "mental delinquents," but his bet was on "organized criminals" as the force behind "the climax of a situation nationwide in scope and co-relative with conditions directly attributable to the Volstead Act," the enabling legislation for the enforcement of Prohibition.[24]

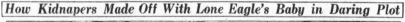

An artist's rendering of the likely kidnapping scenario, from the *New York Daily News*, March 3, 1932.

41

The second assumption was that a woman was involved—who else would take care of the baby? Imaginative depictions of the night of the kidnapping, drawn in comic strip panels, showed two culprits—a man and a woman—skulking in the dead of night. He climbed the ladder and grabbed the child, she quieted the baby and cared for it. The *New York Daily News* referred confidently to "the man and woman who stole the most famous baby in the world."[25]

When not mulling possibilities or conjuring scenarios out of thin air, the press channeled the volcanic fury of an outraged citizenry. "The ravishment of that home by crime becomes a challenge, a personal affront to every decent man and woman, and a disgrace to the nation in which such a thing should occur," seethed the *Washington Evening Star*. The *Philadelphia Record* called the kidnapping a deed so foul "that it overwhelms the mind, bankrupts the capacity for belief . . . [it is] easier to doubt than accept."[26] Could the editors have printed the obscenities snarled in the newsroom, they would have.

Beneath the anger was a deep-dyed, culturewide sense of shame. Depression-wracked, rudderless America had sunk to a new low. A nation that permitted such horror to befall its most cherished couple was nearly as depraved as the kidnappers themselves. "The kidnapping of the Lindbergh baby is a final affront to American civilization," editorialized the *New York Daily Mirror*, seeing a tipping-point moment in the political and moral decline of a once great country. "Federal authorities are powerless before a horde of outlaws bred of Prohibition and financed by malefactors become multi-millionaires in liquor, dope, and other rackets, the last and most profitable of which is abduction for ransom."[27]

The apocalyptic rhetoric fit the temper of the times. Mired in the absolute nadir of the Great Depression, the nation flailed helplessly, free-falling in a downward spiral with no bottom in sight. "Baby Lindbergh has been missing for four days without a clue to his abductors," wrote the *New York Daily Mirror*. "The authorities are floundering." The inevitable conclusion: "There is no use pretending that our existing resources are capable of maintaining law and order."[28] Look no further than the misnamed town of Hopewell for proof that American institutions were dysfunctional, politicians ineffectual, and lawmen impotent.

Yet if the political and social engines of American life were sputtering, the fourth estate was firing on all cylinders. As Walter Winchell noted, New York newsrooms were living up to the stop-the-presses delirium immortalized in *The Front Page*, Ben Hecht and Charles MacArthur's paean to the anything-for-a-scoop ethos of Jazz Age journalism, a Broadway smash in 1928 and a Hollywood hit in 1931. The play inspired a whole cycle of fast-talking newspaper yarns that imprinted the image of a profession of wisecracking cynics for whom nothing was sacred and no means too underhanded to beat out the competition.

In the Lindbergh case, however, the working press did not respond according to type. Frenzy in the newsroom there was, but the usual unbridled glee in covering a juicy story was absent. By all accounts, the hard-boiled cynics were no less heartsick and gut-punched than their readers. "A baby was missing, stolen from his crib on a raw, windy March night," recalled Lorena Hickok. "It didn't matter whose baby—when anything so helpless, so defenseless is missing, people generally react in the same way, and reporters are no exception."[29] In 1936, when memories of the heady days in Hopewell were still fresh, journalist Ishbel Ross reflected, "Reporters are usually impersonal about their work, but this was a story that penetrated the thickest skin."[30] Years later, journalist Quentin Reynolds, who covered the story for INS, also debunked the stock portrait of flippant newshounds cracking wise around the city desk. "It is easy for the cynical to sneer that newspapers and wire services were interested only in breaking what would have been the greatest story of our time, but the attitude of the editors I worked for completely contradicts this viewpoint," recalled Reynolds.[31]

After all, many of the reporters had children of their own.

Kidnappers, Read This

For the Lindberghs, the press served but one useful purpose: it provided a link to the kidnappers. Via the newspapers and radio, the parents could send out a one-way signal they hoped would be picked up by whoever stole their son. The personal communications of the very private couple would be open for all to read, but the self-exposure was the only way to reach the right set of eyes and ears.

The most urgent message concerned the health of the baby, who had been sickly on the night of the kidnapping. On March 2, Anne requested that newspapers print and radio broadcast the items of the baby's diet "in the desperate hope that his kidnappers will follow it":

> One quart of milk, during the day
> Three tablespoonfuls of cooked cereal, morning and night
> Two tablespoons of cooked vegetables, once a day
> Yolk of one egg, once a day
> One baked potato or rice, once a day
> Two tablespoonfuls of stewed fruit daily
> One half cup of orange juice when he awakens in the morning
> One half cup of prune juice after his afternoon nap
> Fourteen drops of Visterol during the day

"If the food is neglected, the results may be serious," warned the *New York Daily Mirror*.[32] "Kidnappers, Read This Diet! Don't Let Baby Die!" begged the *New York Daily News*. "Here, Mr. and Mrs. Kidnapper, is what Charles A. Lindbergh Jr. must have if he is going to live. And, kidnapper of the Lindbergh baby, don't forget the medicine!"[33] Later, Dr. John F. Condon confirmed that the message had reached its intended audience. "We gave him more to eat than we heard in the paper from Mrs. Lindbergh," Cemetery John assured him during their first meeting in Courtland Park.

Two days later, on Friday afternoon, the Lindberghs released to the press another signed, typewritten letter, a facsimile of which ran on the front pages of newspapers everywhere. It was a direct appeal to the kidnappers to make contact. The couple promised to keep the arrangements secret and not prosecute the perpetrators. "Our only interest is in [the baby's] immediate and safe return," they insisted. Shortly after midnight that Sunday morning, also over the couple's signatures, a third letter appointed two shady emissaries to handle the negotiations:

> If the kidnappers of our child are unwilling to deal directly, we fully authorize "Salvy" Spitale and Irving Bitz to act as our go-between.
>
> We will also follow any other method suggested by the kidnappers that we can be sure will bring the return of our child.

Spitale and Bitz were middle-level hoods associated with the recently rubbed-out bootlegger Jack "Legs" Diamond. That America's knight of the air felt compelled to consort with such lowlifes was fresh proof of a fragmenting social order. "No one can blame Colonel and Mrs. Lindbergh for adopting the most practical course for the return of their child," wrote an abashed editorial in the *New York Post*. "That the process should compel the naming of two such envoys as 'Salvy' Spitale and Irving Bitz is one of the most bitter of comments, not upon them but upon American life today."[34]

The other set of one-way communications—the ads put in the *Bronx Home News* and the *New York American* by the mysterious Jafsie—were signal flares too obvious to escape detection by journalists on high alert. Also, Condon was a chronic chatterbox who could not resist dropping hints about his brave and selfless intervention in the case. As reporters examined the Jafsie messages and followed the breadcrumb trail to Condon, word that something Lindbergh-related was afoot circulated in Bronx neighborhoods and New York newsrooms. Still, out of deference to Lindbergh, the reporters kept the lid on. The editor of the *Bronx Home News*, who from the start had been privy to the secret negotiations between Condon and Cemetery John, sent out a calculated piece of disinformation. "There has been nothing to indicate definitely that the 'ads' have any bearing on the Lindbergh kidnapping and their significance is a matter of conjecture," he lied.[35]

Conjecture became near certainty when, after the ransom had been paid and the baby had not been returned, the ads turned panic-stricken. In the *Bronx Home News*, an urgent plea from Jafsie was published repeatedly:

What is wrong? Have you crossed me? Please better direction.

On April 5, through Colonel Schwarzkopf at the statehouse in Trenton, Lindbergh repeated his plea for the press to stand down and allow him to move about freely. Walter Lippmann, the eminent editorial writer for the *New York Herald-Tribune*, gave his colleagues a piece of blunt advice: back off. The newspapers must "call off their reporters and detectives and let Colonel Lindbergh alone."[36]

Newspaper readers agreed in theory, but in fact they were gobbling up whatever Lindbergh news the press printed. Besides, a competitive-by-nature profession could not live long in self-denial. On April 6, W. O. Wood, treasurer of the United States, sent out a circular to the nation's banks asking tellers to be on the alert for a list of serial numbers. The amount of the bills added up to $50,000—the precise amount that had been reported as the

Lindbergh ransom. The press drew the logical conclusion. On April 9, at least two newspapers—the *Newark Evening News* in an early morning extra and the *New York World-Telegram* in its afternoon edition—bannered the news.

Lindbergh panicked: he wanted no news of the ransom exchange published or broadcast. In the ensuing hours, he maneuvered behind the scenes to suppress the information, pleading with the managing editors of the wire services to kill the story.

The mainstream media of the day cooperated fully, quashing a story already transmitted by the wire services. AP, UP, and INS sent out kill notices telling subscribers to stop the presses if need be. AP's message read:

> A story about efforts of the United States Treasurer to trace certain banknotes may be injurious to the Lindbergh search if published. The Associated Press is NOT carrying and suggests the desirability of all papers refraining from publishing.

Compliance was almost universal—almost. The *New York Daily News*, the largest circulation tabloid in the nation, broke ranks. On that Saturday night, April 9, just as Lindbergh thought he had contained the damage, the first edition of its Sunday morning paper was on the streets with the story of the Treasury Department's search for the banknotes.

Lindbergh had no option but to go public. That same evening, at 10 P.M., he released a letter through Colonel Schwarzkopf that formally broke the news and revealed heretofore unconfirmed and unknown facts. On radio and in the newspapers, Americans learned some of what had transpired since Condon received his first letter: that a kidnapper had been in touch ("properly identified as such," though the statement did not say how) and that $50,000 in ransom money had been paid. Lindbergh said he had not intended to have the money traced by federal authorities, but since the baby had not been returned and the kidnappers had not been in touch, he had no alternative but to cooperate with the T-men. He confessed himself "duped" in what the *New York Times* called "a deception as cruel as the crime itself."[37]

Lindbergh did not reveal who had paid the ransom, but the web of secrecy covering the past weeks was unraveling fast. The next day, Lindbergh issued another statement revealing that the ransom note left in the nursery contained a symbol or sign which provided certain identification. He still had not identified Condon as the intermediary, but by then the newspapers were naming him as the Jafsie whose ads had attracted so much notice. The main suspect all but confirmed his identity. "Colonel Lindbergh has told me not to do any talking," Condon said coyly when reporters besieged his home.[38]

Again, it was the *New York Daily News* that broke the wall of silence. Like the *Bronx Home News*, the *Daily News* scented Condon's role almost from the beginning, but when a reporter confronted Condon, he uncharacteristically clammed up. Hearing that his nemesis had the inside scoop, Lindbergh implored Capt. J. M. Patterson, publisher of the *Daily News*, and Frank Hause, managing editor, not to go to press. The negotiations were in a delicate stage; the life of his son was literally at risk.

The *New York Daily News* got the message: even New York's definitive scoop-obsessed tabloid balked at being in any way responsible for harm coming to Little Lindy. The paper withdrew its reporter from the vicinity of Condon's house and kept mum about his role in the ransom exchange.

After Lindbergh's late-night statement on April 9, however, the *New York Daily News* could sit on the story no more. That same night they interviewed Condon for attribution. *Editor & Publisher* reported that, for a period of weeks before the revelation, all the wire services and most New York and New Jersey newspapers had known that Condon was Jafsie but had held the story "out of deference of Colonel Lindbergh's wishes."

On April 10, the Sunday edition of the *Daily News* featured a picture of Dr. John F. Condon coaching a girls' physical fitness class under the caption "This Man Is Jafsie." Condon was quoted as expressing the belief that the kidnappers would ultimately make good on the return of the baby. "Col. Lindbergh will hear from them in a day or so and his child will come back to him, never fear," he predicted.[39]

That same Sunday, the *Bronx Home News* revealed that its regular contributor Dr. John F. Condon was the Jafsie who had placed the cryptic ads and who had acted as intermediary in the ransom exchange. The emergence of Condon, a born ham, was a godsend to the newspapers. The man was a source of endless aggravation to the police, but he made great copy.

Newspaper readers had plenty to pore over in the Sunday papers that day. The night before, the Department of the Treasury made public the serial numbers of the $5 notes and the $10 and $20 gold certificate bills paid out as ransom, all issued in 1928. Newspapers printed the complete list in numerical and denominational order so bank tellers, cashiers, and average citizens could look for a telltale bill. In the *New York Times*, the space allotted to the list occupied more than eighteen columns of figures. "It was an amazing typographical spectacle," said the professionals at *Editor & Publisher*, who had never seen anything like it.[40]

The silence of the press on the ransom notes and the identity of Jafsie was an extraordinary testament to the force of the Lindbergh aura. *Editor & Publisher*, the self-appointed voice of responsible journalism in America, praised the self-censorship and marveled at the restraint and decency of a medium reputed to be run by cutthroat competitors. "For the first time in the history of the American press, a voluntary partial, or case, censorship has been established to aid the poignant cause of a citizen, without regard to the fixed rights of newspaper readers or any of the customary obligations attaching to a free press and in almost total disregard of competitive newspaper practices." For more than forty days, the press had refrained from publishing what it knew out of deference to Lindbergh and out of terror that, should any harm befall his son, it would be held accountable in the court of public opinion.[41]

On the night of April 14, in a public statement issued over his signature, Lindbergh thanked the press for its cooperation and asked it to continue the self-restraint:

> Mrs. Lindbergh and I want to express our great appreciation to those members of the press who in many instances have given us their cooperation often to their own disadvantage. It is of utmost importance for us and our representatives to move about without being questioned or followed, and we are again requesting the complete cooperation of all members of the press to this end.[42]

Under the caution "not for publication," Lindbergh also telegrammed the editors of the wire services with a personal expression of gratitude.[43]

With the floodgates now open, reporters and cameramen staked out Condon's residence—a modest frame house located at 2974 Decatur Avenue in the Bronx—and followed his movements. On April 11, Condon appeared on his front porch and debuted his bizarre persona, waving an American flag over his head and explaining why he would not grant an interview.

The next night, the mercurial Condon relented. "I had contacts with the kidnappers and have direct contacts with them still," he said, the first part of the statement being true, the second part false. "I have never identified them nor said a word against them. I value my life as they value theirs, and I know my life would not be worth anything if I said anything against them." Condon was a wild card, but he seemed sincere when he said, "I would be the happiest man in the world if I could place the baby's arms around his mother's neck."

Lindbergh meanwhile was pursuing other options. Even while Condon was negotiating with Cemetery John, the distraught father was running down another lead. A prominent shipbuilder from Norfolk, Virginia, named John Hughes Curtis claimed to be in touch with the kidnappers, by his account a four-man gang of seafaring Scandinavians. Grasping at any straw, Lindbergh followed Curtis's instructions—implausible as they were—and spent days sailing up and down the coast of Virginia searching for contact men who never materialized.

Through late April and early May, while Condon continued to post increasingly desperate ads and Lindbergh was jerked around by Curtis, the case remained stuck in neutral. Based on a linguistic analysis of the ransom letters and a forensic analysis of the handmade ladder, federal agents put together a rough profile of the suspect, but no solid leads emerged as to his identity or whereabouts.

More troubling, no proof of the baby's life had been offered by either Cemetery John or John Hughes Curtis. Nonetheless, hopes remained high for his safe recovery. Soon after the kidnapping, crime reporter Edward D. Sullivan had cautioned that "only too often *the victim already is dead when the demand for ransom is made*," but that prospect was too terrible to ponder.[44] Whether in print or conversation, Americans seemed to have entered into a shared agreement not to speak the unspeakable. "I am convinced, as this book goes to press, that the son of Charles and Anne Lindbergh is well and safe," declared Laura Vitray on April 12, 1932, in *The Great Lindbergh Hullabaloo*.[45] How Vitray—any more than New Jersey governor Moore—got her health updates on the Lindbergh baby is, as she said of him, a subject of conjecture.

Forced or not, optimism for the eventual return of Lindbergh baby was nearly official public policy. In Schenectady, New York, the city fathers made arrangements for a local celebration once the Lindbergh baby was redeemed: every fire whistle would blow, every church bell would ring, and the townspeople would swarm into the streets for a joyous thanksgiving.[46] Certainly, before too long, Little Lindy would be back in the arms of his mother—safe and "in the pink of health."

Chapter 3
A MEDIUM OF AUDIBLE JOURNALISM

L
ess than an hour after the New Jersey State Police sent out the official teletype at 10:46 P.M., radio bulletins were beaming out word of the Lindbergh baby kidnapping. The "bulletin"—a recent coinage whose roots traced back to the papal bull posted on a Vatican wall—marked a new way of harking to the news. It was a return to the oldest form of communication—the human voice—though the message was not delivered face to face or bellowed by a town crier but transmitted from a central station and sent out to all, "broadcast" like the seeds tossed onto a field by a farmer.

Across the nation, even before headlines were splashed across the pages of the newspaper extras, the shocking news crackled out over the radio airwaves. No extra edition of a newspaper—whose contents had to be typed on a clunky Underwood, typeset, composited, printed, distributed, and hawked by newsboys—could outpace the speed of electricity. No matter how hot off the presses, the news had cooled by the time it hit the streets. Hungry for up-to-the-minute information on the Lindbergh case, Americans switched media allegiances and answered a new calling. Henceforth, when news broke, they no longer rushed to the corner newsstand; they reached for the dial.

The writing—airing?—had been on the wall since the late 1920s. In 1931, Merlin H. Aylesworth, president of NBC, warned his print-based colleagues of the media future, like it or not. "The public insists on hot news," he told a conference at Princeton University. "That is why newspapers use telephones, telegraph, and cables. But the speed of transmission of news has far outstripped the speed of the mechanical processes required to convert it into print for readers. Consequently, if radio broadcasting can serve the public with certain kinds of news sooner than the newspaper, are we to ignore the public's best interests for private gain?"[1]

Not likely—especially when the public's best interests coincided with the private gain of the radio industry. In March 1932, the mature state of the hardware and the magnetic pull of the narrative—the penetration of radio technology into American life combined with a ravenous appetite for information about the Lindbergh case—converged to upend a media hierarchy, a first-place position broadcasting would not relinquish until the rise of digital technology. For the newspaper business, the instantaneous alerts of a radio bulletin and the electric jolt of live reporting were bracing portents of a subaltern future. After the Lindbergh kidnapping, print was yesterday's news.

Radiogeniety

The formal appearance of radio on the American cultural horizon dates from 1920, when KDKA in Pittsburgh launched its broadcasting days with the announcement of the election of Warren G. Harding, a piece of news almost no one, even in Pittsburgh, heard on radio. By 1924, however, the electoral college tally that put Republican candidate Calvin Coolidge over the top was monitored hour by hour over what the *New York Times* called "a new feature in national elections this year," namely "the broadcasting throughout the country of the returns as fast as they were gathered."[2] Early adopters tuned in over temperamental, credenza-size radio sets, perhaps drawn less by the need for news or the sound of music than the thrill of homing in on a remote beacon.

While blasting out a soundtrack to the Jazz Age, radio spread through the American atmosphere with astonishing speed. A blue-chip gold mine, it helped fuel the bull market on Wall Street. In 1925, the stock of the Radio Corporation of America (RCA), the parent company for the National Broadcasting Company, was valued at $11 a share; in 1929, before disaster struck, at $114.[3] To be in the radio business was to be in the money.

The sonic racket from the merging of electricity and sound only grew louder as the Jazz Age played on. Along with the rumble of electronic amplification and the songs from the phonograph, the din from radio made the 1920s America's first sound-crazy decade, a sonic wave of music, voices, and ambient noise coming in at the switch of a dial. On October 6, 1927, with the premiere of Warner Bros.'s landmark musical-melodrama *The Jazz Singer*, the motion-picture medium got in line with Vitaphone's sound-on-disk process, another sign that silence was no longer golden.[4]

What communications scholars call "penetration"—the injection of a mass medium into the bloodstream of a culture—can be measured by statistics and sales, but it can also be pegged to a tipping-point year or linchpin event. Typically, a new media technology prospers by feeding off an item of must-have software, usually an entertainment show, that persuades the consumer to purchase the expensive hardware needed to partake of the tantalizing new diversion. In the late 1940s, Americans bought televisions to watch Milton Berle on *Texaco Star Theater*; in the early 1960s, they bought color televisions to watch *Bonanza*; and in the early 2000s, they bought subscriptions to HBO to watch *The Sopranos*.

For radio, the tipping-point year was 1930, and the must-have software was *The Amos 'n' Andy Show*, a pop cult phenomenon of colossal proportions. Two white men—Charles Correll and Freeman Godsen, a pair of former vaudevillians—built their comedic shtick around the raspy patter of what the trade press called "blackface dialect chatter," a byplay heavy on thick accents, malapropisms, and fractured syntax.[5] The fabricated slang bequeathed catchphrases to the American vernacular ("check and double check" "Holy mack'el!"), idioms that floated infectiously "through the ether," as the phrase went. During its nightly broadcast on NBC from 7:00 to 7:15 P.M., except Sundays, pedestrians strolling down streets in New York never missed a second of the broadcast: radios in every window in every apartment were all tuned in.

But why walk the streets when you could chuckle over *Amos 'n' Andy* in the privacy of your home? Radio soon became a household appliance as desired as—sometimes more desired than—the refrigerator. Not even the stock market crash could halt its incursion into American living rooms. According to NBC's Aylesworth, by 1931 the number of radio receivers had grown to fifteen million sets serving some fifty million listeners, a surge that made radio the sixth largest industry in the United States.[6]

The popularity of *The Amos 'n' Andy Show* accrued to the benefit of other slots on the schedule. Collateral airtime needed to be filled—not just with sitcoms, melodramas, and variety shows, but with a cheap placeholder that was a natural adjunct to entertainment programming—news.

Immediately preceding the most popular show on radio was a fifteen-minute news program hosted by Floyd Gibbons. Based at the *Chicago Tribune*, Gibbons was already a celebrity journalist, globe-trotting adventurer, and best-selling author when radio beckoned. Sporting a white eyepatch over his left eye, lost at Belleau Wood during the Great War, he became the first radio-born glamour boy in the news business, the father of every dashing war correspondent from Edward R. Murrow to Dexter Filkins.

Gibbons's debut broadcast was on Chicago's WGN on Christmas Day, 1925, lured by station manager Quin A. Ryan to talk about the far-distant lands in which he had spent his exotic but lonely Christmas pasts. Five hundred sympathetic listeners were moved to send Gibbons invitations to Christmas dinner. In 1929, Aylesworth recruited him to host a coast-to-coast hookup on NBC. Billed as "The Headline Hunter" and sponsored by the *Literary Digest*, Gibbons covered the news twice nightly in a patented "staccato machine gun like delivery" clocked at 217 words per minute. By 1930, Gibbons had become "a 'name' of prodigious significance on the air."[7]

The key to Gibbons's success—his *radiogeniety*—was the emotional bond he forged with his listeners. He spoke with a fluency and informality new to radio. "Fortunately, he had never heard of the hackneyed speakers of the radio; he had not fallen a victim to the universal notion that broadcast speakers should imitate one another and thus all speak patronizingly or bombastically," recalled WGN's Ryan. "From the radio standpoint, he was a sensation!"[8]

Gibbons had instinctively mastered the art of communication before a radio microphone: not as an orator at a podium pompously exhorting an imagined crowd of thousands but as an intimate friend across the table. Gibbons said that his technique was "to imagine I am just sitting in a circle of my friends, yarning away as the spirit moves me—not giving a prepared lecture—not paying painful attention to precise selection of words—to grammatical construction—to logical sequence—just talking in a conversational flow with people that I know and love and people who feel just as I do about a large number of things."[9] It was a talent cultivated by all the great maestros of conversational radio in the 1930s—whether cordial politicians like FDR and New York mayor Fiorello LaGuardia, soft-spoken raconteurs like Arthur Godfrey and Will Rogers, or the new breed of on-air journalists who were a blend of both.

The Most Important Story In Radio's History

WOR, the independent Newark-based station serving New Jersey and the greater New York area, claimed pride of place for the first on-air bulletin about the Lindbergh kidnapping. *Variety* checked WOR's station logs and verified the claim. "Control room records from the station confirmed that the first mention was made at 11:35 P.M. the night the baby disappeared."[10]

In the days to come, rival radio stations would claim to have beaten WOR on its home turf. WAAB in Boston logged 11:29:30 as the precise time that announcer Don Morton, standing by to give the station's call letters, broke into programming with a twenty-five-word bulletin after receiving a teletype from the *Boston Herald*. WIP-WFAN in New York said it flashed the news thirty seconds later at 11:30, and WGST in Atlanta claimed the earliest time of all, at 11:15 P.M.[11]

At the first alert, the embryonic radio networks marshalled their forces to cover the story in full force. In 1932, two major networks blanketed the nation: NBC, the behemoth, so huge it was divided into the Red and Blue Networks, and CBS, the up-and-coming rival hoping to outhustle the two-headed monster. NBC had an unbeatable entertainment line-up, so CBS counterprogrammed by specializing in news. Being in second—or third—place, CBS was hungry and aggressive.[12]

Shortly after midnight, after CBS got the news from the wire services in New York, a report went out over the entire CBS chain from WBBM in Chicago.[13] At 12:14 A.M., CBS announcer Harlow Wilcox interrupted an orchestra performing at the Granada Café to read the bulletin to the ninety-one-station network. By the next morning, CBS had established remote hookups in Hopewell, Trenton, and Princeton. "When word of the kidnapping first flashed, CBS press relations men, most of whom by sheer coincidence happened to be in the studios, were quick to realize that the most important story in radio's history had 'broken,' " observed *Broadcasting*, the radio-centric trade weekly.[14] CBS president William S. Paley understood that news, especially Lindbergh news, drew listeners to his spot on the dial.[15]

Yet radio was still not secure in its role as a gatherer and disseminator of information. Though CBS had the story nailed and the police in Trenton on the record, the network refrained from broadcasting the news of the Lindbergh kidnapping until a newspaper or wire service had verified the story. (Trenton police logged a telephone inquiry about the kidnapping from CBS at 11:58 P.M. that night; it was the only radio outlet to call for confirmation.[16]) Only after the *New York Times* gave its imprimatur did CBS air the bulletin.[17]

NBC played catch-up, breaking the news shortly after CBS and putting into service the superior hardware of its parent company, RCA. "From the morning of March [2] until 2:00 A.M., March 8, a constant vigil was kept, a period of 148 hours, after which normal operating schedules were resumed," *Broadcasting* reported. "Even then the engineering crews were kept on duty, ready to put dispatches on the air at a moment's notice." NBC assigned William Burke "Skeets" Miller, director of special broadcast events, to the story. Miller possessed sterling credentials: in 1925, for the *Louisville Courier Journal*, he had won a Pulitzer Prize for his reporting on the doomed spelunker Floyd Collins.[18] The first radioman on the scene in Hopewell, however, was NBC announcer Edward Thorgerson, who planted himself in prime real

NBC announcer Edward Thorgerson commands a table at Gebhart's Lunch Room in Hopewell, New Jersey, to broadcast the latest bulletins on the Crime of the Century, March 6, 1932.

estate: a table in the window of Gebhart's Lunch Room, where he set up a remote transmitter for live broadcasts.

Both NBC and CBS deployed mobile transmitting stations mounted on trucks to relay news by shortwave from locations around New Jersey. The trucks roamed the state, driving back and forth from Hopewell to Trenton, broadcasting on a fifty-watt transmitter to receiving and relay stations in Princeton and New York, and thence for broadcast "to the whole anxious world." CBS requisitioned the sound truck from WCAU, its Philadelphia outlet, but its main studio was in a tiny vacant room over Gebhart's in Hopewell. Its other microphones were in Trenton and Princeton. CBS also established quarters near the Lindbergh home, broadcast from planes, and, *Variety* recalled disapprovingly, "did all manner of stunts."[19]

Radio edged ever closer to the source of the news when Col. H. Norman Schwarzkopf permitted WOR to install a microphone on his desk at state police headquarters in Trenton. By the early morning hours of March 2, WOR had set up a remote broadcasting unit that stayed on the air continuously for the next seventy-two hours. By the second night, Colonel Schwarzkopf was speaking live on WOR from his office in Trenton, giving out updates on the case and reading statements from the Lindberghs. "Much of the most important news given out then reached the public through this medium before newspapermen were even summoned to Schwarzkopf's office for the bulletins," gloated *Broadcasting*.[20]

Radio solidified its status as the go-to source for breaking news by interrupting entertainment programs with urgent news bulletins—or at least the interruptions made the bulletins seem urgent. "If a commercial program happens to be on the air at the moment, the news flash is immediately inserted if sufficiently important," *Variety* reported. "So far no advertiser has complained."[21] Nor would they: viewers drawn to radio for Lindbergh news would stick around to hear the commercials. Also, while radio interrupted entertainment shows, it was careful not to step into the airtime allotted for paid advertisements.

"Radio has scooped the daily press on almost all news stories of national and international importance for the past two years," *Variety* pointed out in its first think piece on the media aspects of the Lindbergh kidnapping. "Since the simple procedure of getting a story on the air doesn't include the more involved newspaper process, the element of time gives radio a big edge in high speed dissemination of news."[22] The phrase "big edge" was an understatement. In a business where minutes meant the difference between a hot scoop and a dead letter, newspapers were being left in the dust.

An editorial in *Broadcasting* savored the reversal of media fortunes. "If anyone has any lingering doubts as to radio's rightful claim to being a medium of 'audible journalism,' " boasted the trade publication, the developments in Hopewell "significantly point out the growing stature of broadcasting as a purveyor of news." The evidence was there for all to hear:

> Broadcasters practically cleared their wires and wave lengths for the reports and bulletins on the Lindbergh kidnapping case. Radio reporters, heard via remote controls from strategic points, were accepted by the Lindberghs and by officials on a par with the press reporters who swarmed Hopewell village. When the Lindberghs made their first appeals to the kidnappers in the hope they might be listening in, their statements were given to the radio as well as the press.

The result? "Radio stations occupy much the same place in their communities that newspapers do."[23]

What the newspapers found especially galling was that they were often beaten out by their own reporting. How did radio acquire the news it broadcast? "We swiped it," confessed radio newsman Lowell Thomas.[24] Broadcasters subscribed to the wire services and bought the newspapers, read the teletypes aloud, rifled the pages for headlines and details, and copyedited the prose for broadcast over the air. Newspaper editors were not mollified by the appended afterthought: "For further information and complete details, we refer you to your favorite morning and evening newspapers."

Furious about being outrun on a story they would have owned just a few years earlier, the print press retaliated. On Friday, March 4, the three wire services—AP, UP, and INS—stopped providing news bulletins to NBC and CBS. Finally, said a frustrated newspaper editor, "the news services have awakened to the fact that they were feeding the dogs that bite them."[25]

The petulant wire services should have predicted the blowback from the cutoff. Without copy coming in from the teletype, radio stations were forced to send their own correspondents into the field. "Networks also have their own men at the Lindbergh home now, reporting in by remote control," noted a surprised *Variety.* The reports on radio, *Broadcasting* emphasized, were gathered "not merely by the cooperation of the press but by their own 'radio reporters' on the scene, provided by remote control." The quotation marks—"radio reporters"—highlight the novelty of the job description.

Sensing the ground shifting, newspapers lectured the upstart and headlined its mistakes. "The indiscriminate broadcasting of unverified news has marked radio's activities in the Lindbergh case since its inception," claimed the *Brooklyn Daily Eagle* after a New Jersey station broadcast a false report that the baby had been found. "To put it mildly, these broadcasters went 'haywire' in their effort to outdo competitors in putting out the very latest developments in the case."[26]

A huffy editorial in the *New York Daily Mirror* distilled the complaints of a regime under siege:

> Radio broadcasting, wildly speculative and inaccurate, has done more to complicate the problem and confuse it than any other one element involved in the search. Broadcasters giving ostensible news of the situation at fifteen and thirty-minute intervals have found themselves without information of news value and forced to disseminate purely speculative material, much of it sensational in tone, with the result of creating nationwide hysteria.

The conscientious citizen had but one place to turn for reliable information:

> Nothing could better illustrate the fact that newspapers remain, as before radio broadcasting began, the sole trustworthy media. The Lindbergh abduction is the first really important news story dealt with by radio broadcasting stations, and it is impossible to evade the conclusion that they have muffed it deplorably.[27]

Yet for the print press the hard truth was that radio had not muffed its chance but run with the opportunity. Microphone in hand, portable equipment in tow, radio journalists had elbowed into space that was once the exclusive preserve of print reporters. In December 1933, a short-lived non-aggression pact was negotiated in the press-radio wars, but all attempts by newspapers and press syndicates to stifle broadcast news coverage would be doomed by the expansion of the networks' own in-house news operations.[28]

For radio, the full-immersion coverage of the Lindbergh case had long-term benefits. A breaking news story often presses untested technology into service and stretches both people and machines to new limits. For Lindbergh news, radio not only interrupted regular programming, it extended its broadcasting day into the wee hours. Between 1 A.M. and 7 A.M., radio stations were off the air, their transmitters turned off and cold, neither sending nor receiving signals. Before becoming operational the next morning, the equipment needed to be turned on and warmed up, a process that took around twenty minutes, potentially eating up precious minutes if news broke. To avoid the time lag, in an unprecedented gambit, "the major networks have protected themselves against a press beat in the Lindbergh case by keeping their transmitters going all night," reported *Variety*. "The networks' staffs have been on the job 24 hours a day, the atmosphere closely resembling that of any paper's city room." The trade weekly underlined the takeaway: "The Lindbergh kidnapping which broke shortly after 11 o' clock at night, when all stations were going full blast . . . accentuated the radio edge in news reporting more than previous yarns."[29]

Not least, the Lindbergh case gave radio technicians priceless experience in the skill sets needed—and the seat-of-the-pants improvisations required— for the broadcasting of live news. Especially valuable was the time spent coordinating transmissions from multiple locations. CBS pulled off an historic "four-point broadcast," one from a stationary sound truck and the others from units in Hopewell, Princeton, and Trenton. *Broadcasting* called the remote-control coverage of the Lindbergh kidnapping "perhaps the greatest example of spot news reporting by radio in the history of American broadcasting."[30]

As radio engineers flaunted their technical proficiency, newsmen were honing their reportorial chops. Beset by static, missed cues, and interviewees frozen by "mike fright," they remained calm and unfazed in the flop sweat–inducing pressure cooker of live broadcasting. Studio announcers and on-the-scene reporters learned to think and talk on their feet. They mastered the complexities of the case and assumed the proper tone—serious, concerned, never glib or chipper. No longer blustery orators or hectoring pitchmen, they turned into cool and collected journalists.

For technicians and on-air reporters alike, the hard-won expertise acquired during the Lindbergh broadcasts would be put into service for all the great live-action news stories of the 1930s—the raucous disorder of the national political conventions; the stunning abdication of King Edward VIII, broadcast by shortwave live from Windsor Castle on December 11, 1936; and the menacing bark of Adolf Hitler, sent out from faraway Vienna,

Munich, and Berlin. The urgent tones of the radio reporters and the static glitches in the live feeds would be mimicked to devastating effect for another epochal story emanating from New Jersey—the invasion from Mars as broadcast by Orson Welles's production of *The War of the Worlds* on October 30, 1938.

Commentaries on What Is in Everybody's Evening Newspaper

Though anyone with crisp enunciation might seem worthy of a seat at the radio microphone, a select breed of charismatic vocalists soon emerged from the chorus—spectral audio personalities, heard but not seen, luring in listeners with their seductive tones. Many began as mere announcers—electronic-age town criers—before evolving into true newsmen and commentators—guides who interpreted a complex work and mulled its meaning. A "good special announcer gets the color, the side lights, the human-interest details in the events he's covering," commented Cecelia Ager in *Variety*, taking note of the new species and presuming the gender. "His romantic and imaginative turn of mind supplies him with the incidental high lights so that he doesn't have to repeat himself and so bore his audience."[31]

There was little chance of the Lindbergh case boring radio audiences—and plenty of opportunity for "special announcers" to prove their specialness. Just as the plight of Floyd Collins had propelled Skeets Miller to national prominence and Pulitzer plaudits, the kidnapping would enhance—or make—the career of more than one obscure reporter-commentator.

Radio's prize catch for prestige and dignity was Lowell Thomas. Renowned from his print reporting and books, above all his best-selling *With Lawrence in Arabia*, published in 1924, Thomas first came to NBC in 1930 as a button-down replacement for the hard-drinking, fast-talking Floyd Gibbons. Billed as "the *Literary Digest*'s new radio voice, informing and entertaining you with the latest news of the day," the unflappable Thomas oozed sanity and probity.[32] He kept to a prodigious work ethic and maintained a multimedia profile: in addition to his radio broadcasts, he wrote articles and books, starred in the novelty short series *Paramount Pictorial* (1932), and, beginning in 1934, narrated Fox Movietone News. He greeted his radio listeners with a friendly, even-keeled salutation, "Good evening, everybody."

In 1932, Thomas's radio showcase was *Topics in Brief*, a fifteen-minute news-of-the-day recap broadcast out of WJZ in New York, the flagship station for NBC's Blue Network. "Besides his experience and talents as a spieler, [Thomas] has an unusual background as a traveler, explorer, and adventurer," noted media critic Robert Landry. "He's been places and done things and, like the true citizen of the world, is full of interesting details that fit nicely and neatly into his newscasts."[33]

The day after the Lindbergh kidnapping, Thomas devoted most of his broadcast to the crime.

> I am sorry to say tonight that there is no favorable news about the Lindbergh baby. The mystery of the kidnapping seems to be as blank as ever.
>
> The Lindbergh home near Hopewell, New Jersey, is an isolated house in the country. Last night at seven-thirty the baby was put to bed by his mother and his nurse. At ten o'clock the nurse discovered the child was missing. Sometime between seven-thirty and ten a man stole up to the house and put a ladder to the window of the child's room. His footprints were later found in the soft ground. . . . He took the child, and carried him down the ladder.

Thomas signed off with a simple, melancholy statement of fact: "The world's most famous baby has been kidnapped, and the attention of literally the whole world has been aroused, and in all the civilized countries of this globe, the kidnapping of the Lindbergh baby has caused the deepest sympathy and interest."[34]

Thomas's competition at CBS was the erudite descendent of a German baron, a man who looked and sounded the part, the full-throated baritone H. V. Kaltenborn—the H stood for Hans and the V stood for Von, and using the initials was a smart career move after the anti-German hysteria of the Great War. A former associate editor of the *Brooklyn Daily Eagle* who specialized in fact-finding trips abroad, he nearly matched Thomas in miles logged. In 1922, he got in on the ground floor of the medium with a weekly current-events show on WEAF, billed as a "newspaper of the air." He could improvise an entire show, going on the air without a written script and speaking off the cuff.

In 1932, Kaltenborn hosted three fifteen-minute programs weekly under the title *Kaltenborn Edits the News*. Despite the bombastic cadences and oracular persona, he was a gutsy pundit, more cantankerous and opinionated than Thomas. From 1933 onward, he denounced Nazi Germany for reasons as personal as ideological: while Kaltenborn was visiting Berlin on assignment, his son Rolf was punched in the face by a stormtrooper for failing to raise his arm in the Hitler salute.[35]

The day after the kidnapping, Kaltenborn condemned "the dastardly act" and called for the passing of a federal kidnapping law. He noted that parents—like the Lindberghs—typically prefer to "accede to the ransom demands rather than run the danger of bodily harm coming to their loved ones." Like many newsmen, Kaltenborn was convinced that the kidnapping was the work of an organized gang spawned by Prohibition.[36] As such, the crime was not just an assault on the Lindberghs but "a blot on the country."[37]

H. V. Kaltenborn and Lowell Thomas were already brand names in 1932. Boake Carter was not, but the Lindbergh case would make him one. A Philadelphia newspaper reporter who broadcast on CBS affiliate WCAU, Carter cut a dashing figure and boasted an exotic resumé. Born in Baku, Russia, the son of a British oilman, he had served in the Royal Air Force during the Great War. After the war, he knocked around oil fields in South America and Oklahoma, before landing as a newspaperman in Philadelphia.[38] Despite years in America, he never quite lost—or stopped affecting—his "peculiarly burred English accent."

When the Lindbergh story broke, CBS sent its A-team from New York to Hopewell—where, it turned out, nothing was happening—while the B-team, including Carter, was dispatched to Trenton. At the state capital, Governor Moore and Colonel Schwarzkopf were speaking before every microphone thrust into their faces. Though generating little hard news, they provided reams of broadcast-worthy copy. Trenton, not Hopewell, was the place to score interviews and soak up information.

From March 2, 1932, onward, Carter was heard over CBS's nationwide hookup. His reports kept listeners rapt and faithful. "Looking over the scripts of Carter's Trenton broadcasts now, it is hard to understand why they clicked," puzzled *New Yorker* essayist A. J. Liebling in a profile of the newsman in 1938. Carter favored fatuous expressions like "Great Scott!" and "By jingoes!" and portentous declarations like "That's a very, *very* significant fact." The other signature Carter verbal tick was the chipper British sign off "Cheerio!" "The incongruous valedictory, after a daily record of disappointments, made people remember Carter," noted Liebling, at a loss to explain why.[39]

CBS news commentator Boake Carter in 1936. His passionate broadcasts during the Lindbergh kidnapping made his career.

After a few days in Trenton, with no very, *very* significant facts to report, Carter filled air time by editorializing—decrying the corrosive brew of political corruption, gangsters, and Prohibition that nurtured the epidemic of kidnapping. He also vented his anger at the kidnappers who, "if they had a spark of manhood," would return the baby to his grieving parents. He broke no scoop, but he connected with listeners who craved Lindbergh news and shared his sentiments. Liebling admitted that "the strange quality of the Boakan voice, grave, energetic and British, impressed itself on minds strained to an attention that has not been duplicated since." *Variety* also took note of the curious phenomenon that was Boake Carter. "Carter's address, in a distinct British accent, sounds artificial, but seems to react well with the general public," who showered him with fan mail. "At 7:45 P.M. his news summaries are baked over commentaries on what is in everybody's evening newspaper," continued *Variety*. "Carter merely makes it simpler by analyzing for the listener rather than making him read and figure for himself."[40]

What *Variety* saw as a flaw was precisely what drew listeners into the orbit of the special announcers: not to absorb a just-the-facts recital of information read in a detached monotone, but to hear a reassuring voice that sifted and filtered, that lent emotional valance, that brought order to the chaotic news of the day. No less than the characters in a soap opera, the familiar voices of the radio commentator lent the illusion of intimacy, even if the relationship was only one-sided.

A Kind of Talkie Newsreel: The *March of Time*

The rise of the radio commentators coincided with another landmark innovation in airborne journalism: the introduction of the *March of Time* radio show. Premiering on March 6, 1931, the *March of Time* was the broadcasting arm of Henry R. Luce's *Time* magazine empire and a pioneering venture in media synergy. The show set the template for what became a broadcasting evergreen: the docudrama.

Founded in 1925, *Time* was one of the great publishing successes of the twentieth century. The weekly magazine boasted a loyal and seemingly Depression-proof subscription base of 350,000, and its total readership probably doubled or tripled that figure. Yet Luce wanted to expand, not stand pat.

According to Fred Smith, managing editor of the *March of Time*, the original concept behind the show was to make Americans more "*Time*-conscious" with a "nation-wide radio program which would broadcast from coast-to-coast most effectively the editorial qualities of the weekly magazine which would make people who had not read the magazine conscious of its power."[41] But though conceived as a mere appendage of *Time* magazine, the *March of Time* soon emerged as an autonomous entity—and with wider circulation.

Broadcast Fridays from 8:30 to 9:00 P.M. over CBS and bankrolled by *Time*, the show reported on several stories per episode, a blend of straight news reports and human-interest vignettes. An announcer—first either Ted de Corsia or Harry von Zell, later Westbrook Van Voorhis—provided exposition while a cast of gifted vocal artists impersonated the newsmakers—"ghosting" (in the jargon of the day) the nasal New Yorkese of former governor Al Smith, the operatic bluster of Benito Mussolini, and the patrician tenor of FDR. In the interest of good theater, embellished dialogue punched up the printed record and background music sweetened the mood.

The *March of Time* was an immediate hit—or at least a *succès d'estime*. *Variety* called it "the apex of radio showmanship"; Walter Winchell said "the mag *Time*'s broadcast is a thrill"; and Jack Foster, radio editor of the *New York World-Telegram*, spoke of how the series lingered in his mind as "a kind of talkie newsreel creating vividly in words the tales which have stood beneath the headlines."[42] Its stentorian opening ("The March of Time!") and pregnant-with-import sign-off ("Time . . . Marches On!") became instant catchphrases.

However, as would often prove the case in the history of broadcasting, critical esteem and the devotion of hard-core listeners failed to translate into high ratings and advertising dollars. In February 1932, seeing no spike in revenue, Luce pulled the plug on the show. Thus, during the fateful arc of the Lindbergh case, the *March of Time* was off the air.

Listeners bemoaned the lost opportunities. "What a pity that the *March of Time* was discontinued just at a time when it might have produced an epochal program—a dramatization of the kidnapping of and search for the Lindbergh baby!" complained Harold P. Brown, editor of *Radio Digest*. With CBS crews on the scene in Hopewell and an ensemble of talented performers in the wings, a show devoted to the stricken father and heartbroken mother would have brought the radio audience to tears. "In the Lindbergh case the Columbia System had established its short-wave station right at the scene of the kidnapping and could have connected directly with instant details of this great mystery drama of the hour. The story of how a nation responded to the distress of this outraged family could have been broadcast as a radio epic."[43]

An avalanche of protest followed Luce's decision to cancel the *March of Time*—the first true audience rebellion in broadcasting history. Twenty thousand letters poured into the offices of *Time*. "The worst calamity in the history of broadcasting was the announcement that the *March of Time* broadcast was to be taken off the air," wailed an irate listener.[44]

Luce tried to put the onus on the broadcasting industry with a snooty response: "Should *Time* or any other business feel obliged to be a 'philanthropist of the air' to continue paying for radio advertising it does not want to provide radio with something worthwhile?" CBS president William S. Paley fired back that Luce had no obligation to be a "philanthropist of the air." Moreover, he resented the implication that the *March of Time* was the sole oasis in a vast radio wasteland. "Both Columbia and its advertisers feel a deep sense of responsibility to the public, and the quick assumption of this responsibility has contributed much to the present high standard of American broadcasting."[45] *Broadcasting* also castigated Luce for his "sour grapes" and print-based arrogance. "It is idle even for the brilliant editors of *Time* to believe they have a monopoly on ideas."[46]

Bowing to the firestorm of protest, and seeking to protect his brand, Luce agreed to give the show a second chance. On September 9, 1932, the *March of Time* returned to its old spot on the dial, Friday at 8:30 P.M. on CBS, with a troupe of fifty vocalists, three sound-effects technicians, and a symphony orchestra performing the news of the week.[47]

By then, the search for the Lindbergh baby had come to a resolution that not even the *March of Time* would have dared to reenact.

Chapter 4

NOBODY EVER WALKED OUT ON A NEWSREEL

Ever since that drizzly morning on Roosevelt Field in 1927, the newsreels had abetted the Lindbergh cult. Panoramic shots of rapturous crowds, worshipful close-ups of a noble visage with a faraway gaze, and cozy two-shots of the no-longer-Lone Eagle with his wife and co-pilot Anne—the medium doted on its favorite son and his storybook family. For Americans caught in the Great Depression, the sight of the Lindberghs was a balm.

When the fairy tale ended, the newsreels could not look away. Camera- and soundmen descended on Hopewell and competed fiercely for exclusive pictures of the crime scene. They did not shove cameras and mikes into the faces of the grief-stricken parents, but they did take aside police and eyewitnesses for on-camera interviews, subjects who spoke nervously and self-consciously into the lens, a generation still ill at ease with the mechanical reproduction of self. What the clips lacked in timeliness, they made up for in blunt-force impact. The kidnapping was the first long-term story that the newsreels, only lately equipped with synchronous sound, covered independently of the newspapers. For a time, the medium became what its most ambitious editors had always hoped for, something worthy of the name of motion picture journalism.

Postmortem Surveys of the News of the Day

The newsreels had been an integral part of the motion picture experience since 1914, when the French company Pathé inaugurated news on-screen as a weekly format.[1] By the early 1930s, five newsreel outfits—Fox Movietone News, Hearst Metrotone News, Paramount Sound News, RKO-Pathé News, and Universal Newspaper Newsreel—comprised an essential part of what motion picture exhibitors called "the balanced program," the menu of film offerings made up of cartoons, travelogues, comedy shorts, and feature-length films that defined the cinematic experience in the days before television. Issued twice weekly, clocking in at eight to ten minutes, the newsreel played at the top of the classical Hollywood bill.

On November 2, 1929, the newsreel was promoted from side dish to main course with the opening of the Embassy Newsreel Theatre in the heart of Times Square. For twenty-five cents, moviegoers watched a fifty-minute program made up exclusively of newsreel clips and documentary shorts. "The news of the world in voice, sound, and action," promised the lobby front while display boards outside listed the contents of the current program.[2] The Embassy was an immediate hit, playing fifteen shows a day, often to standing-room-only crowds. No less impressive, the all-newsreel programming proved virtually immune to seasonal and Depression-born drop-offs in attendance. On May 16, 1931, encouraged by the niche market success, the Trans-Lux, a rival newsreel-only theater, opened on Broadway.[3] The two theaters became regular stops on the schedule of screen-oriented news junkies in New York.

According to exhibitor Fred S. Mayer, moviegoers watched the newsreel with more dedication than they read the newspaper. "From the days the newsreel first made its bow, I cannot recall a single instance of when a patron walked out during its showing," averred Mayer, calling on his twenty-two years of experience in the motion picture business. "Folks may disapprove of any part of the program but"—and here he capitalized his expert opinion—"NOBODY EVER WALKED OUT ON A NEWSREEL."[4]

Mayer was overselling the goods. Not quite everybody sat entranced before the newsreel portion of the balanced program. Static military parades, posed ceremonies, and stiff politicians droning into a camera lens made up the kind of screen fare that propelled many moviegoers into the lobby for a cigarette break. "Half the material that constitutes the present so-called newsreel" wasn't even news, H. E. Jameyson, a prominent Midwest exhibitor, pointed out in 1932. "You can't rush a ton of batteries, a mile or two of cable, [and] a truck of electrical gadgets to a three-alarm fire and expect to get anything but the dying embers of what might have been a news picture."[5]

Jameyson nailed the problem: not that a filmed report was old news but that the newsreel camera missed the action shot. Having read about the story in the newspapers or heard about it on radio, audiences already knew the news in the newsreels; what they wanted were moving images of the event, a visual complement that, barring dumb luck, almost always eluded the medium. The most spectacular of all newsreel imagery from the 1930s—the jaw-dropping footage of the zeppelin *Hindenburg* exploding into a fiery ball in full-frame close-up—was pure happenstance: the newsreel cameras were already set up to film a routine mooring at Lakehurst, New Jersey, on May 6, 1937, when the ship ignited. Except for such "lucky accidents," as *New York Herald Tribune* critic Joseph C. Furnas callously put it, the newsreel relied on stationary "set pieces" which "can be spotted weeks ahead, planned for as carefully as a surgical operation, and duly photographed when the calendar gives the signal."[6]

Despite the built-in limitations, the place of the newsreel on the motion picture bill was secure. Though always more of a loss leader than a profit maker, the newsreel waved the studio flag and lent the motion picture medium, still suspect and condescended to by elite critics, some of the cachet of its parent medium, the newspaper. "A very large part of the screen's status has been built by the newsreel," *Motion Picture Herald* asserted in 1931. Its quasi-journalistic aura made the newsreel the "one expression of the screen which has been the least subject to attack, censorship measures, and the strictures imposed by the foes of art."[7] Legally, it was not sheltered by the First Amendment, but the rollout of segments in any given issue—news, human interest, entertainment, and sports—was enough like the layout of a newspaper for the format to be granted informal constitutional dispensation.[8] State and civic censor boards clipped and banned the entertainment items on the balanced program with impunity, but they tended to give the newsreels extra leeway—up to a point. Venture too far into political controversy or partisan advocacy and the scissors came out.

Not that the newsreels wanted to stir up trouble. Though never subject to formal regulation by the Motion Picture Producers and Distributors of America or, after July 1934, the strict oversight of the MPPDA's Production Code Administration, the newsreels operated under a policy of "voluntary restraint" that could be just as onerous as official oversight. With exhibitors preferring happy talk and state censors ready to pounce, the newsreels tip toed carefully around culturally incendiary topics—and avoided the most combustible material entirely. Sensitized to the limits of what could be shown and said on screen, newsreel editors seldom overstepped the bounds.

Little wonder the medium suffered from an identity crisis: was it a species of journalism, like the newspaper it resembled, or a warm-up act for the feature film, like the cartoons and comedy shorts it accompanied? While adopting the codes and categories of the newspaper, the newsreel had to be cheerfully effervescent and universally acceptable, else too downbeat a tone might depress moviegoers and alienate exhibitors. The abrupt shifts in mood and material from segment to segment—the assassination of foreign royalty followed by a man playing songs on his hands—reflected the schizoid personality. Critics encouraged the newsreel to get serious; exhibitors wanted nothing more than an appetizer that would not leave a bad aftertaste.

Of course, being jealous of its purview, the print press also preferred that the newsreels stay in their lane as entertainment and not become journalistic competition. "People appear never to grow tired of the two-headed calf, the infant prodigy, oldest veteran, fattest girl, tallest giraffe, and all the other dime museum numbers," observed *Editor & Publisher*, the trade paper for print journalists, admonishing the newsreels to focus on the freak shows and know their place.[9]

Newsreel editors groused about the need to dumb down their coverage and waste precious screen time on trivialities. "The newsreel, which is probably for many millions quite as much a vehicle of the news as the printed page, is in the eyes of the law and the tradition of the courts, merely a part of the entertainment business," complained Martin J. Quigley, editor and publisher of *Motion Picture Herald*, the trade magazine that kept the closest watch on the newsreels. The momentous but decidedly grim stories of the 1930s—the march of Japanese imperialism in Asia, the rise of fascism in Europe, and the blight of the Great Depression at home—tended to be buried under the upbeat frolic of madcap antics, fashion parades, athletic contests, and, after May 28, 1934, the growth spurts of the Dionne quintuplets. Why upset Depression-battered audiences who had come to the movies for two hours of escape from the anxieties of the world outside? "We will not run on the screen of our theater any talks on 'depression' or any pictures pertaining to the subject and I think it is time that the newsreels realized that what we want is one hundred per cent entertainment," decreed Sophie K. Smith, manager of the Little Picture House in New York, an opinion shared by many managers of the big picture houses.[10]

The main exception to the chipper tone of the newsreels was in the coverage of crime. The exploits of the colorful gangsters of the early 1930s made for a perfect alignment of the sensational and the moralistic. Shielded by a crime-does-not-pay voiceover—especially when the gangster was laid out on a slab (John Dillinger) or crumpled in a cornfield (Baby Face Nelson) as an object lesson in the wages of sin—crime was too much a mainstay of the American pageant to be denied priority. Universal Pictures even offered a $5,000 reward for the capture of John Dillinger—but only if Universal Newsreel were tipped off in advance to record the moment for posterity.[11]

No one tracked the journalistic progress, or lack thereof, of the newsreel more closely than Terry Ramsaye, vice president and general manager of *Motion Picture Herald*. As a former newsreel editor himself, he well understood the nature of the business and the limitations of the technology. Too often, Ramsaye admitted, the material in the newsreels was "synthetic and reduced to post-mortem surveys" of the news of the day. Yet the potential for a union of "real reporting and real showmanship" remained an untapped resource. The newsreel was "taken too much as a matter of course within the industry and is classified quite too much as a mere entertainment item by laymen and legislators," he complained. The neglect explained why "newsreels, plainly and frankly, have been much in the doldrums of late."[12]

In the doldrums at the moment, perhaps, but not for long. Written less than two days before the kidnapping of the Lindbergh baby, Ramsaye's bleak assessment of the state of screen journalism was soon nullified by the biggest newsreel story since Lindbergh's flight to Paris.

Watch for Him Everywhere

In the early morning hours of March 2, 1932, newsreel editors in New York were rousted out of bed and tracked down in speakeasies. Packed into sound trucks, sleepy and/or hungover cameramen and technicians joined the caravan of reporters speeding out to Hopewell. On the way, they checked their equipment, counted up film stock, and cursed the darkness that made filming impossible.

The veterans anticipated trouble from the man at the center of the story. Fox Movietone's Charles Peden frankly admitted that Lindbergh was "heartily disliked by every cameraman and soundman in the business." The feeling was mutual. A long history of bad blood tainted relations between the medium and its most desired close-up. Lindbergh "does not mind posing for pictures, but when a microphone is around, he gets sore," said Peden. "He seems to have a phobia for the mike."

In fact, the onset of sound seemed to have increased tensions. On one occasion, having granted a print reporter a private interview, Lindbergh discovered a microphone concealed behind a hotel curtain. Furious, he tossed the device out of the hotel window. "It is very likely that cameramen heartily dislike Lindbergh because he is one the very few prominent persons who has gumption enough to stand upon his own rights and regard the cameramen as the pests that they are," editorialized a sympathetic newspaper. "He is to be applauded for throwing the mike out of the window. He should have thrown it upon some newsreel man's head."[13]

The enormity of the present tragedy put all that in the past. Soon after the story broke, Peden expressed the universal sentiment. "There is not a single person covering this story that doesn't pray for the safe return of that cute little baby."[14]

The crew from Universal got to the crime scene first, arriving on the Lindbergh grounds at 2:30 A.M. to question police and locals. By dawn, more than fifty newsreel men and more than a dozen sound trucks had congregated around the Highfield estate, ready to shoot film with the coming of daylight. Light meters came out, tripods were set up, and cameras whirred. Chartered planes circled overhead to obtain aerial footage of the house and grounds; a Pathé News crew was nearly knocked out of the sky by a plane sent up by the New Jersey police. During the first frenzied week, the five newsreel outfits shot more than sixty thousand feet of film, from which each culled five hundred feet (about five and a half minutes of screen time) for a typical segment.[15]

That morning, March 2, the footage was rushed to developing laboratories and editorial offices back in New York, and by afternoon, Broadway audiences were viewing the first filmed reports. The footage showed New Jersey state troopers searching cars, interrogating witnesses, and patrolling the grounds while curious onlookers milled about and cars jammed the road to Highfield. Agitated voiceovers and exclamation-pointed title cards related the sparse details. An insert of Charles and Anne showed distraught faces and stiff body language—an instructive example of the Kuleshov effect because the shots were from 1929 when the newlyweds reluctantly posed for the newsreels.

The newsreel was also reporting on the news media, with shots of the swarms of newspaper and radio reporters on the scene—and self-referential glimpses of the newsreel crews. Paramount showed reporters on telephones frantically dialing their editors, cooking wieners in an ash can fireplace, and shooting craps on the frozen ground. "Paucity of developments in the police investigation of the kidnapping caused a battery of newsreel photographers to turn on their newspaper associates this morning as subjects to 'shoot,'" observed the *Philadelphia Inquirer.* "They turned a café into a Hollywood studio, made up a cast of men and women reporters, and had them 'do their stuff,' in pounding out stories of the kidnapping. This finished, the radio announcers, their microphones conspicuously in front of them, gave samples of the

Turning the lens on itself, the news media cover the coverage of the news media in the Lindbergh case, as press and cameramen set up camp outside the Lindbergh home in Hopewell, March 8, 1932. (Courtesy of the Borowitz Collection, Kent State University) (electronic image)

73

news bulletins they are sending forth to the listening world."[16] When news was scarce, journalists were learning to make news by reporting on themselves.

The singular newsreel coup in the Lindbergh case—and the most poignant moment in all the early newsreel coverage—was three hundred feet of home movie footage of the baby in his crib, shot in 16mm, taken the previous fall (not, as initial reports said, a few weeks earlier). Strangely, when newsreel men first asked Lindbergh about the existence of motion picture footage of his son, he said he knew of none, but Fox Movietone contact man J. C. Brown recalled having heard that the family had taken home movies of the baby. Perhaps the footage might help moviegoers recognize the child? "Lindbergh's face brightened at the suggestion, and he put a call through to [the Morrow estate at] Englewood to locate the film," recalled Charles Peden. "[The film] was there, and soon prints were being made of the baby, showing it playing in its crib, and various angles of it creeping about."[17]

The newsreel men tried to persuade Lindbergh to make a personal appeal on camera to the kidnappers, arguing that a direct address from the parents would have greater impact than an appeal printed in the newspapers. At that, however, Lindbergh balked.

The task of blowing up the 16mm home movie footage to 35mm for theatrical release fell to Pathé, "which may or may not explain how that reel happened to be the first into New York theaters with the baby's pictures," commented *Motion Picture Herald* archly. Developed and distributed with unprecedented speed, the first pictures of the child appeared the very next day, Wednesday, March 2. However, Paramount News, not Pathé, was first with national distribution: its Wednesday release got to moviegoers in Chicago that Friday, March 4, and to Los Angeles that Sunday, March 6.

The footage of the Lindbergh baby was a newsreel first: never before had an amateur home movie been projected on the motion picture screen and sent out as an all-points bulletin. "In making his own pictures of the child available to the newsreels, Lindbergh paid one of the highest tributes to the reels ever paid them as public service agencies," observed *Motion Picture Herald*. "His act was a testimonial to his belief that the making public of these pictures of the child would do more to bring about its return than any other publicity medium."[18] A trade critic said the home movie scenes looked "as though they had been taken by an expert cameraman."[19] Newspapers requested frame enlargements from the home movie footage and published multiple images on their front pages.

Just as the newspapers put extras on the streets and increased print runs of regular editions, the newsreels made up approximately a thousand additional prints highlighting the prize footage. "Watch for him everywhere," urged Universal Newsreel announcer Graham McNamee. "Bring him back to his mother's arms." In 1930, Universal had tapped McNamee, a popular radio announcer, to be the first of the "talking reporters" or "spielers" hired to narrate the newsreels, a practice soon adopted by its four competitors. Over images of New Jersey police stopping and searching cars, McNamee described "the greatest manhunt in the history of modern crime" undertaken "in the search for the most famous baby in the world, innocent, blue-eyed, twenty months' old son of the Lone Eagle and his mate, the victim of as cruel and fiendish a crime as any human can be guilty of." Of the home movie footage, he explained that "these photos are enlargements of small films photographed by Colonel Lindbergh himself, and show the youngster in the last pictures ever taken of him."

After checking out the coverage of all five newsreels, exhibitor Fred Mayer believed that McNamee "created a feeling of sympathetic understanding not equaled in any other expressed method of screen or press."[20] McNamee channeled both the anger ("I'd sure like to have that kidnapper alone for just about four minutes," he growled) and hopes ("Well, come back soon, Little Lindy, our hearts are with you") of his audience.

Fox Movietone, which had tracked Lindbergh from Roosevelt Field onward, felt a proprietary interest in its first star. Watching Fox's initial report on the kidnapping at the Embassy Newsreel Theatre, Tom Waller, *Variety's* man on the newsreel beat, gave a detailed rundown:

> A close-up of the parents after plane views of the house are shown. Sen. Roscoe C. Patterson (R-MO) and Rep. Mary Norton (D-NJ) both advocate capital punishment for kidnappers. The Lindbergh message to the abductors is then flashed, after which it is read by a police officer. Fox even shows the placement of the ladder and the spot where footprints were detected.[21]

Fox's unbilled narrator is not content to let the pictures speak for themselves. "The sympathy of the world goes out to Colonel Lindbergh and his devoted wife in their supreme anguish as the entire nation stands aghast at the kidnapping of their baby son, Charles Augustus Lindbergh Jr.," he says.

Charles Lindbergh Jr. in a frame enlargement from the all-points bulletin screened in the newsreels, released on March 2, 1932.

The centerpiece of the Fox report is the home movie footage, the newsreel exclusive. "To aid in the search, the most recent photographs of the stolen child is [*sic*] given to cameramen for distribution throughout the world," says Fox's man, before the big reveal: "And here are motion pictures of the baby taken by members of the family and given out by Colonel Lindbergh to aid the public in recognizing him."

Deputized in the search, motion picture audiences are given strict instructions:

Listen carefully to this description of the baby and try to memorize it. He is twenty months old. When stolen, he was dressed in a white sleeping suit. His hair is fair and curly. His complexion is light. Is able to walk a little and prattle a few simple words such as a child just beginning to talk would know. He weighs about thirty pounds and is two feet nine inches tall. He resembles his father allowing for the chubbiness of his baby face.

Like McNamee, Fox's announcer vents the public anger:

> All America has demanded with one voice that the inhuman abductors of
> this innocent child shall not escape their just fate.

Fox Movietone makes two common assumptions: that the kidnapping was
the work of more than one man ("one of the kidnappers," "inhuman abductors") and that the baby will soon be safely returned. "It may be that when
these pictures are shown the baby will have been found, but nothing can wipe
out the dreadful sorrow and suffering that this shocking crime has inflicted
upon the child's father and mother."

Audiences reacted to the footage of the adorable, frolicking child with
gasps of sympathy and distress. Women were especially moved, sometimes
to tears.[22]

So long a mere headline service parroting the print press, the newsreels
offered what the newspapers and radio could not: home movies of the baby,
aerial footage of the estate, filmed interviews with police and bystanders, and
from-the-screen expressions of pent-up rage.

Seizing the moment, newsreel editors covered the Lindbergh kidnapping with the zeal of reporters working for a metropolitan daily. Like radio
reporters, their usual practice was to wait for a newspaper report or teletyped
bulletin to point the way and verify information. With the Lindbergh case,
editors and camera crews were on-site, questioning the police, interrogating
witnesses, and persuading the very private Lindbergh to turn over his family
album to aid in the search. They were no longer waiting for the news to break,
but breaking it themselves.

Paramount Sound News went a step further, touting not only its journalistic enterprise but its role as an auxiliary to the police. Promising to stand
"fully prepared to get the first visual news of developments and also to aid by
every means in its power in the nationwide search for the kidnapped child,"
the newsreel posted crews just outside the grounds of the Hopewell home, at
the Morrow estate in Englewood, in Trenton, in Newark, in Philadelphia, and
in New York, both at police headquarters and at Paramount's central offices.
"All these units will remain at their posts until the child is found," pledged
the newsreel sleuths. "The men on duty sleep in three shifts so that one with
each unit is always on the alert for the latest news and ready to rouse his com-
panions in case there are developments in the section his group is covering."[23]

The trade press lauded the new hustle in the step of the medium. "Never in their history have newsreels had more dramatic and universal appeal," wrote *Film Daily* publisher Jack Alicoate. "We have had several folks tell us recently that their regular visits to the cinema were because of these screen animated newspapers." Indeed, given the drawing power of the Lindbergh newsreels, Alicoate wondered why the studios skimped on publicity. While newspapers hyped their scoops and sold tens of thousands of extra copies, the newsreels were "allowed to slumber peacefully for the lack of enthusiastic exploitation."[24]

MGM's *Distributor*, the studio's in-house sales organ, seconded Alicoate's complaint. "The theater has in its projection room a newsreel giving marvelously INTIMATE details of this remarkable event . . . presenting them more dramatically and convincingly than the newspaper does . . . making a special subject of them . . . yet offers this epochal material in habitual silence . . . as if it were something for which it should apologize."[25] Why lump the newsreels in with cartoons and comedy shorts when they were outperforming the rest of the bill for emotional impact? At the *New Yorker*, film critic John Mosher scanned the list of feature films then in release and concluded that no motion picture entertainment "however adroit or novel, could compete in interest with that brief strip of the Lindbergh baby at his play or with those scant views of activities at Hopewell. . . . Against such actualities of the world itself, fiction at best is feeble, and the four new pictures [currently being advertised] are but thin stuff to distract our minds."[26]

Actually, many exhibitors fully appreciated the drawing power of the Lindbergh newsreels. "Watch Pathé News Lindbergh Baby Kidnapping," urged a marquee that put the newsreel in the same size type as the feature film.[27] Audiences not in the mood for either Marlene Dietrich in *Shanghai Express* (1932) or Joan Bennett in *She Wanted a Millionaire* (1932) were lured by come-ons such as "Another RKO Scoop! Authentic Newsreel Pictures. Lindbergh Kidnapping. See the Scene from which Little Lindy was Stolen" and "Kidnapping of the Lindbergh Baby. Fox Movietone News on the Spot."[28]

Yet after the coup of the home movie footage and the jolt of the first title cards, the newsreels were again relegated to being a follow-up medium, providing after-the-fact visuals to news already reported by the print press or radio. Neither Charles nor Anne Lindbergh was talking to the newsreel cameras, and those who were—Governor Moore, Colonel Schwarzkopf, alleged experts, and dubious witnesses—had nothing of consequence to say.

"In addition to the clumsy interview with Mrs. Antonia Chowlewsky on a red-hot inside Lindy tip, with [the] aged foreign woman speaking with an accent and seeing no reason why she should tell the newsreel boys anything, [the Trans Lux] house shows what it calls first picture of Henry (Red) Johnson, long held as a suspect," wrote a weary report in *Variety*, about two red herrings made temporarily notorious—she an eccentric lady butcher who owned a shack in the Sourlands, he the luckless boyfriend of nurse Betty Gow, an innocent Norwegian sailor detained by police.

Like the newspapers and radio, out of deference to Lindbergh and fear for the baby's safety, the newsreels kept quiet about the behind-the-scenes maneuvering in the case. "Any newsreel cameraman covering the Lindbergh kidnapping will tell you that much of the 'real inside' has yet to be published by newspapers which to date have devoted more space to the incident than to any news story since the Armistice," whispered trade reporter James Cunningham, also keeping what he knew of the 'real inside' to himself.[29] Little wonder the trade papers detected a "tapering off" of interest by exhibitors: the newsreels had nothing new to unspool.[30] So unnewsworthy was the newsreel news that both the Embassy and the Trans-Lux took a break from Lindbergh coverage.[31] Why remind audiences of stasis and dead ends—and the limitations of the medium?

The newsreels could not long abide the blackout; they were, after all, in the motion picture business. Soon enough, they reverted to type. "Pathé gives the Lindbergh case and [the] Depression bright touches by consulting a Florida soothsayer," *Variety*'s Tom Waller reported just two weeks after the kidnapping.[32] Of all the media, only the newsreel would feel compelled to give two of the great tragedies of the 1930s a "bright touch."

Chapter 5

GET THE LINDBERGH KILLERS!

The most famous man in the world—his fame surpassed even that of Charles Lindbergh—got the news of the death of the Lindbergh baby by ship-to-ship wireless aboard the steamer *Terukuni Maru* as he was sailing to Japan, where moviegoers, like moviegoers everywhere, knew on sight the silhouette with the bowler hat, baggy pants, and floppy shoes. He had built his global renown on silent comedy, a universal language that required no translation, but he was never just a mugging clown doing pratfalls: he had the preternatural ability to turn on a dime from slapstick to sentiment, to yank viewers from laughter to tears.

But standing at the deck rail of the *Terukuni Maru*, the warm humanitarian felt no compassion. Charles Chaplin was seething with anger, sputtering with rage, cursing the bastards who had killed the son of his friend. "I'd throttle the breath out of their dried-up rotten souls," were the mildest words overheard by a fellow passenger.[1]

The body of Charles Augustus Lindbergh Jr. had been found. On the afternoon of Thursday, May 12, 1932, a forty-three-year-old African American laborer named William James Allen walked into the Sourland woods on the Mount Rose Hill in New Jersey to relieve himself. He spied a form he first thought was a dead animal half buried in underbrush. Then he saw a skull and a baby's foot sticking out of the ground.[2]

The child had been dead for some time, doubtless since the night of the kidnapping. His body had been dumped less than five miles from the Lindbergh home, not far from where emergency telephone wires had been strung along the ground only a few days before. The remnants of clothing on the body matched the garments known to be worn by the Lindbergh baby. A hasty autopsy conducted by the county coroner at the morgue in Trenton determined the cause of death: a fractured skull due to external violence.[3]

By late afternoon, rumors that something terrible had broken in the Lindbergh case were already rippling through police, and therefore journalistic, ranks. AP newshound Francis Jamieson was again the fortunate point man, in the right place at the right time. In the AP office in Trenton, he detected the molecular shift in the wind. At 5:45 P.M. Jamieson sent out a confidential alert to AP's subscribers:

> An announcement regarding the Lindbergh case is expected within the next several hours from New Jersey State Police. There has been no indication as to whether it will be of a routine nature or otherwise. You will be kept advised of developments. The Associated Press.

The early warning gave editors time to mock up headlines for extra editions, which would be ready to roll off the presses after getting the official flash from Jamieson. The news, they suspected, would not be good.

Knowing that Governor A. Harry Moore was making an address in Newark, Jamieson tried first to reach the governor there. No luck. He then called the governor's home in Jersey City, repeatedly, until he got an answer. Moore told Jamieson he knew nothing but said that Colonel Schwarzkopf had been trying to reach him. Jamieson asked the governor to call him first thing after speaking with Schwarzkopf. Jamieson had commandeered the governor's office, adjacent to AP's headquarters, and was calling from the governor's desk, so Moore knew the number.

Interminable minutes ticked by before the phone rang. "I have sad news for you," said Moore. "The Lindbergh baby has been found dead." As the governor confirmed the death notice, Jamieson shouted the news into another telephone he was keeping open to the AP office in New York. At 6:10 P.M. the flash went out over the AP wires:

> Flash—Gov. Moore announces Lindbergh Baby Found Dead.

AP passed the exclusive on to its subscribers, including radio stations, who, wary of broadcasting the bulletin even with AP's imprimatur, hesitated to blurt out the dread news on air. Editors frantically telephoned police contacts for confirmation.[4]

Earlier, at around 5:00 P.M., before the AP report was sent out, Colonel Schwarzkopf had summoned reporters in Hopewell and Trenton to the Lindbergh home for an "important announcement" that could mean only one of two things. The journalists drove to the destination through a steady rain. Upon arrival, they were herded into the garage at Highfield, which since the morning after the kidnapping had been used as a makeshift police headquarters. They seated themselves at a long table before a battery of telephones.[5]

For nearly two hours, the journalists were kept waiting, incommunicado, sensing the grim tidings in the air. Colonel Schwarzkopf wanted to make sure that every authorized reporter was present. At 6:45 P.M., assured that all were accounted for, he ordered the doors to the garage locked. Sequestered inside, the print press had not heard the news being broadcast on radio—with one exception: AP's Jamieson, having raced down from Trenton, was among the group, the only reporter present who knew for certain the reason for the summons.

Schwarzkopf cleared his throat. In a crisp monotone, as rain pattered on the ceiling of the garage, he read the official statement. The room was dead silent, the faces of the journalists frozen and expectant. "We have to announce that apparently the body of the Lindbergh baby was found at 3:15 P.M. this afternoon," began Schwarzkopf.

At the word "body" the reporters made for the doors to telephone their editors with the news.

"No! No!" Schwarzkopf barked. "Not a man will leave this room until I have read all my statement." He recited the bare facts—who had discovered the body, where it lay, and how the identity was confirmed to the satisfaction of the police. The news had already been broken to Mrs. Lindbergh and Mrs. Morrow, both in seclusion in the house, just feet away from the garage. "That's all, boys."[6]

Schwarzkopf ignored the shouted questions. "I will answer no questions and say nothing until I issue my regular bulletin at 9:00," he decreed before backing through the doors, followed by reporters who leapt into their cars and raced to the nearest telephones in Hopewell—all except Jamieson and his colleague Sam Blackman who had made arrangements with their new friend the baker, about a mile's dash from Highfield, to use his telephone.

By then, the news had already been broadcast on radio. As with the announcement of the baby's kidnapping, Newark-based WOR scooped the competition, going on the air at 6:12 P.M. after station manager Alfred J. McCosker received a personal call from Governor Moore. Once the story had been confirmed by their own reporters, NBC and CBS interrupted programming to broadcast the news at 6:30 P.M.[7]

A listener in Schenectady, New York, described the stomach-churning disorientation, sonic and emotional, of hearing the bulletin on radio. It was the first, but not the last, of America's broadcasting-induced traumas, when the lulling sound of mundane programming is shattered by the sharp retort of a real-world shock to the system: a serene symphony interrupted by the attack on Pearl Harbor, a banal soap opera cut into by shots fired in Dallas, a chipper morning chat show jump-cutting to smoke billowing from the Twin Towers.

> Orchestras were toddling out the usual dinner hour tunes. The "toompah bu dump" was broken short. "Announcement has just been made that the Lindbergh baby has been found," came the voice of an announcer. More tooting. Several minutes later it was revealed that the child was dead when discovered.[8]

Throughout the night, bulletins and updates were read over the air, breaking into regular programming. Newspaper offices were swamped with calls from listeners seeking confirmation of what they had heard on the radio, unwilling to believe the new medium without verification from the old.

Again, United Press was left flat-footed by AP's hustle. At 6:34 P.M., the also-ran syndicate sent out a pathetic nonbulletin from Trenton:

> A report gained wide circulation here today, without confirmation from the Lindbergh family, that the kidnapped Lindbergh baby, Charles A. Jr., had been found dead.

By that time, AP subscribers already had extras on the street.[9] Even before that, some newspapers had the headlines posted on bulletin boards outside their buildings. New Jersey's *Plainfield Courier-News* posted the news at 6:17 P.M.[10]

The *New York Daily News* was on the street within thirty minutes of the first flash with a two-word headline that needed no surname. Hundreds of

DAILY NEWS

The net paid circulation for April exceeded
Daily.. 1,425,000
Sunday 1,780,000

Copyright, 1932, by News Syndicate Co., Inc. Reg. U. S. Pat. Off.

NEW YORK'S PICTURE NEWSPAPER

Entered as 2nd class matter. Post Office, New York, N.Y.

RAIN

Vol. 13. No. 276   68 Pages   New York, Friday, May 13, 1932*   2 Cents IN CITY LIMITS | 3 CENTS Elsewhere

BABY DEAD

newsboys fanned out across the city, the papers snatched up by pedestrians struck dumb by the front pages and by drivers whose cars screeched to a halt when they heard the boys shout: LINDY'S BABY DEAD! "Shocked readers everywhere cleaned out newsdealers' supplies of extras faster than they could be replenished by the speeding presses," reported *Editor & Publisher.*[11]

Around the country, the newsrooms of medium-size cities were no less speed-minded, the citizens no less horrified as they grabbed for the extras. In Lubbock, Texas, newsies were set upon with such ferocity by passing motorists that the police had to break up the traffic logjam.[12] In Iowa, the *Ames Daily Tribune* put out its first extra since the death of Warren G. Harding in 1923.[13] Michigan's *Port Huron Times Herald* claimed to have made the race from teletype to the street in twenty-two minutes. The proud editor sent AP a scrawled chronology that clocked the minutes from first flash to printed papers:

AP flash:	6:11 P.M.
AP bulletin:	6:12 P.M.
Ad[justing copy]	6:14 P.M.
Edition carrying story closed in composition room:	6:28 P.M.
Papers on the street at	6:33 P.M.

As with all AP stories, the coverage of what was now the Lindbergh baby murder was very much a team effort, but it was Jamieson who won the Pulitzer Prize—and the $1,000 that went with—for "the best example of a reporter's work" that year. He edged out Blackman because of his persistence and enterprise in running down Governor Moore.[14]

Stunned disbelief, inconsolable grief, universal mourning—the news of the death of the Lindbergh baby hit the nation like a dagger to the heart. "A great many Americans whose memories of other events of the decade are vague can recall just where and under what circumstances they first heard that piece of news," recalled the cultural historian Frederick Lewis Allen in 1939, speaking for his generation.[15]

In Times Square, crowds gathered in the rain to look up at the electric sign flashing bulletins across the *New York Times* building. The first ribbon stretched around the building moments after the AP flash at 6:10 P.M. A collective gasp went up from the stricken spectators. "Despite an intermittent and drenching rain, crowds stood and waited for further bulletins," wrote the normally dispassionate *New York Times*, one stranger drawn to another "in mutual expressions of astonishment and condemnation."[16]

Business at motion picture theaters and vaudeville houses cratered. Sick at heart, in no mood for a fun night out, theatergoers with tickets called to cancel reservations at the legit houses and restaurants. "Thoughts of amusement were far away from the minds of all people who heard the news of the culmination of the brutal crime which had shocked the world for 10 weeks," reported the *Billboard*, unconcerned for once with the bottom line.[17]

Women reporters, often consigned to female-centric beats and denigrated as "sob sisters," did not have to strain to wring tears from their readership. "The hearts of millions of mothers in every corner of America—yes, and all over the world—are bleeding for Anne Lindbergh, and for that bonny, sunny-haired, murdered baby found in the Sourland woods," wrote Marguerite Mooers Marshall in the *New York Evening Journal*.[18] Not that only mothers were shedding tears. "The kid of Anne's and Lindy's—the Nation's child, the World's baby—is dead," mourned Floyd Gibbons. "Poor helpless little duffer. He never hurt anyone."[19]

The elegies were laced with righteous anger and steely determination. "The most despicable crime every perpetrated in the history of the country," said New York mayor Jimmy Walker. The mayor heard the news while at WOR, where he was scheduled to speak from 6:45 to 7:00 P.M. about a scheduled "Beer Parade," a march against Prohibition by the city's thirsty wets, planned for the next day. He departed from his prepared remarks to pledge that the city's entire police force would work tirelessly "to run down what I consider to be the most miserable criminals and scoundrels in the annals of criminology."[20] New York governor Franklin D. Roosevelt promised that "every agency at my command has been instructed to bring the fiendish murderers to justice." At noon the next day, the sober Beer Paraders stopped for a minute of silence in sympathy with Anne and Charles.[21]

At the White House, President Hoover said the murder of the Lindbergh baby must be made "a live and never-to-be forgotten case, never to be relaxed until these criminals are implacably brought to justice." He ordered all federal law enforcement agencies, upward of 28,000 agents, to hunt down the killer.[22] "The Federal government does not have police authority in such crimes but its agencies will be unceasingly alert to assist the New Jersey police in every possible way until this end has been accomplished," he promised.[23]

Attorney General William D. Mitchell did not bother to pay lip service to the firewall between state and federal police authority. "Several of the executive departments of the Federal Government have investigating forces whose aid you may desire to invoke," he informed New Jersey governor Moore, "and in order to avoid confusion, it has been suggested that Mr. J. Edgar Hoover, of the Bureau of Investigation of the Department of Justice, co-ordinate such services as the Federal agencies are called upon to render."[24] Taking the suggestion as a mandate, Hoover barged into the case—and planted himself before the cameras—as the dauntless paladin of federal law enforcement.

Nonetheless, though chastened by the blistering criticism in the press (how could the police have overlooked a corpse so close to the scene of the crime?), Colonel Schwarzkopf and his troopers continued to stiff-arm the federal authorities. The high-handed Schwarzkopf refused even to provide Hoover's men a copy of the ransom letters for forensic and handwriting analysis. The cost to the reputation of the New Jersey State Police and to the competence of local law enforcement when measured against federal expertise would be high. Only late in the game did Schwarzkopf realize that it might be wise to spread around the responsibility—and the blame.

Like the newspapers, the newsreels rushed to release special issues on the discovery of the body. Paramount Sound News flashed the news on title cards on New York theater screens just as the newsboys outside on Broadway were hawking the first extras. Paramount also got the jump on its competitors with a complete pictorial history of the kidnapping.[25] The edit had been in the can, ready to go, for weeks, whatever the outcome of the case.

Both the newspapers and the newsreels spared audiences extant crime scene photographs of the child's decayed corpse. However, they did make the man who discovered the body into a short-lived celebrity. When William James Allen and his companion Orville Wilson turned up for work as usual at 7:00 the next morning, cameramen were waiting. Both men repeated their stories several times: how Allen had found the body and summoned Wilson, and how the pair had then driven to Hopewell to report the discovery. "I don't know any more to say than that," shrugged Allen.[26]

So disturbing was the news that some theater managers pulled the newsreels from their programs for fear of upsetting patrons. Surveying the coverage at the Trans-Lux and the Embassy Newsreel Theatres, the two flagship newsreel theaters in Times Square, *Variety*'s reviewer Tom Waller noted that, at the Trans-Lux, Pathé covered the story with scenes of the "spot where the body was found and views of the Negro who made the discovery as well as principals in the case," but that at the Embassy "no reference at all to the Lindbergh climax" was included in the program.[27]

As newspapers and radio sounded the death knell, one American was not in hearing range. Colonel Lindbergh was at sea, aboard the yacht *Marcon* off the coast of New Jersey, on the cruel wild goose chase hatched by the Norfolk shipbuilder John Hughes Curtis. Not until midnight did a radio call get through to the ship to inform Lindbergh of what most of America already knew.

To his old nemesis, the press, Lindbergh was gracious in grief. "I will never forget the wholehearted and splendid way in which newspapermen have cooperated with our request that they leave the farm and leave us entirely alone," he said in a statement of gratitude. "I am sure no similar request on a story of such wide interest had ever been made before and acceded to. When the newspaper people understood how important it was that we not be followed or disturbed in our work, they left us alone. Their spirit has been fine all the way through."[28]

The next day, Friday, May 13, Lindbergh drove to the morgue in Trenton to confirm the identity of his son. The body lay under a sheet on a table. Lindbergh asked that the sheet be removed. "I am perfectly satisfied that it is my child," he said, his cheeks flushing.[29]

Lindbergh soon had good reason to repent his praise of the fine spirit of the newspaper people. After his identification, photographers gained entrance to the morgue and snapped pictures of the shriveled, blackened corpse on the slab. He never forgot, and he never forgave.[30] *

That afternoon, the body of twenty-month-old Charles Augustus Lindbergh Jr. was cremated at the Rose Hill Cemetery in Linden, New Jersey, not far from the Morrow home in Englewood. No religious service was conducted, and only Lindbergh watched as the flames consumed the remains

---

* Lindbergh claimed that "the photographers broke through the window of the Trenton morgue to open my baby's casket and photograph its body," but the official police report of the incident by Lt. D. J. Dunn demurs. "In the room where the remains of the Lindbergh baby had been, [I] examined both windows and found no signs of forcible entry. Neither did the door show any signs of being forced. The shades on the windows had been drawn down and secured by tacks. There were no signs of these shades having been torn." Lt. Dunn admits that an unlocked door leading from the garage to the morgue could have been the means for photographers to have gained entrance to the morgue undetected.

of his son. Later, Lindbergh went aloft and scattered the ashes in the clouds, an act that would inspire endless conspiracy theories and a succession of impersonators who popped up over the years—sometimes at the Lindbergh doorstep—to claim their birthright as Little Lindy.

For Will Rogers, who just three months earlier had spent a happy day with the Lindbergh family at the Morrow estate in Englewood, the loss was devastating. "One hundred and twenty million people lost a baby," he wrote. "One hundred twenty million people cry one minute and swear vengeance the next."[31]

As usual, Rogers voiced the raw feelings of his fellow Americans. In the space of a broken heartbeat, the mood shifted from grief to vengeance. "The damnable fiends, the inhuman monsters," railed the *New York Daily News*, searching for language that could be printed in a family newspaper. "A heart-sick nation, shocked as it has seldom been shocked before, bows with the parents of the Lindbergh baby under the weight of a terrible tragedy," declared the *Literary Digest*. "But under the chorus of sympathy a deep and ominous rumble is heard: 'Get the Lindbergh killers!' "[32]

Who Killed Lindy's Baby?

In January 1934, the British novelist Agatha Christie, a writer whose name was already synonymous with middlebrow detective stories featuring well-man-nered murderers swanning through well-appointed drawing rooms, pub-lished *Murder on the Orient Express*. Her ratiocinator was not from Scotland Yard but from Belgium, the brilliant, fastidious, wax-mustached Hercule Poirot. The plot of Christie's latest mystery was suggestive.

Aboard the famed locomotive, a passenger line redolent of romance, intrigue, and class privilege, an American gangster is found murdered, slain by multiple stab wounds to the chest. While the train is snowbound in the mountains, M. Poirot strives to smoke out the perpetrator from a lineup of a dozen suspects, each of whom has good reason to murder the hoodlum. Was the killer the Russian countess, the British military officer, the pretty govern-ess, or perhaps even the flighty American matron?

Christie's plot twist is inspired: they *all* did it. Their common motive? The gangster had kidnapped and murdered the baby daughter of a famed

American hero, a man beloved by all. The blackguard had escaped the arm of the law, but not the retribution of the friends and family of the victimized parents.

Murder on the Orient Express was a transparent expression of wishful thinking and vicarious catharsis: who wouldn't have guiltlessly joined in stabbing to death the man who had murdered the Lindbergh baby? And what officer of the law would have denied the rough justice of the vigilante action? The coldly logical, by-the-book M. Poirot lets the murderers go free and continue their journey aboard the Orient Express.

Americans would have to endure a long wait before feeling the satisfying closure delivered by Christie's fiction. "Who killed Lindy's baby?" asked a disbelieving *New York Evening Journal.* "Who COULD have? Who WOULD?"[33] For nearly two and a half years, the anguished questions went unanswered. The trail for the killer was not quite cold, but the leads always fell short of netting the prey.

During the interregnum, an authentically odd and headline-grabbing event occurred. On June 10, 1932, a British maid at the Morrow estate with the film noirish name of Violet Sharpe committed suicide by swallowing poison just as the police were pulling up into the driveway to interview her. Was she a hysterical female terrified of public disgrace? A guilt-wracked accomplice?

Meanwhile, Great Depression America was undergoing a peaceful revolution. On March 4, 1933, Franklin Delano Roosevelt assumed the office of the presidency and launched the New Deal, a massive centrifugal initiative that vacuumed power from cities and states into Washington, D.C. The legislation passed during his storied first one hundred days spawned a blizzard of bureaucracies that expanded the scope of federal authority and ballooned the size of the national government. FDR's multifarious "alphabet agencies" established codes for farming, manufacturing, and banking and regulated everything from the slaughter of poultry to the painting of post office murals.

No three letters in the New Deal alphabet would be printed more indelibly into the national psyche than the initials of the Federal Bureau of Investigation, formally consecrated by federal legislation in 1935. The face of law enforcement was no longer the town constable or the state district attorney but the bulldog countenance of J. Edgar Hoover, "the nation's number one G-man," high sheriff of the FBI.

At noon on November 1, 1933, Attorney General Homer S. Cummings gave J. Edgar Hoover formal authority over the Lindbergh case; henceforth all matters pertaining to the investigation would be coordinated by the FBI. Government moving vans carted the dozens of boxes of case files over from the Treasury Department and other agencies. Files neatly arranged in cabinets, occupying acres of hallway space, were already defining Hoover's *modus operandi*.[34]

Yet a federal agency under a different set of letters was doing the shoe-leather detective work that ultimately cracked the Lindbergh case. Agents of the U.S. Treasury—T-men, not G-men—were tracking the serial numbers on the telltale gold certificate notes Dr. John F. Condon had turned over to Cemetery John on the night of April 2, 1932. Not only had Treasury agents insisted the numbers be recorded, but they were farsighted enough to envision that the bills would soon be bright markers of complicity.

Among FDR's economic initiatives was a currency reform that took America off the gold standard. Paper currency bearing the motto "payable to the bearer" in gold, known as gold certificates, were withdrawn from circulation. Though the bills were still legal tender, they became rarer and more conspicuous, especially after May 1, 1933, the last official grace day for holders of gold certificates to exchange their bills for Federal Reserve notes.

Due to the smarts of the T-men, the bulk of the Lindbergh ransom money paid to Cemetery John by Condon consisted of $10 and $20 gold certificate notes. After the ransom exchange, when it became clear Condon had been double-crossed, the complete list of serial numbers was released to the newspapers. Across America, bank tellers and cashiers looked for the serial numbers when they closed out their registers. Ordinary citizens lucky enough to get hold of a $10 or $20 bill did likewise.

The bills provided a luminous paper trail. Sometimes, too, a description of the man who passed the bill might be obtained from an alert witness, giving police sketch artists the outlines of a profile. Cecile Barr, a ticket seller at Loew's Sheridan Theater, recalled the man who handed her a $5 bill on the night of November 26, 1933, and offered a description that matched Condon's: 30ish, clean-shaven, medium build and height.

As sightings of the bills trickled in from stores and banks, the police dotted a map with a pin at every point the money turned up. Gradually, the pins clustered in the area of the Bronx.

Little of the progress of the ongoing criminal investigation made the news of the day. At the request of law enforcement, the press kept quiet about the telltale bills. If the kidnapper thought the coast was clear, he might get careless, and the police might get lucky.

Detectives also quietly worked the evidence left at the crime scene. None was more tenacious than Arthur Koehler, an expert on wood grains and lumber from the U.S. Forest Products Laboratory in Madison, Wisconsin. An obsessive-compulsive of superhuman fixation, Koehler doggedly tracked the wood grain from the ladder found on the Hopewell grounds to a lumber company in the Bronx. From there, the trail went cold.

Initially, despite the lack of new developments to report, public interest in the Lindbergh baby murder remained intense. "Audience reaction to anything about the case proves that it is far from being a dead issue with the newsreels," wrote *Variety*'s Tom Waller when the New Jersey police released photostats of the ransom notes. The newsreels lingered over close-ups of the distinctive scrawl and the Germanic spelling and syntax. Perhaps a sharp-eyed moviegoer would recognize the penmanship.[35]

As the months dragged on, however, with no breaks in the case and the incremental progress embargoed by the press, the fever pitch cooled. During the Great Depression, Americans had plenty of other troubles to occupy their attention.

An Epic Passage in Modern Detective Work

On the morning of Saturday, September 15, 1934, an alert gas station manager named Walter Lyle felt a little hinky about a customer. A man in a dark blue Dodge sedan had pulled up to the pump at the Warner-Quinlin filling station at 2115 Lexington Avenue in Harlem. He handed Lyle a $10 bill for 98 cents worth of gas. It was a gold certificate note.

"You don't see many of these anymore," said Lyle.

"No," said the customer. "I guess you don't. I've only got a few of them myself—'bout a hundred."

Lyle studied the man's face, noting the distinctive pointed chin and more than a trace of an accent—a German accent.

As the Dodge drove away, Lyle wrote the license number on the back of the bill. "There's something screwy about this business," he said to his assistant John Lyons. Lyons agreed and walked three blocks to the Corn Exchange Bank Trust Company to turn in the day's payroll.[36] The next Tuesday morning, while tallying up receipts, a bank teller checked the serial number against the list of Lindbergh ransom notes and got a hit. He turned the bill over and saw the license plate number Lyle had scrawled on the margin on the reverse side.

The car was registered to a man named Bruno Richard Hauptmann. He fit the profile and looked the part: an illegal German immigrant, a carpenter, a resident of the Bronx, and a clean-shaven man with a pointed chin. On Wednesday morning, September 19, the police cased the house and watched nervously as a man got into a blue Dodge sedan and began driving toward the city. They followed for just thirty minutes before pouncing. The driver was brought in for booking and interrogation at the Greenwich Street Police Station in lower Manhattan.

Officially, the biggest news story of the year was being kept secret as the police grilled the suspect, but journalistic grapevines were soon buzzing with reports of unusual activity at the Greenwich Street Station. High-ranking police officials—including Colonel Schwarzkopf, whose presence meant one thing, New York police commissioner John F. O'Ryan, and J. Edgar Hoover—were spotted on-site.

By late afternoon, a mob of reporters was packed inside the station house, trying to push into the jail area, including first among equals Walter Winchell. The syndicated columnist and radio star had an intricate web of high-placed tipsters—none higher than J. Edgar Hoover, for whom Winchell served as pro bono PR man.

Whether tipped off by Hoover or the local cops, Winchell was already hot on the trail. Three days before Hauptmann pulled into the gas station, Winchell suspected the net was closing in around a suspect. "The federal men are convinced that they will break the most interesting crime on record—the Lindbergh snatch," he announced in his column of September 12, 1934. "A squad of hand-picked aces still are working on it—24 hours every day . . . I hear they have collected some definite clues, which is encouraging." Winchell stroked the ego of his most important source. Hoover's G-men "would have broken the case speedily if they had been called in promptly," but the hidebound "New Jersey Sherlocks" kept them at bay. Fortunately, thanks to the recent change in federal law, "whenever a kidnapping case breaks nowadays, the federals don't wait for instructions. They go to work on the case at once—knowing that it will be laid at their doorstep long after matters have been bungled."[37]

Winchell and Hoover both understood that the Lindbergh case was a transformative moment for the FBI. During Prohibition, the G-men were known mainly for busting up barrels and bottles of America's favorite beverages. Loathed as mirthless "dry snoopers," they were in serious need of an image makeover. "The lads are sure that the breaking of the Lindbergh case would do more to reinstate them in the public heart than anything else," commented Winchell, after being led through the new building built by the Department of Justice to house FBI headquarters in Washington, D.C.—"the first newspaperman, they said, to see it inside," he couldn't resist adding.[38]

On September 16, Sunday night, during his popular NBC broadcast, Winchell informed Mr. and Mrs. North America and all the ships at sea that Lindbergh ransom money was turning up all over Manhattan and the Bronx. "Boys," he said, addressing the city's bank tellers, "if you weren't such a bunch of saps and yaps, you'd have already captured the Lindbergh kidnappers."[39] His column that day also reported the news about the ransom money—and printed the insult. "For the first time in a year some of the Lindbergh ransom money (gold certificates) bobbed up in local banks last week," he revealed. "So sappy were the bank tellers, you'd think they would have detained the passers, considering gold certificate hoarders were threatened with imprisonment last year."[40] Later, Winchell would claim that his jibe at "sappy" bank tellers caused an insulted teller, William R. Strong of the Corn Exchange Bank, to redouble his vigilance. Strong told Winchell that on Monday morning a customer confronted him with a taunt: "Winchell says you're a sap!" He resolved to prove Winchell wrong and the next morning came across the incriminating bill tagged by gas station attendant Walter Lyle. "Imagine the beat of his heart when the next morning he matched the ten spot and discovered it was ransom money!" exclaimed Winchell, who figured the nation should give "1½ cheers for Lyle and 1½ cheers for Strong"—and presumably three cheers for Walter Winchell.[41]

So, when Winchell arrived at the Greenwich Street Police Station, he felt entitled to go right to the top. "Tell Hoover that Walter Winchell would like to see him," he instructed a cop guarding the entrance to the jail area. As his colleagues bristled, Winchell was beckoned into the inner chamber, where a beaming Hoover invited him to dinner.

That evening, the reporter and the lawman shared a leisurely meal at Hoover's New York residence. Hoover told him everything—the name of the suspect, the nature of the incriminating evidence, and the certainty that the federal government had collared the right man. "I think this is the man who did it," Hoover informed Winchell, who was already imagining the banner

Gas station manager Walter Lyle (right) and attendant John Lyons (left), the men whose suspicions led to the arrest of Bruno Richard Hauptmann, photographed on September 20, 1934. (The "masking" of the heads is a compositor's mark to set off the heads in cropped reproductions of the photograph.)

The press melee at the Greenwich Street Police Station after word leaked that a break was pending in the Lindbergh baby kidnapping case, September 20, 1934.

headlines—and the byline "Exclusive to Walter Winchell"—when Hoover shattered his fantasy. "Of course, all this is off the record."

"But, God, man!" Winchell pleaded. "I'm in the racket of helping my boss sell papers. If I've got a story, I've got to use it."

"Not yet," said Hoover.

Winchell bit the bullet, figuring to pocket the marker for later use. "OK, it's off the record."[42]

The next day, September 20, late in the afternoon, Commissioner O'Ryan, flanked by Schwarzkopf and Hoover, waded into the melee at the Greenwich Street Police Station and formally announced the capture of the suspect.

We have in custody the man who received the ransom money. His name is Bruno Richard Hauptmann of 1279 East 222nd Street [in the Bronx]. He came to this country a stowaway eleven years ago. He is an alien, unlawfully in the country.

O'Ryan then went over to the NBC studios at Radio City Music Hall and from 5:25 to 5:40 P.M. read the statement over the air, adding new information: that Hauptmann was married and had a child ten months old, that he was arrested at 9:00 the previous morning on Tremont Avenue in the Bronx, and that $13,750 of the ransom money was found in his garage. That night, O'Ryan issued a second statement, expanding on his earlier comments and making clear that the authorities believed "the mystery of the Lindbergh kidnapping" was at long last solved. He thanked Hoover and Schwarzkopf and insisted the solution of the case was a result of the "unrelenting and closely coordinated effort" of the police agencies of New York, New Jersey, and Washington, D.C.[43]

"Lindbergh Kidnapper Jailed" was the banner in the *New York Daily Mirror* the next day, with only the slightest equivocation included in the caption

Col. H. Norman Schwarzkopf (left), head of the New Jersey State Police, Commissioner John F. O'Ryan (center) of the New York City Police Department, and J. Edgar Hoover of the Bureau of Investigation of the Department of Justice, at the Greenwich Street Police Station, announcing the capture of Bruno Richard Hauptmann, September 20, 1934.

on the front page photo. "With the seizure of $13,750 of Lindbergh ransom money yesterday and arrest of Bernard R. Hauptmann [sic], solution of famous kidnap-murder is believed near."[44] The identical headline in the *New York Daily News*—"Lindbergh Kidnapper Jailed"—also confirmed that the case had moved "swiftly toward a solution" with the capture of the man already being typed as a cold Teutonic villain.[45]

Not stinting on self-praise, the newspapers lauded their prior restraint. "Meanwhile, the aid of the newspapers was enlisted and editors agreed not to publish anything concerning the finding of the money," reported UP, neglecting to mention Winchell's items. "Soon, [the bills] were appearing at the rate of $20 to $50 a week and the detectives needed nothing else to tell them that the kidnapper, seeing nothing in the papers, believed he could spend without detection."[46]

Though the newsreels had also abided by the blackout, the editors had put the time to good use, going through their archives to stitch together a capsule review once a suspect was arrested. "Moving with the speed which was almost comparable to that of the newspapers' rotary presses, the five newsreel companies late last week brought to the screens one of the most dramatic stories of the decade—the breaking wide open of the Lindbergh baby kidnapping case," trumpeted *Motion Picture Herald*.

Pathé News editor C. R. Collins gave a minute-by-minute account of the production process:

> On Thursday, September 20, about 3:00 P.M. we were officially advised of the arrest of Bruno Hauptmann and learned of his being held and questioned in the Greenwich Street Police Station. We immediately rushed two sound crews with an electrician and lights to the station house where, after considerable difficulty, we succeeded in inducing authorities to permit us to photograph Hauptmann being questioned, to photograph the pile of ransom money found at his home, [and] we recorded a talk by Police Commissioner O'Ryan, who posed with J. Edgar Hoover of the Secret Service [sic] and Colonel Schwarzkopf of the New Jersey State Police.

An excited Collins continued his rundown of the timeline:

> About 4:00 P.M. we learned where Hauptmann lived in the Bronx and had the first crew on the scene making pictures of the home, garage where the

money was found, Hauptmann's Dodge car with its telltale license plates, policeman digging up the ground surrounding the home looking for money and so forth.

By the time the newsreel crews arrived at Hauptmann's home, daylight was beginning to fade, but despite the handicap, cameramen "managed to get shots of the guards there [and] the digging around the garage where the ransom money was concealed."[47] (A location shot denied the newsreels was of Hauptmann's hometown of Kamenz, in the Saxony region of Germany. Nazi propaganda minister Joseph Goebbels banned the export of any footage from Hauptmann's fatherland.)[48]

By 10:00 that night, just hours after the announcement of Hauptmann's arrest, "newsreel shots of the questioning of the suspect, interviews with police officials, and neighbors of Hauptmann were being shown in theaters along Broadway." Universal, whose regular release went to bed on Thursday night, held up their shipment for twenty-five minutes in order to turn out a "Universal Special."

The next day, September 21, the crews took shots of Hauptmann in a police lineup and during arraignment and jailing, scenes edited into updated issues. "For the first time the New York police lineup was photographed when Hauptmann was dragged down there under the big lights for questioning," marveled *Variety*.[49] Universal Newsreel editor Allyn Butterfield emphasized that the newsreels were on the spot for "the hot news" that was the "the arrest of Hauptmann and the dramatic events which led to his capture."

Hot news it was, the film being just "out of the soup," in the jargon of the lab workers who developed and printed the negatives. In the interim between the crime and the capture of the culprit, the turnaround for motion picture news had accelerated appreciably. "The speed records established by the newsreels in the Hauptmann capture are generally reported to have exceeded those of the original kidnapping in 1932," noted *Motion Picture Herald*.[50]

Indeed, for the first time ever, the turnaround speed put the motion picture screen neck and neck with the printing press, at least in midtown New York. Berner J. Rybak, vice president of the Trans-Lux Newsreel Theatre on Broadway, gloated that the newsreels had beaten the newspapers "at their own game." Rybak savored the reactions the night the news of Hauptmann's arrest first broke:

I believe there was a greater demonstration from the audience when the title was flashed on the screen than there ever has been for any other subject we have played. There was considerable clapping of hands and stamping of feet. I would judge that the majority of the audience hadn't even seen this in the newspapers and it came as a complete surprise to them.[51]

The raucous response at the Trans-Lux was a window into the media future: breaking news gleaned from a screen, seen and heard at the same instant.

As Hauptmann was interrogated—none too gently—at the Greenwich Street Station, details of his biography and alibi emerged. Neither reflected favorably on him.

Born in 1899 in Kamenz, Germany, Bruno Richard Hauptmann—his friends and wife called him Richard, the press called him Bruno because it sounded more foreign—was a combat veteran, convicted criminal, and illegal immigrant. While still a teenager, he had served in the Great War as a machine gunner and claimed to have been gassed and knocked senseless by an artillery shell. Mustered out, he turned to crime and accrued a rap sheet that included home burglary and the armed robbery of two women wheeling baby carriages. Both crimes, for which he served four years in prison, seemed germane to the Lindbergh kidnapping. In 1923, after being captured and deported twice, he slipped into the United States and melted into the supportive German colony in Yorkville in upper Manhattan. In 1925, he married Anna Schoeffler, a waitress in a Bronx bakery; in 1933, the couple had a son, Manfred, named for the German air ace Capt. Manfred von Richthofen. Hauptmann was nominally a carpenter, but at the time of his arrest he had no visible means of support. Still, he seemed to live well, particularly after April 2, 1932.

The residual image of the bestial German Hun in the American imagination, imprinted by lurid Great War propaganda, and Hauptmann's military occupational specialty as a machine gunner, manning the weapon that had mowed down American doughboys, made him a mug shot the nation was ready to despise. Perhaps, too, buried in the cultural memory was the notorious scene in *The Heart of Humanity* (1918) in which a Prussian officer, played by Erich von Stroheim, while trying to rape a Red Cross nurse, tosses a crying baby from a second-floor window.

Yet as the layers of Hauptmann's personality were revealed, he came to better fit a newer image of the German, not a bloodthirsty Hun ruled by bestial passions but a cold, ruthless automaton, the *übermensch* of the Third Reich. Reports that Hauptmann had spoken admiringly of Adolf Hitler—or maybe just the fact that he was an illegal German immigrant accused of an unspeakable crime—compelled Rep. Samuel Dickstein (D-NY), founder in 1934 of the original House Committee on Un-American Activities, to investigate the Hauptmanns for possible distribution of Nazi propaganda in America. Dickstein labeled Hauptmann's circle of German friends, many of whom were active in the pro-Nazi Friends of the New Germany, "a nest of aliens." For their part, Nazi sympathizers in America insisted Hauptmann had refused to join their groups. They pointed out a disqualification for membership: he was close friends with a Jewish furrier named Isidor Fisch.[52]

In fact, the mysterious Isidor Fisch was Hauptmann's alibi. Hauptmann told the police that the ransom money on his person, in his garage, and

Flanked by Assistant District Attorney Andrew C. McCarthy (left) and his attorney at the time Bernard Meisels (left), Bruno Richard Hauptmann is arraigned at the Bronx Magistrate's Court on a charge of extortion in the Lindbergh baby kidnapping case, September 24, 1934. "Police were taking no chances that the prisoner would attempt suicide, as the absence of his belt and necktie indicates," read the original caption.

concealed in his house came from a box that had been given to him for safe-keeping by Fisch, a former business partner. When the astonished Hauptmann discovered the wads of cash in the box, he had no idea the windfall was Lindbergh ransom money, but since Fisch owed him $7,500, he felt entitled to dip into the cash and spent it incrementally. Fisch had conveniently gone back to Germany in 1933 and even more conveniently died there in 1934.

Journalists snickered at the implausible "Fisch story."

Radio reinforced the image of a taciturn German spouting an unbeliev-able alibi on the signature showcase for dramatizations of the news of the day, the *March of Time*. On enforced hiatus during the kidnapping in 1932, the show had become a radio institution since its return to the air on September 9, 1932, Fridays at 9:00 P.M. on CBS.[53] The inescapable Walter Winchell called the rejuvenated *March of Time* "the only noticeable achievement in radio since Marconi invented it."[54]

On October 5, 1934, the premiere of the new season, the capture of Bruno Richard Hauptmann received the full *March of Time* treatment.* The question posed at the top of the segment ("Does the evidence prove Hauptmann committed the kidnapping and the murder?") is answered in the affirma-tive, not by direct assertion but by Hauptmann's dull stonewalling. He has no explanations, only denials.

"Bruno Richard Hauptmann, you are indicted for extortion, suspected for kidnapping and murder," barks an investigator voiced by Edwin Jerome.

"I am innocent," replies a feeble voice with a German accent, the tone exhausted and emotionless, almost drugged out.

The voice belonged to the vocal chameleon, Dwight Weist, who was tapped to ghost everyone from FDR to Adolf Hitler. Weist did not know it at the time, but on and off for the next eighteen months he would be the spectral personification of Bruno Richard Hauptmann on the *March of Time*.

Hauptmann's pathetic response to each accusation makes a solid case for the prosecution:

"The handwriting on the first ransom note left on the windowsill of the baby's room the night of the kidnapping has been identified in the criminal labora-tories of the Department of Justice as your handwriting."

---

* The episode of October 5, 1934 seems to be the only extant episode of the many *March of Time* reenact-ments of aspects of the Hauptmann case.

"I do not know anything about it."

"In your house was found a German-American dictionary with the pages turned down where it appears the most difficult words in that note found on the sill—?

"I am innocent."

"The ladder used to enter the Lindbergh nursey was constructed from lumber taken from a lumber yard in which you once worked."

"I do not know. I was never in Hopewell."[55]

Confronted with item after incriminating item, Hauptmann brushes off or denies the evidence. By the end of the segment, listeners had little doubt that the case was airtight, the suspect stone guilty.

If the radio and the newsreels now had a villain in focus, they also had a hero: the relentless hunter who had run the outlaw to ground, or so he said. Initiating a long-term media love affair, Pathé News concluded its segment on the latest developments in the Lindbergh case with an homage to J. Edgar Hoover and his cache of records at FBI headquarters. Paramount News competed with Pathé for FBI fetishism by embarking on what *Variety's* Roy Chartier called a "very enterprising journey through the Federal Bureau of Investigation in Washington where fingerprint and other records are kept."[56] Hoover and his records—floor upon floor of file cabinets and desks and typists and detectives and microscopes and laboratories—were caressed by the cameras and cooed over by the narrators.

For wide-eyed Hoover boosterism, however, Walter Winchell remained unrivaled. In column after column, as the Hauptmann case moved speedily from arraignment in the Bronx to extradition to New Jersey, he extolled the FBI chief and his G-men as "the citizen's best friend in time of serious crime." In turn, Winchell was rewarded with scoops on the Hauptmann case. "Flash! Exclusive!" he exclaimed in his column of December 10, 1934. "Jersey's 'ace' evidence against Bruno Hauptmann for the murder rap will be this astounding fact hitherto unpublished," namely that a plank of wood from the ladder used in the kidnapping fit precisely into a space in the attic floor of Hauptmann's Bronx home. "Winchell has been doing yeoman's work on the Lindbergh case and digging up scoops right and left," admitted an envious competitor without access to Winchell's FBI tipster.[57]

Winchell was not the only reporter who printed the Hoover legend. "It was not until the Department of Justice entered the case as the sole arbiter of procedure late last year [November 1933] that the smoke screens of jeal-ously, of viciousness, of insanity and glory-grabbing gave [way] to a scientific re-study of all the evidence and a uniformly directed search for the culprit and his blood money," averred the *New York Daily News*.[58] Broadway colum-nist Ed Sullivan also shilled for the new heroes of American law enforcement. "The Government men did splendid work on the baffling mystery," he wrote, emphasizing "the excellence of the Government investigators" and praising the spot-on profile they had drawn up: "Their reconstruction of the figure, coloring, his speech and general characteristics of the Lindbergh kidnapper long before they actually laid hands on him, will forever remain one of the epic passages of modern detective work."[59]

The newspapers, the radio, and the newsreels all agreed: the G-men—not the Jersey boys, not New York's finest—were the modern detectives who cracked the Lindbergh case.

Chapter 6

HOLLYWOOD AND THE LINDBERGH KIDNAPPING

For Hollywood, the story of the Lindbergh kidnapping might have seemed an irresistible scenario, a surefire attraction literally as timely as the day's headlines. Whether as straight adaptation or *film à clef*, it offered fertile territory for heart-tugging melodrama, pulse-pounding tension, and—in the end reel, certainly, unlike the real case—the satisfaction of the perpetrators punished and the child delivered back into the arms of his joyous parents. As further incentive, the crime of kidnapping possessed a built-in appeal to Hollywood's prime demographic target: women, always suckers for tales of endangered children rescued from harm.

Or so it was thought. The "snatch racket" never inspired a full-blown Hollywood genre, not even a minor cycle. A few kidnap-themed films slipped into the production pipeline, but plans to ride the Lindbergh case to box office gold ran into a solid wall of opposition—from the highest levels of the motion picture industry, from state officials wary of films that highlighted the haplessness of the police, and from critics who felt the plotline was too harrowing for the local Bijou. A sustained backlash from industry, government, and the press made kidnapping the crime Hollywood could not commit to the screen.

A Menace to Public Welfare

From Edwin S. Porter's *The Great Train Robbery* (1903), the starting gun for American cinema, to last weekend's blockbuster heist flick, crime has been good business for the motion picture industry. No less than the tabloid press of the 1830s, the first popular medium to discover that a blood-soaked head line pumped up circulation, Hollywood in the 1930s thrived on first-degree murder and armed robbery. The crime-does-not-pay message that the films paid lip service to belied their besotted infatuation with the outlaws.

Abetting the symbiotic relationship was a fortuitous bit of historical timing. In the 1920s, the nascent studio system met another aborning industry, the business of organized crime. The proliferation of urban lawlessness and the rise of gangland kingpins during Prohibition—above all, mobster Al Capone, underworld overlord of Chicago, a city already notorious as the *locus classicus* of American crime—fit Hollywood like a pinstripe suit. In embryonic mobbed-up films like Josef von Sternberg's *Underworld* (1927) and Tod Browning's *The Big City* (1928), the frontier desperado of the Wild West was transported onto the mean streets of the gin-soaked Jazz Age.

Yet only with the onset of sound and the turmoil of the Great Depression did the gangster film find its guttural voice and cultural resonance. The genre templates—William Wellman's *The Public Enemy* (1931), Mervyn LeRoy's *Little Caesar* (1931), and the most sensational of the trio, Howard Hawks's *Scarface: The Shame of the Nation* (1932), a thinly veiled biopic of Al Capone—all trafficked in social rebellion and political insurrection. Willing accomplices, Depression audiences went along for the ride, shrugging off the lethal comeuppance meted out in the last reel.

The meaning was not lost on lawmen and politicians. In the darkest years of the Great Depression, the twisted morality of the gangster films—the allure of colorful violence and rough vengeance exacted by virile alpha males— made the genre a cultural powder keg. Moral guardians and civic leaders condemned Hollywood for celebrating a deviant criminality that might lead audiences, especially susceptible juveniles, on the road to perdition. "Pictures which depict and glorify gangs and crimes," warned a typical newspaper editorial, were "a menace to public welfare in that they are witnessed by immature, impressionable children" liable to mimic in life "the criminality displayed so minutely on the screen."[1]

For agents of the state, an equally troubling aspect of the gangster film was the subtext of police incompetence. The gangster film, wrote journalist Alva Johnston in a widely quoted piece in *Vanity Fair* in 1931, "indirectly exposed the feebleness of federal, state, and city governments." As such, Johnston felt the genre performed a laudable if inadvertent public service. "The gangster

At the end of Howard Hawks's *Scarface: The Shame of the Nation* (1932), gangster Tony Camonte (Paul Muni) lies dead, but not before leading a glamourous life of crime.

picture is, on the whole, the most meritorious and socially valuable achievement of Hollywood: it has stung and shamed the country into a campaign against racketeers."[2] That was dubious praise.

Whether racketeers or lone wolves, the gangsters who made money at the ticket window also made trouble for an industry subject to state regulation and community approval. Understanding the cultural stakes in seeming to traffic in magnetic lawlessness, the Motion Picture Producers and Distributors of American (MPPDA), the cartel that represented the major studios, clamped down hard on Hollywood's gangster fixation. The rakish bank robber John Dillinger—who blazed across headlines in 1933–1934 before being gunned down in front of Chicago's Biograph Theater on July 20, 1934, after watching the gangster-friendly *Manhattan Melodrama* (1934)—was banned by name from a cinematic *homage* on the grounds that "presenting a jailbird on the screen was detrimental to the best public interest."[3]

Even more detrimental to the public interest was the kidnapper. As a criminal subspecies, he had none of the glamourous élan and gun-crazy machismo that made the gangster so viscerally thrilling, but he too highlighted the ineptitude of the police and the economic desperation of the times. Well before the Lindbergh baby was slain, the wave of sensational kidnappings that beset America in the early 1930s had been seen as evidence of a nation in moral collapse and political crisis. Not too far under the surface, the brutal exchange of human beings for cash operated as a metaphor for the blood-sucking financial transactions that had plunged the nation into the Great Depression.

Nonetheless, like the bootlegging and speakeasies spawned by Prohibition, the crime of kidnapping saturated too much of the atmosphere, especially after March 1, 1932, for Hollywood not to exhale the fumes. Sensing profits from a presold property, a few filmmakers defied the decrees from the MPPDA and the criticism in the press to venture into the cultural minefield of a Lindbergh-inspired kidnapping scenario. The films slipped through a brief window of opportunity before the opening slammed shut.

This Particular Dastardly Crime

Any Hollywood studio seeking to turn elements of the Lindbergh case into a feature film confronted a formidable set of obstacles. The highest was internal. The official ranks of the motion picture industry—the men who set official policy and controlled the cash flow—were united in opposition to even the faintest shadow of the Lindbergh baby darkening the screen.

The outfit tasked with quality control over motion picture content was the Hays office, the all-purpose signifier for the yoke of Hollywood censorship. Officially an in-house arrangement, it was named after Will H. Hays, the strait-laced Presbyterian elder who had been the face of probity for Hollywood since 1922, when the heads of the major studios formed the Motion Picture Producers and Distributors of America to burnish their image and beat back demands for federal censorship. Connected to both Capitol Hill and Wall Street, Hays led the motion picture industry from scruffy adolescence to well-scrubbed maturity. A crucial part of the makeover was a system of self-regulation that kept Washington out of the business of Hollywood censorship.

To placate the bluenoses and busybodies accusing Hollywood of pagan designs on Christian America, Hays promulgated a list of "Don'ts and Be Carefuls," an informal set of namby-pamby caution signs for motion picture scenarios, and established a modestly staffed agency called the Studio Relations Committee (SRC) to monitor compliance by the major studios. Col. Jason S. Joy, a loyal Hays lieutenant, headed up the office from 1927 to 1932, when Dr. James Wingate, formerly head of the Motion Picture Division of the New York State Education Department, took the reins from 1932 to 1934.

In 1930, while the SRC struggled to bring moral equilibrium to a topsy-turvy screen world, a stricter, more comprehensive set of guidelines was adopted in the form of a momentous document known as the Production Code. Written by Daniel A. Lord, a starstruck Jesuit priest, from an original idea by Martin J. Quigley, a devout Catholic layman and editor of *Motion Picture Herald*, the Code was designed to place Hollywood cinema under a moral canopy. Explicit sexuality, gruesome violence, and dozens of lesser offenses to Victorian sensibility were prohibited by the Code, but above all the document sought to imbue the screen with a deeply Catholic faith in a transcendent order presided over by God in heaven and His representatives on earth.

Unfortunately, first for Colonel Joy and then for Dr. Wingate, the SRC had no enforcement mechanism, no coercive penalties to exact if a producer defied the Code commandments. Joy and Wingate might cajole, browbeat, and threaten—but they could not demand, order, or intimidate. Pledges of fidelity to the Code notwithstanding, the Hollywood studios might violate its letter and spirit with impunity.

To film scholars, this period of relative screen freedom—a blip that would last four years, from 1930 until 1934—is known as the pre-Code era. The timeline coincides with the kidnapping and murder of the Lindbergh baby and the nationwide hunt for his killer. Taking advantage of the lax policing, a handful of kidnap-themed films rushed through the red lights flashed by the Hays office. The scofflaw productions incited consternation—and sometimes near panic—within the ranks of the MPPDA.

Knowing the causal relation between tabloid-friendly crime stories and Hollywood knockoffs, the Hays office tried to act preemptively, almost as soon as the first headlines of the Lindbergh kidnapping were typeset. "In Hollywood it's understood there's a dictum against kidnapping film yarns," *Variety* reported. "Major studios [are] giving thumbs down on kidnapping stories." Lest creative energy be expended needlessly, mercenary screen-writers "pounding out abduction yarns, inspired by the Lindbergh case, of course" were informed that their scripts "will probably get 100 percent rejection from censor boards which believe it would plant ideas in the wrong heads."[4]

The statement referred to the state and municipal censor boards that inspected the movies seeking entry into their territories. In the early 1930s, and for most of the classical Hollywood era, a honeycomb of censorship boards inspected, cut, and banned Hollywood releases. Empowered to clip offensive scenes or ban films outright from their jurisdiction, the boards bedeviled the industry with eccentric demands, making the distribution of motion pictures a tortuous and expensive coast-to-coast gauntlet. In a letter to Hays, Colonel Joy had the state and city censor boards in mind when he cautioned: "It seems to me that it would be utter folly for any company to attempt to make a picture paralleling the Lindbergh kidnapping."[5]

To head off trouble, Hays and Joy consulted with representatives from the major studios to arrive at an accommodation for the common good. Lacking authority to dictate compliance, the pair entered into a good faith "gentle-man's agreement" whereby the studios would voluntarily forswear kidnap-ping scenarios. The verbal contract would soon confirm the Sam Goldwynism about not being worth the paper it was written on.

Within days of the discovery of the body of the Lindbergh baby, Uni-versal inserted a kidnapping subplot into *Okay, America!*, a film originally conceived to cash in on the white-hot celebrity of Walter Winchell without actually hiring Winchell to star. Alarmed, all levels of the Hays office—from the SRC on-site in Hollywood on up to Will Hays in MPPDA headquarters in New York—tried to dissuade the studio from a project that could only incite bad publicity and political blowback.

Colonel Joy and SRC staffer Lamar Trotti called an emergency meeting with Universal producer Henry Henigson to communicate "why, in our opinion, the story based on kidnapping and paralleling the Lindbergh case should not be undertaken by a picture company." Reporting to Hays on the meeting, Joy informed his boss that "the chief worries are that [first, the] story too closely parallels the current reported kidnapping case and second shows law enforcement agencies utterly helpless before [the] menace."[6] The second point—that the depiction of inept lawmen undercut respect for state authority—cut to the heart of the matter.

However, the trouble looming over *Okay, America!* was not Joy's only woe. Even as he was jawboning Universal, he was blindsided by a fait accompli from Warner Bros., a gritty melodrama about a trio of gal pals titled *Three on a Match*.

A quintessential expression of the Warner Bros.'s house style, *Three on a Match* (October 1932) follows three woman from Jazz Age girlhood to Great Depression adulthood: a fun-loving flirt and future showgirl (Joan Blondell), a studious good girl and future bespectacled secretary (Bette Davis), and a snooty rich girl (Ann Dvorak) who seems to have it all—a wealthy husband, an adorable little boy, and a lifestyle of privilege and leisure. Yet the bored and feckless high-society lady tosses the sweet life away and runs into the arms of a handsome cad. When their adulterous life hits the skids, the boyfriend hatches a plot to kidnap her young son and extort ransom from the father. Gangsters muscle in on the shakedown, and the scheme goes sideways. To keep the child from talking, the gangsters hand the boyfriend a knife and tell him to "take care of" the kid. The desperate mother sacrifices her life to alert the police and save her child.

Three on a Match depicts the details of the kidnapping in chilling and instructive detail: how the boy is lured away from his governess by a familiar face, how the ransom demand is made, how the child is hidden and mistreated, and—most disturbingly—how the child's life is threatened by a gleaming knife. All were clear violations of the gentleman's agreement between the studios and the SRC.

Reaction from critics and censors was swift and scathing. "Warner-First National have apparently decided—after exhausting the possibilities and popularity of the general gangster and racketeer field—to commercialize the Lindbergh tragedy and start a cycle of baby-kidnapping epics to edify the motion picture public," wrote critic Harold Weight in *Hollywood Filmograph*, appalled at the way "the kidnapping sequences so closely aped the Lindbergh case." He was particularly exercised over the fact that the kidnappers were not shown being punished, "not simply to quiet various censor boards—although we know that there are several who have girded themselves to fight the glorification of kidnapping on the screen"—but because it frustrated "the natural desire of a normal audience to see such beasts, as these men are made out to be, get theirs.'"[7]

Pete Harrison, the publisher-editor-critic behind *Harrison's Reports*, an independent newsletter for motion picture exhibitors, blasted *Three on a*

The child kidnapping scenario injected into the pre-Code melodrama *Three on a Match* (1932) appalled the Studio Relations Committee and state censor boards. Here the faithless wife and repentant mother (Ann Dvorak) tries to shelter her child (Buster Phelps) from (left to right) craven boyfriend Lyle Talbot and gangsters Humphrey Bogart, Allen Jenkins, and Jack La Rue. (Courtesy Photofest) (electronic image)

Match with a venom that must have made MPPDA officials blanch. "Sensitive people will not be able to watch it, especially the situation in which the abductors decide to murder the child when they realize they are trapped," Harrison asserted, before making the obvious connection: "The horror of the Lindbergh kidnapping is still vividly imprinted in the minds of the American people."[8] Why reimprint the horror at the neighborhood theater?

Colonel Joy was of the same mind. "It was with considerable surprise that we saw your picture *Three on a March* yesterday [August 22, 1932], as the script—and the re-writes—had not prepared us for the details of a baby-kidnapping, involving a brutal threat against the baby's life, and [the] accompanying actions of the kidnapper," he informed Darryl F. Zanuck, head producer at Warner Bros. "I'm frank to say I am at a loss what to say about it.

While there has been no signed agreement among the studios not to make child-kidnapping pictures, the general impression here has been that no one would follow the Lindbergh kidnapping with a picture dealing with the kidnapping of a baby for ransom. With the present fear on the part of parents as a result of the Lindbergh tragedy, the public resentment is apt to be strongly against such a picture." Zanuck's ungentlemanly double-cross infuriated Joy, but, knowing he held no cards, he ended on a conciliatory note, suggesting to Zanuck, "I think we ought to get together, with Mr. Hays if possible, to discuss what, if anything, ought to be the policy."[9]

Joy's plaintive tone was a perfect illustration of why the pre-Code regulatory setup was so ineffectual. A headstrong producer like Zanuck could simply roll over the SRC by filming whatever he wanted—and renting the print to any exhibitor who wanted to book it. Joy could squawk, but he could not prevent distribution.

For his part, Zanuck could defy the SRC, but he could not dodge the state censor boards. Upon examining *Three on a Match*, boards in Pennsylvania, Ohio, and New York all eliminated scenes of the actual kidnapping before clearing the film for exhibition. However, the boards warned Vincent G. Hart, head of the New York branch of the SRC, that any subsequent kidnap-themed pictures would be banned outright.

Hart immediately wired the West Coast studios about the ultimatum. Propped up by the threats from the state censor boards, Joy entered into *another* "gentleman's agreement" with the major studios whereby they again pledged to refrain from making kidnapping pictures.[10]

Joy had better luck in softening the kidnapping trope in *Okay, America!* "The major suggestion made to Universal was to divorce the kidnapping from anything associated with the Lindbergh case, and with ordinary kidnapping cases, by substituting a situation in which the girl would simply be held as a hostage," he reported to Hays. "This, of course, gets away from the idea of a deliberate kidnapping for money, adds a new motive to the situation, and, in our opinion, would entirely take this out of the Lindbergh affair." Pressed from on high and persuaded that the MPPDA was correct about trouble with the state censorship boards, Universal complied—sort of.

Okay, America! stars Lew Ayres—imitating Winchell's patented rapid-fire nasal delivery—as newspaper and radio show scandalmonger Larry Wayne, whose must-read Broadway column dishes the dirt on high-society dames and low-rent racketeers alike. Gangsters have kidnapped the (adult) daughter of a wealthy cabinet officer who, contrary to Joy's understanding, pays a ransom of $100,000 for her release. "If Americans can't live safely in America, it isn't much of a country, I say," Wayne tells his radio listeners, before citing the apt example: "No atrocity in the World War was more horrible than the theft and murder of a child of our national hero." The plot ambles wildly through the loony, free-fire zone that is pre-Code Hollywood before wrapping up with the girl being released unharmed, Wayne killing the gangster mastermind, and the gangster's goons murdering Wayne on live radio.

Despite Universal's compromises, the MPPDA was nervous about the reception of *Okay, America!* (September 1932). "This is the first kidnapping story we have had and I don't know what the temper of the censors or of the public is since the Lindbergh tragedy," Joy wrote in an internal memo. "If the picture had come along even two months sooner, I doubt if it could have been shown." On the plus side, "certainly everything in the picture works to the ends of justice and upholding the law."[11]

Exacerbating the fears of the MPPDA was a more serious regulatory threat on the horizon. From March 1933 onward, under the authority of the National Recovery Administration (NRA), FDR's New Deal was implementing a set of restrictive economic codes regulating private business—including the motion picture business. Suddenly, the federal government possessed the power to control pricing at the ticket window, cut the inflated salaries of stars and executives, and limit studio profit margins. The Production Code could be finessed or ignored; the NRA codes were the law of the land. With Washington set to turn the economic screws, the MPPDA had good reason to suppress scenarios that showed a crime wave sweeping over impotent agents of the state.

The best proof of how seriously the MPPDA took the cultural backlash was the personal involvement of Will Hays. "The public relations and legislative relations affected by the kidnapping theme are obvious," Hays informed Dr. Wingate, Colonel Joy's successor at the SRC. "Following the publicity incident to some famous kidnappings, there were suggestions of the use of the kidnapping theme in pictures, but this was avoided, properly."[12] Hays was referring to the scenario Universal had softened in *Okay, America!* and forgetting (or choosing to forget) Zanuck's defiance with *Three on a Match.* Concurring fully with the MPPDA line, Vincent Hart in New York based his opposition on the united front put up by the state censorship boards, all of which "were averse to such themes because of the Lindbergh kidnapping." Unlike Hays, Hart had not forgotten the controversy over *Three on a Match.*

The studios got the message—with one exception. "Despite topical nature of kidnapping as picture material, all major studios with the exception of Fox have shied at snatching stories fearing censorship frowns and the objections from the Hays office," reported *Daily Variety* in September 1933. "Fox has injected kidnapping into *The Mad Game* though the picture is not entirely based on the racket."[13]

Actually, the whole plot of *The Mad Game* (released October 1933) was based on the "snatch racket," which made sense since the original story was by Edward Dean Sullivan, whose alarmist 1932 book helped popularize the term. A streamlined description of the convoluted plot finds bootlegger Edward Carson (Spencer Tracy) conscientiously restricting his criminal activities to illegal liquor before the feds send him to prison for income tax evasion. Meanwhile, on the outside, the end of Prohibition having dried up revenue, his former partner in crime decides to diversify into kidnapping. For very personal reasons (his own daughter had been kidnapped and murdered), Carson persuades a sympathetic judge to parole him so he can infiltrate his former gang and break up the kidnapping racket. When the newlywed son and daughter-in-law of the judge are snatched, Carson frees the victims, guns down his former partner, and dies a hero.

The responsible, pro–law enforcement approach taken by *The Mad Game* satisfied some critics. "There seems hardly a chance that this pioneering kidnapping picture will encounter the objections with which the initial gangster films met," commented *Motion Picture Herald*, a bastion of conservative opinion. "Rather, being always on the side of law and order, it is a definite adjunct to any public safety campaign." Moreover, "no kidnapping methods are illustrated. . . . In every phase the picture comes within the provisions whereby the production of kidnapping stories is permitted."[14]

Thus encouraged, and sensing that the atmosphere that had made the kidnapping theme so toxic in 1932 was dissipating, the studios decided to test the waters again. The first ripples were detected at the Title Registration Bureau, a branch of the MPPDA that served as an early warning sign for Hollywood's sense of the Next Big Thing. When a new catchphrase entered the language or an exploitable plotline hit the headlines, studios rushed to the Title Registration Bureau to stake a claim to a marquee-friendly title. A registration by a member studio did not have the force of copyright law; it was (another) gentleman's agreement binding any member in good standing to respect a prior claim on nomenclature.

In September 1933, when Paramount registered the titles *Snatched* and *Miss Fane's Baby Is Stolen*, Title Registration Bureau chief J. M. Kelly informed the studio that kidnapping themes were discouraged by the MPPDA and summarized the official policy:

> We decided that kidnapping, per se, as an element of crime, cannot be barred. The record as to kidnapping you are familiar with—i.e., that we prevented the cycle after the Lindbergh case and we have kept out, generally speaking, any quantitative element of kidnapping [that is, the payment of ransom] and, we think, we have kept out entirely the matter of kidnapping of children. I don't think we can take the position that no kidnapping can be used but it must be handled with great care.[15]

Ultimately, the problem of kidnap-themed titles landed on the desk of Maurice McKenzie, Hays's executive assistant and all-purpose troubleshooter. Alert to the "dangerous ground" Paramount was straying into, McKenzie told Dr. Wingate that "with the approval of Mr. Hays" the two titles would "be held in abeyance until the entire subject matter can be discussed at an early meeting of our Board of Directors."[16] After due consideration, the board decided to approve the titles, leaving in reserve the right to reject the actual scenarios.[17]

Though willing to toe the official line, McKenzie himself was not averse to kidnapping scenarios. While Hays and Wingate opposed *all* kidnapping plotlines, McKenzie cautioned: not so fast. He reminded Wingate that "the crime of kidnapping has long existed, it is now almost one of this country's major industries, a subject of importance and constant discussion everywhere," and asked a reasonable question: "Are we going to take the position that no picture shall touch that subject even though the story would be on the side of law enforcement and in accord with the thought of decent people— that those who engage in the crime of kidnapping are the scum of the earth, that officers of the law, juries, everybody ought to leave nothing undone to wipe out the practice?"

Shortly after writing Wingate, McKenzie consulted with Dr. Carleton Simon, a prominent criminologist who served as special adviser to the Hays office. Dr. Simon disagreed with McKenzie, and McKenzie had the good grace to pass on the opposing view. "[He] says I am wrong—that no matter how well we might make kidnapping pictures the public at large would accuse of us inspiring crime, that the farther we keep away from kidnapping the better off we are."[18]

Dr. Simon's reading of the public mood came to determine MPPDA policy. In October 1933, the Hays office abandoned the behind-the-scenes palavering and took matters in hand by issuing a strict set of guidelines for any Hollywood producer who might "attempt a kidnapping yarn." *Variety* delivered the memo-cum-ultimatum in four parts:

> First, the screen must not show how the kidnapping is done. There must be no pay off of ideas which would foment in the mind of some moron with abduction inclinations.

The next two edicts were designed to squelch the kind of validation by stylish portraiture that had made gangsters such flashy role models:

> Second, the kidnappers must not be handsome, aggressive, glamorous types. They must be depicted as mean and slinky and the kind which only a crook, which filmdom couldn't influence anyway, could desire to emulate.
>
> Third, it must be stressed throughout the story that there is no monetary reward for the kidnappers. He or she must not be well dressed or expensively housed. Overalls for costume and a garret or cellar for domicile are preferred.

The final caution really was needless to say:

> Fourth, it must be established beyond a peradventure of doubt that all kidnappers are punished; that their wind up is miserable, being either from the gallows or life-long stay behind bars.[19]

Nonetheless, despite the MPPDA's attempts to lay down the law, the lax enforcement mechanisms of the pre-Code era allowed a flagrant breach of industry policy to reach the screen. Making good on one of the titles it registered, Paramount green-lit production of *Miss Fane's Baby Is Stolen*. It would be the only scenario to exploit in connect-the-dots fashion the national anguish over the kidnap-murder of the Lindbergh baby.

On December 13, 1933, Joseph I. Breen, by then de facto head of the SRC, previewed the final print of *Miss Fane's Baby Is Stolen*. After being reassured that the Miss Fane of the title was not an unwed mother, Breen told A. M.

Botsford, assistant to Paramount production head Emanuel Cohen, that the film passed muster. Fixated on the text of the Code, which had not yet formally incorporated explicit anti-kidnapping language, Breen deemed it "satisfactory under the Code" and complimented "the studio on the way in which they have handled this story." However, he cautioned that the film still faced obstacles from state censorship boards. "We trust, however, that the fact that the picture is unmistakably an attempt to arouse the public conscience to the necessity of stamping out this particular dastardly crime, and that the entire story is on the side of law and order, will weigh heavily in its favor, both with censor boards and audiences throughout the country."[20]

Released in January 1934, *Miss Fane's Baby Is Stolen* was based on a short story by Rupert Hughes, a grim piece of pulp fiction in which the snatched baby was slain. "Fearing censorship reaction to the recent kidnappings and particular[ly] in respect to its closeness to the Lindbergh case, Paramount

Baby LeRoy and Dorothea Wieck in a publicity still for Paramount's pre-Code thriller *Miss Fane's Baby Is Stolen* (1934), the only connect-the-dots *film à clef* exploiting the Lindbergh baby kidnapping.

has changed the end of *Miss Fane's Baby* so that the kid is eventually returned to his mother," reported *Daily Variety*.²¹ Hays office or not, the murder of a kidnapped baby was an ending no sane Hollywood producer would have ever committed to celluloid.

Directed by Alexander Hall and scripted by Adela Rogers St. Johns, whose day job was as a reporter for the *Los Angeles Herald Examiner* and who would later have a front-row seat during the judgment phase of the Lindbergh case, *Miss Fane's Baby Is Stolen* stars Dorothea Wieck, a recent import from Weimar Germany, as the mother in distress, a widowed motion picture star.

The film opens with Miss Fane at work, on location for a Hollywood costume drama. Gracious to her adoring public, she bonds with a dazzled admirer named Molly Prentis (Alice Brady). Miss Fane is all aflutter about returning to her Beverly Hills mansion where a certain "lucky fellow" awaits her—presumably her romantic interest. When Miss Fane darts breathlessly into her palatial home, arms outstretched, a cutaway shot reveals that her beau is none other than her eighteen-month-old baby boy Michael (Baby Le-Roy). "He's the most remarkable, intelligent, adorable and charming young man in the world!" she gushes. With the help of a nurse, Miss Fane tucks Michael in for the night and retires to sleep.

The next morning, the baby is gone—stolen from his crib. The poised Miss Fane goes totally to pieces. "They've stolen my baby!" she wails. "My baby!" Afraid to contact the police, she frets that the kidnappers do not know Michael's special baby formula. After an agony of waiting, a ransom note arrives with a piece of the baby's night gown enclosed. Miss Fane raises $90,000 in ransom money, but when she arrives at the rendezvous site, the kidnappers are scared off before she can close the deal.

Miss Fane finally calls in the cops. Tramping through her house, the police discover that the kidnapper entered the baby's second floor nursery by climbing up a trestle. When Miss Fane informs the police that she has taken home movies of the child, the chief detective vows, "We'll run them in every theater in America! We'll set the whole country on the hunt for your little boy." As the cops preview the home movie footage—showing little Michael swimming, eating, playing on the lawn and in his crib—a hysterical Miss Fane runs up to the screen, arms outstretched. "Don't cry, darling!" she sobs. "Mommy's coming!"

The FBI having not yet risen to abbreviation renown, the Los Angeles police are confused about what federal law enforcement agency to call in

("Contact the Department of Justice—we need the Secret Service!" barks a detective), but they know the media can galvanize an outraged public. Supplementing the newsreel clips, all-points bulletins are broadcast on radio in the form of emotional appeals by Miss Fane and groups of concerned women. Mothers across America are instructed to look for Miss Fane's baby and join together to "make the death of another child impossible in these United States." An NBC announcer calls for a federal law making kidnapping a capital crime.

Miss Fane's baby is safe, for the moment, but he is in mortal danger. Concealed in a wooden shack in the Hollywood Hills, little Michael is in the clutches of two brutal men and a coldhearted woman.

By screenwriterly design, however, Miss Fane's biggest fan—Molly Prentis, from the opening reel—lives in a shotgun shack down the road from the kidnappers' hideout. Molly grows suspicious of her secretive neighbors and discovers the truth. Alarmed, the kidnappers prepare to flee the hideout but not before getting rid of the evidence. No line of dialogue articulates their cruel design, but a man grabs a shovel and begins digging a grave in the backyard of the shack.

Sensing the imminent danger, Molly grabs the baby and flees in her jalopy. Outracing a hail of tommy-gun fire from the kidnappers and picking up a police escort along the way, she careens though the streets of Los Angeles and pulls up to Miss Fane's mansion. Michael waddles over to Miss Fane and says his first word: "Ma-ma."

For the captured kidnappers, justice is swift: they are indicted, tried, judged, and sentenced in a single day. The judge looks down in disgust as he delivers the verdict. "As I now complete the duty laid down upon me by the law, my only regret is that I haven't the power to send you to the gallows!" Life imprisonment without parole will have to suffice.

Virtually every review of *Miss Fane's Baby Is Stolen* mentioned the crime that inspired it. "Written around a sensational theme and undoubtedly inspired by the Lindbergh kidnapping, the drama gets off to a slow start, gradually speeds up, and ends with a series of suspenseful situations that will have them yelling," predicted the *Film Daily*.[22] The *Chicago Tribune* detected "a tolling reverberation from the Lindbergh case that awakens vivid, heartbreaking memories" and judged the picture "tragic and moving."[23]

But many critics saw *Miss Fane's Baby Is Stolen* as unsettling and exploitative. "It is a harrowing experience to sit through the kidnapping of Miss

Fane's baby," wrote the *New York Daily News*. "It brings back too vividly the horror of those dark days when the country waited breathlessly and despairingly for news of the Lindbergh baby."[24] The kidnap-averse Pete Harrison expressed a widespread revulsion. "The entire action revolves around the kidnapping of a child, and it is too harrowing for the average audience; it cannot be classified as entertainment," he stated. "Mothers will feel frightened and even have nightmares over the possibility of such a thing happening to them."[25]

No exhibitor wanted to be accused of giving nightmares to the mothers of America. The film faded from view and sank into obscurity, never revived and seldom seen.

Miss Fane's Baby Is Stolen was the last of the kidnap-themed films of the pre-Code era. On July 15, 1934, a new in-house censorship regime opened for business in Hollywood, the Production Code Administration (PCA). Overseen by the no-nonsense Joseph I. Breen, the PCA would henceforth vet all Hollywood scenarios for conformity to the tenets of the Production Code. Unlike the SRC, its word was law and its enforcement mechanism had teeth: without PCA approval, Wall Street denied the studios up-front financing for production. The cajoling and confusion of the pre-Code era gave way to the strict regulations and inviolable boundaries of Hollywood under the Code. The crime of child kidnapping would no longer be permissible as a motion picture plot point—period, no argument, no exceptions.

Chapter 7

THE GREATEST MURDER TRIAL THE WORLD HAS EVER KNOWN

The Hunterdon County Courthouse in Flemington, New Jersey, was a forbidding brick-and-mortar structure, built to intimidate defendants, guilty or innocent. It dated from 1828, when the tenets underpinning the American criminal justice system owed more to Puritan retribution than Progressive rehabilitation. Within these walls, sinners and malefactors were convicted and sentenced. Had a motto been inscribed above the entranceway it would have said, "Abandon hope, all ye who enter here."

A courtroom invites comparison with a theatrical venue—it is, after all, a stage built for ritual performance featuring actors, critics, and spectators playing assigned parts in an unfolding story with a surprise finish—but the overworked metaphor was never more apt than on the morning of January 2, 1935, when the Crime of the Century gave way to what was billed, with no expectation the title would ever be surrendered, as the Trial of the Century.

The proceedings lasted six weeks, ending on February 13 with a verdict that condemned the man in the dock to death in the electric chair. By the next morning, the media caravan had moved on, never to return, leaving the whiplashed residents of Flemington with memories of a brief moment in the sun and a few enduring transformations, such as the new dry-cleaning business started up to service the newsmen who needed their suits cleaned and pressed. The price gouging and fast-buck making came to an end for the short-lived boomtown enjoying "an economic windfall from the fourth estate."[1] Local farmers who had charged $5 a day for opening their homes to teletype machines and extra telephones returned to less remunerative work in the fields.

When court was in session, crowds of as many as a hundred thousand packed the streets to gawk at the dramatis personae, purchase macabre mementos (souvenir toy ladders—only twenty-five cents), and partake of Lindy-themed local color (a downtown restaurant served up a special "Trial Menu" of Lindbergh steak, Hauptmann beans, Trenchard roast, Bruno gravy, and Gow goulash).[2] "Without benefit of any of the Broadway impresarios," *Variety* reported in its customary mercenary style, "this small hamlet, 19 miles from Trenton, the state capital, has raised the curtain on one of the most publicized, sensational, and profitable dramas in the nation's history—the Hauptmann trial."[3] Even the staid *New York Times* spoke in huckster terms of "a criminal trial which most people would call the most sensational in the memory of man."[4] Broadway columnist Ed Sullivan, playing hooky from his usual beat, traveled to Flemington to soak up the local color and review "the most compelling drama ever acted out on any stage."[5] To the multihyphenate scribe Adela Rogers St. Johns it was, hands down, "the greatest murder trial the world has ever known."[6] *

Almost every top-line and on-the-make journalist in the newspaper game traveled to Flemington for a syndicated dateline: besides Sullivan and St. Johns, name brands like Arthur Brisbane, Damon Runyon, Walter Winchell, and Alexander Woollcott rubbed elbows with uncredited unknowns hoping to ride the trial to the big time. "The greatest galaxy of writers, reporters, artists, and columnists ever to show up for a murder trial in America" is how INS's James K. Kilgallen dubbed the assembly. Kilgallen modestly omitted himself from the constellation, but not his twenty-one-year-old daughter Dorothy, playing second fiddle to William Randolph Hearst's favorite gal reporter, featured soloist St. Johns. "The Hauptmann trial drew more than 300 reporters who wired 11 million words during 28 days, thereby breaking all existing records for a murder case," figured a modest tally that omitted the estimated 150 telegraphers on hand to send the copy out over the wires.[7] Whatever the precise numbers, only one precedent matched the scale of

---

* In a common misattribution, H. L. Mencken is often quoted as calling the Hauptmann trial "the greatest story since the Resurrection," but he actually used the line ("the best story since the Resurrection") in 1936 to describe the abdication of King Edward VIII to marry American divorcée Wallis Simpson.

coverage. By common consensus, the Hauptmann trial "has been the biggest newspaper circulation builder since the World War."[8] That meant it surpassed the astronomical numbers amassed by coverage of the kidnap-murder of the Lindbergh baby in 1932.

The journalists up against a daily deadline were joined by a more leisurely class of writers, slumming for a fat paycheck, but also drawn by the novelistic aspects of the case. The best-selling author Fannie Hurst, a specialist in plucky female protagonists who rose above working-class roots and shiftless men to achieve financial success if not romantic bliss, checked in for the *New York Times.* She was joined by Kathleen Norris, the socially conscious author and journalist, and Ford Madox Ford, the upper-crust British novelist and critic. Edna Ferber, the hugely successful novels-into-films author of *Show Boat, Cimarron,* and *So Big,* weighed in for the North America Newspaper Alliance chain. Waxing florid and mulling sagely, the novelists tended to overwrite and overthink. "Trained seals," sneered the job-of-work journalists, who better understood the nature of the beat and the most effective prose style: terse, straight from the shoulder, subject-verb-object blunt. The drama, tragedy, and twists of the Lindbergh case never needed rhetorical embroidery. "At a murder trial you simply sit still and write down what happens," advised Joseph Mitchell, who covered the case for the *New York World-Telegram.* "A newspaper can have no bigger nuisance than a reporter who is always trying to write literature."[9]

For moments of tear-jerking drama and pulse-pounding emotion, the trial did not disappoint. The bereaved parents testified, attorneys grandstanded, experts explicated, and witnesses plucked from obscurity savored their moment in the spotlight. The sight of Anne Lindbergh on the stand broke hearts. The identification of Hauptmann by Colonel Lindbergh and Dr. John F. Condon, both of whom were certain that the defendant was Cemetery John, electrified the courtroom. The voice of the man of mystery, a petulant tenor with a thick German accent, was heard in public and, thanks to the sound newsreels, not only in the courtroom. As with any trial, long stretches of lawyerly tedium—wrangling over admissible evidence and droning on about legal precedents—ate up hour after interminable hour, but the *longueurs* seemed to heighten the bursts of fire and revelation. Even the jargon-ridden testimony of experts in arcane fields might hold the courtroom spellbound. When wood expert Arthur Koehler recounted his obsessive two-and-a-half-year quest for the source of a plank of lumber from the ladder left below the second-floor nursery, judge, jury, reporters, and spectators leaned forward, transfixed.

The jury—eight men, four women—sat on the original hand-carved seats from 1828, on the Calvinist theory that an uncomfortable pew kept a congregation alert. "They sit like sideshow performers on a platform while the acts in the main tent go on," observed newbie INS reporter Dorothy Kilgallen, working the go-to metaphor.[10]

The director of the show—or stage manager—was Justice Thomas W. Trenchard, a jurist of the old school, formal, dignified, not to be trifled with. He received near-universal praise for his even-tempered and fair-minded rulings. The judge was old school in another habit he brought to the bench, hence the cuspidor under his desk. "Although he always bends down to see that his aim is correct, he hasn't any cause for worry," noticed columnist Sheila Graham. "Like the Canadian Mounties, the Judge never misses."[11]

Brooklyn's flamboyant Edward J. "Big Ed" Reilly led the defense team, his fee paid in part by William Randolph Hearst in exchange for exclusive access to Hauptmann.

A boozer who had seen better days, the tabloid-christened Bull of Brooklyn snorted, pawed the ground, and played to everyone but his most important audience, the jury of Hunterdon County locals who were unimpressed by the slick interloper from the big city sporting an incongruous white carnation in his lapel. "Reilly is a ponderous, fleshy man with a bald, high-domed forehead where gray stubbles of hair curl despite the barber's oil," observed James Cannon at the *New York Evening Journal*, unconcerned that his boss was footing the bill.[12] The vainglorious Reilly ordered new office stationery to reflect his current job title. In lieu of an office address, it read: "The Lindbergh-Hauptmann Trial, Flemington, N.J. Office of Edward J. Reilly, Chief Defense Counsel." On the left side of the sheet, running down the length of the page, was a sketch of a ladder in red ink.[13]

Also in Hauptmann's corner was C. Lloyd Fisher, a local Flemington lawyer more in tune with the temperaments of his townspeople, who was considered the more effective if less mediagenic attorney. Fisher took over cross-examinations whenever Reilly, who never shut up if a microphone was in range, contracted laryngitis.

Representing the state was thirty-nine-year-old David T. Wilentz, who knew that the case was an express elevator to a topflight political career. A first-generation American success story, born in 1894 in Latvia to Jewish

New Jersey District Attorney David T. Wilentz (left) and defense counsel Edward J. Reilly have a friendly encounter on the twentieth day of the Hauptmann trial, January 29, 1935.

parents who emigrated when he was an infant, Wilentz possessed the requisite pedigree (a graduate of Perth Amboy High School, a veteran of the Great War, with a law degree from New York Law School), a flair for sartorial elegance ("tailored for the last degree of the quieter Broadway perfection, in a plain brown suit all cut in angles" noted a fashion-conscious admirer), and an eye for the jugular.[14] Brittle, sardonic, ready to get right in the face of a witness, the wiry bantamweight was determined to be the tribune of justice who strapped the despicable murderer of the Lindbergh baby into the electric chair. The Hauptmann prosecution was the first criminal case Wilentz had ever tried.

In addition to putting Reilly on the payroll, Hearst bought access to Hauptmann's loyal wife Anna, steadfast in her belief in "my Richard's" innocence, paying a $7,500 retainer for exclusive rights to her story. To protect his investment, he assigned Jeannette Smits of the *New York Evening Journal* to be Anna's round-the-clock body woman. Smits was "to literally sleep with the wife of the defendant, this being part of an 'exclusive' which Hearst tied up with her," reported *Variety*. "They live, eat, and sleep together so that if anything happens the Hearst papers will have it first."[15]

Smits was known as the best sob sister in the business. As Anna cried on her shoulder, she scribbled notes and shared the anguish of the devoted hausfrau. "She looked grey and worn with the strain of a heart-stabbing experience," Smits wrote of Anna after the first day of courtroom testimony, when Hauptmann had cried out to her, "Have faith in me!" The couple's fourteen-month-old child, "little Manfred Hauptmann," was a prominent supporting character in Smits's entries, but his presence may have served less to humanize the parents than to remind readers of what the kidnapper had taken from that other set of parents.[16]

As Hearst's subvention of the defense team made clear, the press was not just a passive onlooker but an active participant in the Hauptmann trial. The self-reflexive—if seldom very self-critical—eye the media cast on itself was an enduring legacy of the Lindbergh case. When the trial got slow, reporters filed sidebars on the role of the press, the antics of their colorful colleagues, and themselves. "So high, in fact, has the state of journalistic excitement risen that it has become a part of the news itself and we are presented with photographs of news photographers photographing and stories by reporters about the reporting of other reporters," scoffed the Communist weekly *New Masses*, painting the media circus as just another capitalist plot to distract the workers while plutocrats picked their pockets.[17]

The carnival atmosphere disturbed even the performers on the midway. "It was difficult to tell after the first day whether the 1935 cloak of justice was a black robe or a joey [clown] suit," scolded *Billboard*.[18] The *Newark News* called upon "the newspapers, the lawyers, [and] the moving-picture companies not to profane the temples of justice" and issued a heartfelt plea: "Let us be civilized and not make judicial processes a barbaric spectacle."[19]

Barbaric spectacle or solemn ritual, the show was the hottest ticket in town. Seating was at a premium. The newspaper boys—and girls, for the tabloids knew the female angle was a potent draw—were accorded privileged access and granted, officially, 141 reserved seats, but Sheriff John Henry Curtiss, presiding over the courthouse, crammed as many as 200 into the space allotted, not including telegraphers. Three hundred seats were reserved for spectators, distributed on a first-come-first-served basis, or so said Sheriff

The gentlemen and women of the press take notes and write copy as Bruno Richard Haupt-mann confers with Egbert Robecrans, a member of his defense team, during a break in the trial, January 11, 1935.

Curtiss, who fielded more than fifty thousand requests from around the world. "More than 10,000 persons have made personal application for seats, and hundreds of others are coming in daily," said the overwhelmed lawman turned usher.[20] Of course, a celebrity face or a cash tip moved a petitioner to the front of the line.

Radio journalists were given the coveted press credentials, but their equipment, per Governor Moore's edict, was denied admission. To compensate, radio stations broadcast regular recaps and interrupted commercial programming with urgent (and not so urgent) bulletins. They also hired prominent lawyers to comment on the trial's progress and vocal artists to reenact testimony.

Oddly, however, a bulkier medium was granted conditional access to the courtroom. The presence of newsreel cameras in the temple of justice—and the subsequent decision of their operators to violate its sanctity—would precipitate the most controversial media-centric brouhaha of the entire trial.

Let's Go to Press

The newspapers owned the Hauptmann trial. Radio was denied a signal, the newsreels were blinkered and delayed, and still photographers were shut down. A rude shutterbug who snapped a picture of a grieving Anne Lindbergh on the stand was reprimanded by Justice Trenchard, who then demanded the negative be destroyed in his presence.[21] With the visual media blocked and the electronic media banned, the print media had a clear field. At least for the duration of the Hauptmann trial, the newspapers regained some of the ground lost to the networks and the newsreels.

The print press fully exploited the advantage. Every major newspaper devoted front-page, above-the-fold coverage each day the trial was in session, and the copy continued from page one deep into the interior. Page after page was given over to verbatim transcripts of the cross-examinations and attorney statements, supplemented by human-interest vignettes, wire photos, and sketched illustrations. Diagrams showing the layout of the Lindbergh home and the grids of the Bronx and facsimiles of the ransom notes and Hauptmann's handwriting were laid out for close textual examination by armchair detectives. Readers mastered the minutiae of the forensic evidence and learned new vocabulary words: dendrology, the study of wooded plants; and graphology, the study of handwriting.

On-the-spot interviews with attorneys for the defense and prosecution, all very available, brightened up the pallid patches. Occasionally, too, a brief encounter with the main attraction yielded a quotable utterance. On January 4, Universal Services reporter Lou Wedemar stepped in front of Hauptmann as he was being escorted out of the courtroom and asked, "How's it going?"

"Fine," Hauptmann replied.

"Do you think things are going in your favor?"

"Oh, yes, the witnesses—"

At which point the deputy sheriff accompanying Hauptmann body-blocked Wedemar and sent him reeling.

Hauptmann looked back and completed his comment: "I believe the jury is already convinced I am innocent!"

And then, to Wedemar's delight, Hauptmann winked and turned away with a grin. "He actually winked me!" blurted out Wedemar, who got an entire column out of the ten-second exchange.[22]

The queen bee of the press corps was not interested in being winked at by Bruno Richard Hauptmann. Former Hearst scribe and current Hollywood screenwriter Adela Rogers St. Johns had been lured back into harness by a personal appeal from "the Chief" himself, whom she could never say no to. Not that she took much persuading: St. Johns was waiting by the phone, thankful to be rescued from studio system drudgery and summoned to cover what she knew would be the story of her life.

St. Johns was among a select band of star reporters for the Hearst empire, and Hearst insisted his stars look the part. He provided her a fashion consultant and a generous expense account for an *haute couture* wardrobe. "I could wear the clothes but I couldn't always select them," recalled St. Johns, who waltzed into the courtroom each day dressed to the nines in one of five dresses "of heavy slipper satin, damn-all elegant, in dark and lighter blue, beige, silver gray, and black . . . coats to match in fine wool lined with soft fur and a series of custom-made soft brimmed hats, tailored but flattering."[23] St. Johns was worth every penny: she hammered out 1,200 words or more each day of the trial and left behind the best you-are-there record of the courtroom action. More than one city editor waited by the teletype machine at night to read her copy as it came in hot off the wire.

William Randolph Hearst's ace reporter Adela Rogers St. Johns, who wrote the best day-by-day chronicle of the Hauptmann trial, here seen deplaning on assignment in Topeka, Kansas, August 28, 1935.

St. Johns's boon companion was the legendary Damon Runyon, something of a clotheshorse himself. Better known as a short-story writer, sketching romanticized tales of New York City's colorful dese-and-dem underworld, Runyon hit pay dirt when sound came to Hollywood and brought with it a market for cityside patois: the film version of his sentimental short story *Little Miss Marker*, with Shirley Temple as the orphaned collateral to a gruff bookie, was a huge hit for Paramount in 1934. Hearst papers ran St. Johns's and Runyon's columns in tandem, a one-two punch no other syndicate could match. Determined to bury the competition, Hearst's *New York Evening Journal* engaged the largest single staff of reporters on-site.

Hearst's other big-name byline, septuagenarian Arthur Brisbane, sat near the jury box, scribbling notes with the "diligence of a cub reporter," as a bemused onlooker noted. Considered an over-the-hill prima donna, he was despised by St. Johns as a pompous desk jockey. Brisbane had something to prove, but he was roundly throttled by his more courtroom savvy and emotive female colleague.

The biggest media star in the courtroom, who turned the heads of celebrity watchers almost as much as the Lindberghs and Hauptmann, was Walter Winchell, the man who invented the mélange of gossip, news, and commentary that has come to define American journalism.[24] Instantly recognized by byline, voice, and face, he was in a class by himself, as famous as the movie stars whose press agents begged for his seal of approval. His syndicated gossip-cum-news column was devoured throughout New York, Hollywood, and across the hinterlands; the tempo and tagline of his highly rated radio program on Sunday nights at 9:00 was ripe fodder for impressionists, amateur and professional, who mimicked the adrenaline-fueled agitation of Winchell's voice firing off copy as if read fresh from a crackling ticker tape: "Good evening, Mr. and Mrs. North America and all ships at sea, let's go to press!" Winchell's prose was spattered with glibber-than-thou lingo that sometimes entered the "slanguage": "pro-and-conning" (giving both sides), "Garbo-ing" (being alone), and "Ratzis" (Nazis).

Winchell reveled in his big-dog status, dining most evenings and motoring into Flemington from Trenton most mornings with David Wilentz. Winchell's columns referred to his dining companion and chauffeur as "the brilliant lawyer for the state."

Winchell's status as first among equals was confirmed on the first day of the trial during the jury selection process, when each member of the pool was asked:

Do you read Walter Winchell's column?
Do you listen to Walter Winchell on radio?

Anyone conversant in Winchell-ese was excused from the jury.

Winchell's name also occasioned one of the biggest laugh lines of the entire trial. On January 21, Cecile Barr, the observant ticket taker at the Loew's Sheridan Square Theatre in Greenwich Village, testified that Hauptmann was the man who had handed her $5 in Lindbergh ransom money for a forty-cent movie ticket on the night of November 26, 1933.

What was the film being played? asked Wilentz.

Walter Winchell's *Broadway Through a Keyhole*, she replied to gales of laughter.[25]

Even Hauptmann took notice of the celebrity competition. "Where is dot Vinchell zitting?" he asked the reporters sitting behind him. "He should not be allowed here. He is not a nice man."[26]

Newspaper columnist and radio commentator Walter Winchell in his heyday, August 13, 1934.

A Dramatic Serial with a Flemington Dateline

The reporters did not have to wait long for a showstopper. On January 3, 1935, the second day court was in session, the appearance on the stand of Anne Lindbergh reminded everyone that the circus was in town because of a murdered baby. Anne herself did not cry, but she was the exception. During her heart-wrenching testimony, many in the gallery tried to stifle sobs; many others wept openly, without shame.

Adela Rogers St. Johns melted at the sight. "We who sit in the courtroom at the trial of Bruno Hauptmann for the murder of Charles Augustus Lindbergh Jr. have seen something we will never forget," she wrote, "a great woman and a great lady courageous in sorrow, gallant in grief—a slim young thing in black who will never again be happy." Though she did not fit the job description, St. Johns wore the sob sister label as a badge of honor. Herself the mother of a boy she adored, she tugged hard at the maternal heartstrings and laid it on thick:

Did you ever put warm, woolly sleepers on a baby you loved very much? There is something about them, about the silly, foolish little feet, about the smell of them, about the little pants that button across the back, that makes your heart go soft in the happiest moments. . . .

She had put that little woolly sleeping thing on her baby the night of March 1, 1932. She had buttoned it about him, and you knew that as she did so, she'd held him close and kissed the top of his head and probably tickled him inside his woolly sleepers. And he had laughed and snuggled against her. She said:

"I never saw him again."

As she looked at his woolly sleepers, she knew that after they left her mother's hands, they were torn from the little eagle with the merciless cruelty of a hawk.[27]

Defense attorney Reilly wisely decided not to prolong Anne's ordeal. "The defense feels that the grief of Mrs. Lindbergh needs no cross-examination," he said gallantly.[28]

Scheduled to follow her mistress to the stand, nurse Betty Gow had become too distraught to testify. In her place, Wilentz called Colonel Lindbergh. Gently, respectfully, he led the first of his two star witnesses through the identification of Hauptmann as the man whose voice he heard shouting from the interior of St. Raymond's Cemetery on April 2, 1932, the night he drove Dr. Condon to the ransom exchange.

That night in the Bronx cemetery, asked Wilentz, whose voice did you hear yell "Doktor! Over here, Doktor!"

"That was Hauptmann's voice," Lindbergh stated firmly.

"It took my breath away," wrote St. Johns. "It was the biggest moment of the trial so far."[29]

The evidence against Hauptmann was largely circumstantial—overwhelmingly so, but still circumstantial. Lindbergh was the first witness to accuse the defendant to his face, fitting in place the first layer of the brick-by-brick case Wilentz was building.

The next day, January 4, Reilly cross-examined Lindbergh in what St. Johns deemed "probably the most exciting day ever spent in an American courtroom." In seeming to badger the heartsick father, Reilly made him, again, a hero.

Under Reilly's skeptical interrogation, Lindbergh explained why he had grasped at any lifeline that might lead to his child, why he delegated two gangsters to act as intermediaries, why he believed the cruel hoax hatched by the disturbed Norfolk shipbuilder John Hughes Curtis, why he trusted the eccentric Condon, and why he followed the orders of Cemetery John to the letter. "You see," he said quietly, "I figured out that after such an event and in such a situation, nothing could be normal. I knew that I couldn't judge anything by the usual things that I knew about life."[30]

Reilly's aggressive posture was a serious tactical error, especially his insinuation that the father of the murdered baby was somehow deficient in his paternal duties. St. Johns, who had been in courtrooms since the age of eight, tagging along with her beloved father, Earl Rogers, the best defense lawyer of his time until alcohol brought him low, couldn't believe how badly Reilly had misread the room. "Within ten seconds, [Lindbergh] had brought the courtroom almost to its feet," she wrote. "Within ten minutes, he had evoked a wild round of applause from the spectators and you knew except for the stern eye of the judge and the black-robed dignity of the court, we'd have all been on our feet cheering."[31] Under fire by a glowering Reilly, Lindbergh became once more the dauntless Lone Eagle, calm, forceful, utterly trustworthy. "He was the best witness I ever saw," marveled St. Johns.[32]

Lindbergh attended every day of the trial, packing a revolver strapped under his arm because of death threats from the crazies. "With his right hand sometimes tight around the outlines of the gun where it bulged in his pocket,

Charles Lindbergh and Col. Norman Schwarzkopf enter the lobby of the Hunterdon County Courthouse on the opening day of the Trial of the Century, January 2, 1935.

the world hero sat only eight feet away from Hauptmann," wrote Martin Sommers, correspondent for the *New York Daily News*, not the only person in the courtroom ready to render a verdict of justifiable homicide had Lindbergh gunned down the defendant.[33]

The morning after the Lindberghs' testimony, Justice Trenchard was angered when he opened his newspaper and saw, in defiance of his orders, photographs of Anne and Charles on the stand. "I very much regret that I have to speak of a matter this morning which relates to the matter of talking photographs here while the court was in session," he said at the opening of court. "I thought it was perfectly understood between the court and the photographers and everybody else, that no photographs were to be taken here while the court is in session." Glaring at the culprits in the press section, he ordered, "Now that must not occur again." If it did, he would be obliged "to take such measures as the court deems expedient."

The judge was not joking. A few weeks later, when the most famous photojournalist in America strolled into court, brazenly set up her tripod, and begin clicking away, he ordered Margaret Bourke-White ejected from the courtroom.[34]

Betty Gow's testimony was eagerly awaited: she was pretty, an ordinary mortal, and under something of a cloud because the baby had been kidnapped on her watch. "Was she as watchful of baby Lindbergh as she should have been?" asked Dorothy Kilgallen, speaking aloud what many thought.[35] St. Johns, who switched easily from hard-boiled crime reporter to sister under the mink, assumed a maternal solidarity with Anne's devoted nurse-nanny. "Now, we all guard our children, we are all kidnap-conscious," wrote St. Johns, but "before the thing happened, I don't imagine that such an idea entered the mind of any human being in the Lindbergh household as even the vaguest possibility." For failing to imagine the unimaginable, "we ought not to feel any underlying prejudice against Betty Gow."[36]

Gow made a strong appearance and absolved herself. Immediately afterwards, drained from her ordeal, she fainted—a theatrical moment the reporters loved.

On January 9, the star witness for the prosecution, Dr. John F. Condon, the redoubtable Jafsie, testified about the German-accented phantom with whom he had rendezvoused in two Bronx cemeteries.

Condon was a blowhard, but he knew how to tell a story. The courtroom hung on his every word, riveted by the gothic atmospherics of the cemetery meetings: the jump over the graveyard fence, the footrace down 233rd Street, the side-by-side conversation with Cemetery John on the bench at Courtland Park, and, at the second meeting, the sudden appearance of Cemetery John materializing like an apparition behind a headstone at St. Raymond's

Cemetery. "In the dark, lonely night, in cemeteries, with the very smell of corpses in our nostrils, we saw that criminal crouching behind a hedge, reaching up his hands for the blood money," shivered St. Johns. "We saw him climbing like an animal over iron gates, shrinking from the light and from his fellow man."

Wilentz fed Condon his lines. "Who was the man you spoke to then between the gates?"

"John, as given to me by himself."

"And who is John?"

Milking the drama, Condon wagged his finger at the defendant and, parsing out the words, declared: "John is . . . *Bruno. . . . Richard. . . . Hauptmann!*"

"I tell you, it was an experience I do not want to repeat again as long as I live," confided St. Johns. "It is a figure I never want to see again, that man prowling through dark nights, that man taking money, that man asking the one question that stirred his emotions, 'If the baby is dead, will I burn?'"

"Yes, he'll burn!" St. Johns answered. She did not encounter "one person, when [Condon's] cross examination was half over, who did not believe him."[37]

During the cross-examination, Reilly had tried to rattle Condon by implying he was part of the kidnap plot, but the old man was unshakable. To most observers, Jafsie was just what he appeared to be. "Studying [Condon's] background as I have, I fail to see how anyone can accuse him of anything more baleful than an old man's yen to stick his nose into matters of importance," observed Broadway columnist Louis Sobol, who, like most entertainment journalists, strayed from his usual beat to comment on the actors in the greater show.[38]

Though not as intrinsically electrifying as the face-to-face identifications by Lindbergh and Condon, the testimony of scientific experts in esoteric fields was even more incriminating. Graphologists matched Hauptmann's handwriting to the ransom notes, U.S. Treasury officials analyzed his finances, and—most devastatingly—Arthur Koehler, the specialist in wood identification from the U.S. Forestry Service, nailed Hauptmann to the rails of the ladder used in the kidnapping.

Koehler, "a bald, middle-aged, keen-looking man with a professional manner," as *New York Times* reporter Russell Porter described him, was an unlikely attention grabber. Yet as he painstakingly retraced his step-by-step search for a plank of lumber that matched the grain of wood from the kidnap ladder, the courtroom was mesmerized. He asserted unequivocally that a board from the kidnap ladder was taken from the same plane of wood as floorboards in Hauptmann's attic. "Hauptmann knows I am right," Koehler said in a low voice, eyeing the defendant. "He of all people in this courtroom knows. He knows I traced the wood in the ladder from the tree in which it grew to the attic in his room. He is a carpenter—and even though he is a bum one, he knows that wood does not lie."

Koehler's performance on the stand received rave reviews from a press corps amazed that planks of wood could be made so fascinating. "He is a wizard of wood—a mental blood hound who can trace a toothpick home to the tree from which it was nicked," rhapsodized James Cannon in the *New York Evening News*.[39] UP's Sid Whipple was only slightly less effusive. "Arthur Koehler went to the stand to tell the most fascinating detective story ever unfolded before a living jury," he wrote. "He told it as a scientist with calm, cold impartiality. But when he had finished, he had made his inanimate blocks of wood shout to the jury their condemnation of the prisoner."[40]

It was Koehler's lucid, plank-by-plank testimony—not Lindbergh's ear-witness identification, not Jafsie's eyewitness identification, not the hand-writing of the ransom notes, not even the ransom money found in Haupt-mann's garage—that was the decisive evidence, the damning smoking gun. "In that moment," wrote St. Johns, she and everyone else in the courtroom "fought back the sick horror of believing that this man was the Lindbergh kidnapper—of knowing it." She looked over at the defendant. Their eyes met, and her "heart was sick with certainty," the dead certainty that Bruno Richard Hauptmann had murdered the Lindbergh baby.[41]

The Granite Mask of Bruno Richard Hauptmann

INS reporter Dorothy Kilgallen sat in seat number 13, right behind Haupt-mann. Occasionally, she would lean over and ask him a question, but mostly she just stared at the back of his head and wondered what went on inside.[42]

She was not alone. Getting inside Hauptmann's head was the favorite after-hours parlor game of the courtroom reporters, his iceman demeanor an incessant source of comment and speculation. "Inscrutable automaton," he was called, "silent alien." Damon Runyon, who knew all the types, sized him up as "the cold silent morose type of the old-world criminal."[43] "He's a wooden Indian, I tell you," said Deputy Sheriff Harvey Low, who escorted Hauptmann from the jail to the courtroom each day.

The impenetrable exterior only accentuated Hauptmann's allure. "Staring at him, as the testimony against him goes on, he becomes the outstanding figure in the courtroom," wrote Adela Rogers St. Johns. "He looms on a huge screen. I cannot take my eyes off him."[44]

On the first day of the trial, during a recess, St. Johns got up and walked in front of Hauptmann, boldly looking him up and down. "He does not carry a head upon his shoulders," she noticed after her first good look. "It is a skull. I have never before seen such an effect upon any human being. You can see the bones of that skull so plainly through his flesh that it startles you once or twice, in the cold winter sunshine, it gave you the feeling of a death's head carried about by a living man." The sunken eyes, the curve of the bone socket, the sloping brow, and the stark jaw—she saw the skull beneath the skin.[45]

Occasionally, the mask cracked. When Lindbergh identified Hauptmann as the voice of Cemetery John, the defendant "was visibly affected by the words which may send him to the electric chair," wrote Joseph F. Driscoll of the *New York Herald Tribune*. "His sunken eyes blinked, his jaw dropped, his

Three views of the cold Teutonic villain, Bruno Richard Hauptmann, in the law library adjacent to the courtroom in the Hunterdon County Courthouse, January 6, 1936.

Hauptmann and his wife Anna talk in German during a break in the trial testimony, as Deputy Sheriff Hovey Low (in glasses) and New Jersey state trooper Lt. Allen Smith look on, January 21, 1935.

ears reddened, he breathed heavily and his body stiffened." Within ten seconds, Hauptmann had recovered his "icy poise and glared defiantly back at his accuser."[46] After Condon made his emphatic identification, UP reporter Sid Whipple thought he detected involuntary muscle movement. "I saw his neck muscles grow taut, and color creep up his neck and into his sallow cheeks," observed Whipple, who like every reporter with a clear view was laser-focused on the defendant.[47]

Arthur Koehler also got under Hauptmann's skin. As the dendrologist explained the fine points of wood grain, the blood drained from Hauptmann's face. "His muscular frame sagged in his chair between his guards, and his pale face was whiter than ever," noted Russell B. Porter at the *New York Times*.[48] When Koehler matched a plank from the ladder to a plank in Hauptmann's attic, "Hauptmann's head went forward an inch, as though a rope around his neck had jerked it," observed St. Johns, again previewing his execution.[49]

On the rare occasions the iceman spoke, the press was all ears. On January 8, Joseph Perrone, the Bronx taxi driver who delivered a letter to Dr. Condon's house, positively identified Hauptmann as the man who stopped him near Van Cortlandt Park and gave him a dollar. When Perrone put his hand on Hauptmann's shoulder and said "This is the man," Hauptmann snarled at him: "You're a liar!" When Wilentz introduced the ramshackle ladder as evidence, Hauptmann ventured a snarky wisecrack: "If I built that ladder, I'm a second-hand carpenter, yah?"[50]

The *New York Evening Journal* tapped its drama critic, John Anderson, to review Hauptmann's performance and its sports columnist, Bill Corum, to size up his physical fitness. "Questions eddy and swirl about this Gibraltar of mysteries, mount and pile up upon each other as if to topple it all in—but there it stands in the granite mask of Hauptmann himself, unshaken," overwrote Anderson.[51] Corum fell back on the pugilistic language of the sports pages. "Guilty or innocent, the guy can take it," he admitted. "This thing is certain—you could freeze the Madison Square Garden skating rink with the blood that flows in the veins of the German ex-machine gunner."[52]

Percy Winner, yet another reporter working for the *New York Evening Journal*, dissented from the conceit of the granite mask, or at least refined it. After watching Hauptmann "at close range for a period of many hours," Winner concluded that "far from being a granite mask, Bruno Hauptmann's face is a mirror—a double mirror with two surfaces, one opaque and recessive, into which his emotions disappear darkly, the other luminous and revealing, in which violences flare out boldly and in which shy, almost boyish charm at moments seems to give the lie to the outer sullen gloom."[53]

As the trial went on and the evidence piled up, St. Johns discerned a gradual erosion of the arrogant, inscrutable front. After the Lindberghs and Betty Gow testified, "he began to change. The wooden figure came to life. The death's head began to grimace and smile and talk."[54] Kilgallen agreed, sort of. Though as "strange and cold-eyed and unfathomable as ever," Hauptmann sometimes twisted his face into "a laughing mask, smirking grimly like the face of a comedy on a theater curtain."[55]

St. Johns best expressed the motive behind all the psychological probing and amateur phrenology. "Only Hauptmann knows what really happened. Locked inside that skull is the secret of his own guilt or innocence."

When she met what she assumed was the window into his soul, she tried to look inside:

> As I gazed straight into Hauptmann's eyes, I wished that for one moment God would give me the power to see into his mind, to turn on a magic ray and hear his thoughts as one turns on a radio, or see them as one watches a teletype.[56]

Listen as she might, stare as she might, St. Johns picked up no signals.

"Will He Break?"

On January 24, heedless of the bitter cold and snowdrifts, crowds waited in line outside the Hunterdon County Courthouse to get in to see the most anticipated testimony of the entire trial. The defense team had no choice but to roll the dice and trust the fate of their client to the man most concerned with it. Shortly after ten o' clock, Bruno Richard Hauptmann was called to the stand. Adela Rogers St. Johns asked the question on everyone's mind: "Will he break?"

For nearly two full days, Edward J. Reilly led Hauptmann—nonchalant, speaking in a strong clear voice, legs crossed, fingers intertwined—through a prolonged exercise in exculpation. Virtually any resident of the eastern seaboard was a more likely kidnap-murderer than the hardworking immigrant, faithful husband, and doting father who was Bruno Richard Hauptmann. Only the treachery of the New Jersey police and the ambitions of an unscrupulous prosecutor could explain the persecution of a man who was, in fact, another victim of the Lindbergh tragedy. The whole thing—ladder, ransom money, ransom letters, eyewitness identification—was a pathetic frame-up by lawmen pressured to close the case and collar a suspect, any suspect.

Hauptmann's deflections, denials, and obfuscations were interrupted by a singular instance of misfired wit. Asked by Reilly if he had built the rickety kidnap ladder placed in evidence, Hauptmann scoffed, "I am a carpenter," repeating on the stand the wisecrack he had earlier tried out from his seat. "It looks like a musical instrument."

Though usually a sucker for a glib line, Alexander Woollcott, the acerbic wit writing for the *New York Times*, was not amused. "His wisecrack hung in the chill air unrewarded by the response usually indicated in the stenographer's notes as 'laughter in the court,' " commented Woollcott. Nor did Woollcott think the offhand use of the nickname "Lindy" by both attorney and witness was appropriate. "The atmosphere was one in which whimsies could scarcely be expected to flourish."[57]

On the second day of direct examination, Friday, January 25, at precisely 4:11 P.M., as dusk began to fall, an exhausted Reilly turned the witness over to Wilentz. "He looks supremely confident," wrote William Weer of the *Brooklyn Daily Eagle*, who had kept a closer eye on Wilentz than Reilly. "On his face is a cat-about-to-eat-the-mouse grin."[58]

The cat wasted no time in pouncing. Wilentz ripped into the witness and, for the next thirty minutes, kept up a relentless barrage.

"Wilentz waded into Hauptmann with the killer instinct of a Jack Dempsey," wrote Joseph Mickler of the *New York Evening Journal*, watching from his ringside seat. "Those 30 minutes in the hands of a dapper young prosecutor who filled a merciless cross-examination with as much fire and fury as any inquisition ever held left the Bronx carpenter a confessed criminal and a confused liar and toppled the edifice of innocence he had spent long hours in rearing."[59]

Hauptmann was visibly rattled. "Lightning struck Hauptmann on the witness stand, and he shriveled under it, cowering, grasping, livid," wrote St. Johns, enjoying the meltdown. "Those of us in the courtroom shrank from the sight of a man who was being electrocuted before our very eyes."[60]

At 4:45 P.M. Hauptmann was saved from further pummeling when Justice Trenchard adjourned court for the day. The defendant would have the weekend to recover.

By Monday, January 28, prosecutor, defendant, reporters, jury, and gallery had all rested up for the rematch. So had Hauptmann. He looked rejuvenated and cool, no longer the cornered animal of the previous Friday.

Primed by serial radio and Hollywood melodrama, spectators hoped for an emotional end-reel outburst. Would Hauptmann break down on the stand, confessing tearfully and explaining everything? After nearly three years of waiting, would the mysteries of the Lindbergh kidnapping be revealed in an explosive catharsis?

For two full days, Wilentz and Hauptmann sparred. On the first day, during five hours of brutal cross-examination, Hauptmann remained steadfast—but not unshaken. So long bland and waxen, he became by turns angry, smug, and loud. His eyes blazed with fury and hatred: this was a man, thought many in the courtroom, who could murder a baby in cold blood.

"In all my many years of courtroom experience, I have never known anything quite like what is happening now," wrote St. Johns of the action during the second round.[61] Few doubted Hauptmann's guilt any longer; what the gallery craved was resolution, the answers to the questions that had haunted everyone since the night of March 1, 1932.

Wilentz struggled to land a knockout blow, but Hauptmann stuck with the improbable "Fisch story" he had told since the day of his arrest, explaining that a now-deceased friend named Isidor Fisch had left the ransom money in his house for safekeeping. "I am innocent!" he protested, his English failing him. "That keeps me the power to stand up!"

As the grudge match dragged on, Wilentz and Hauptmann edged physically closer to each other, Wilentz boring in and wagging his finger, shouting and berating; Hauptmann, tense, slashing the air with his hand. So palpable was the eye-to-eye hatred between the two men that at any moment St. Johns "expected them to leap at each other's throats."

Of course, a defendant has good reason to hate a prosecutor trying to put him in the electric chair and a prosecutor has good reason to hate a defendant whom he believes murdered the twenty-month-old baby of a national hero, but the duel between the two men radiated an ideological and ethnic subtext that pulsed just below the surface—if not for the men themselves then for the crowds in their respective corners. The malefactor was an ice-cold German who had spoken favorably of Adolf Hitler. The prosecutor was an American Jew who embodied the best hopes of his people. For the one, Hauptmann was a victim of Jewish American perfidy. For the other, Wilentz was an avenging warrior and a symbol of vicarious payback.

The Jewish press beamed with pride on its kinsman. The *Wisconsin Jewish Chronicle* hailed "the unquestionably dapper, youngish David T. Wilentz" as one of the year's "most important Jewish newcomers," in a class with such luminaries as *New York Times* publisher Arthur Sulzberger and playwright Clifford Odets.[62] Wilentz was spoken of—in Yiddish and English—as "the man responsible for bringing justice to bear in the tragic Hauptmann affair, and who deservedly has earned the approbation and indeed admiration of millions of people throughout the world."[63]

The combat by proxy worked both ways. German American groups rallied to Hauptmann's side, contributing money to his defense fund and holding rallies to proclaim his innocence. Much of the nationalist solidarity took inspiration from Hauptmann's home country. Walter Winchell reported that "Nazi contributors" funneled enormous sums of cash into the Hauptmann defense coffers. "Did you ever eat dinner up in Yorkville?" Winchell asked, referring to the German American enclave in upper Manhattan. "Try it sometime and you'll find an extra twenty-five cent charge tacked on to your bill. Ask 'em to explain it and they'll say it's for the Hauptmann Defense Fund."[64]

Part of the strategy for Hauptmann's supporters involved slurring the prosecutor. Wilentz was assailed as a Talmud-quoting, Cabala-practicing agent of the Elders of Zion, the mythical star chamber of Jewish illuminati bent on world domination.[65] For his part, Wilentz was reported to be keenly aware of what the *Jewish Ledger* called "the delicate Nazi-Jew angle," but he kept the equation strictly defendant-prosecutor.[66]

Not so the Nazis, foreign and domestic, who advanced a novel theory about the kidnap-murder of the Lindbergh baby, a scenario that absolved Hauptmann by promulgating a libel as old as European Christianity: that American Jews had kidnapped and killed the Lindbergh baby to use his blood in the performance of their Passover rituals. "The Lindbergh baby was killed in a ritual murder," stated leaflets circulated at Hauptmann defense rallies. "Now Hauptmann will be the next ritual victim."

The leaflets cited the authority of Julius Streicher's Nazi propaganda sheet *Der Stürmer.*[67]

Chapter 8
INTO THE ETHER

The trial of Bruno Richard Hauptmann would have been perfect for radio. A stationary event built around verbal byplay with ready-made breaks in the action for spot commentary and commercial sponsorship, the real-life courtroom drama might well have beaten the ratings of the usual daytime programming, the serial melodramas recently dubbed soap operas. Even the dead air would have had listeners (as another recent coinage had it) glued to the set.

And why not? In the years since 1932, radio had spread out across America to become the most intimate and pervasive of the media, a siren call beckoning at arm's reach. In 1936, a CBS survey—the most extensive and scientific ever done, far more reliable than the widely criticized survey by the federal government in 1930 that placed the number of homes with radio at twelve million—found that seven out of ten American households owned a radio. In a population of nearly 130,000,000, an estimated 21,500,000 families gathered around the electronic hearth, not counting homes with second or third sets or the nearly 1,800,000 automobiles equipped with radio. Even the CBS survey was thought to lowball the numbers.[1]

Radio technology had also advanced apace, facilitating movement away from the confines of the studio to remote locations for on-site "spot coverage." Portable transmitters, shortwave hookups, and cleaner audio signaling gave the network behemoths—the NBC Blue and Red networks, CBS, and Mutual Radio, the last a fourth-place consortium of affiliated stations launched in 1934—the means to transmit the entire proceedings of the Hauptmann trial coast to coast, live, clear as a bell. With months of advance notice, technicians could have descended on Flemington and turned the Hunterdon County Courthouse into a state-of-the-art broadcasting facility. Hour after hour, the sounds of the courtroom—the gavel of the presiding judge, the interrogation of witnesses, the hubbub from the gallery—promised a spellbinding sonic spectacle.

The prospect of gavel-to-gavel coverage of the Hauptmann trial was not wishful thinking. Radio had already made tentative inroads into the chambers of American jurisprudence. Early in the medium's history, on September 10, 1924, during the verdict phase of a previous candidate for the trial of the century, radio aired the shocking decision by Justice John Caverly that the child murderers Nathan Leopold and Richard Loeb had been sentenced to life imprisonment, not death. Although microphones, transmitters, and announcers were deemed too disruptive of courtroom decorum to broadcast during testimony and arguments, the judge permitted WGN, the *Chicago Tribune*'s radio arm, to wire the courtroom for the reading of his decision.[2] In 1931 in Los Angeles, Superior Judge Harry W. Falk went further, allowing local stations to place microphones in his courtroom for the murder trial of former deputy district attorney David H. Clark. The judge reasoned that, when the public interest was at stake, airing the trial served the noble cause of civic education. "I predict that within ten years, American citizens will be able to sit in their homes and by radio and television not only hear but see public events, including trials," he prophesied.[3]

The farsighted jurist was about fifty years off. Less open-minded judicial gatekeepers blocked the entrance of radio into their august chambers; the officers of the court were tribunes of justice, not stage actors. In 1932, at the annual convention of the American Bar Association, the live broadcasting of murder, divorce, or other sensational trials was roundly condemned as a "breach of decorum" and "an interference with the administration of justice." The lawyers adopted a resolution:

> All judicial tribunals, and particularly those which determine the liberties and at times the lives of those accused of crime, are the most serious of human institutions. It would seem incredible that an invasion of the sanctity of a court room, such as that referred to [radio broadcasting], could be thought to be compatible with the dignity which should surround the administration of justice according to law.

To the graybeards of the legal profession, who were fond of quoting Lord Bacon's line that "the place of justice is a hallowed place," the courtroom was the secular equivalent of a cathedral. The intrusion of radio disrupted the grandeur of a sacred ceremony.[4]

Nonetheless, when news of Hauptmann's capture flashed across the wires on September 20, 1934, radio programmers hoped that the judges would bend to the will of a public eager to listen in. Surely, every American deserved to sit with the jury and hear the evidence in the tragic case that had touched so many hearts.

Of course, the performance of a civic duty was not the only incentive. A surprise ratings hit that coincided with the Hauptmann arrest and indictment had proven the drawing power of live courtroom drama. On September 8, 1934, the *Morro Castle*, an ocean liner sailing from Havana to New York, caught fire off the coast of New Jersey, killing 137 passengers and crew before running aground near Asbury Park. The disaster was a gripping life-or-death tale of survival on the high seas, packed with novelistic details (the captain had died of a heart attack the night before) and stories of heroism (passengers rescuing each other) and cowardice (the crew panicked). Fortuitously too, at least for the newsreels, the story was within the field of vision of the motion picture camera: close to New York and visible above water. From their central offices, the newsreel companies chartered planes to circle the crippled ship and captured spectacular aerial shots of the smoking vessel.[5]

To investigate the cause of the disaster and the conduct of the crew, the Department of Commerce convened a board of inquiry in Room 426 of the New York Federal Building. Beginning on September 10, 1934, and concluding on September 28, 1934, WMCA broadcast the proceedings live. Listeners were riveted by the accounts of dauntless courage and lucky escapes, disgusted by the cowardice and incompetence of the crew, and horrified at the fiery deaths and watery graves.

In the final days of the *Morro Castle* investigation, the story of the arrest and arraignment of Bruno Richard Hauptmann was playing out downtown at the Greenwich Street Police Station and across the river in the Bronx. Suddenly, radio had a surplus of broadcast-worthy news.

After Hauptmann was perp-walked around the Greenwich Street station, radio stations in New York made tentative plans for live coverage of his trial in the Bronx County Courthouse at Third Avenue and 161st Street. "Recent excitement occasioned by the *Morro Castle* hearings which resulted in

Joseph Welch, a seaman from the SS *Morro Castle*, testifying at the inquiry into the disaster at the federal courthouse in the Bronx, broadcast live on radio, September 13, 1934.

WMCA getting plenty of listeners prompted all metropolitan stations to cast eyes at the Hauptmann trial," noted *Variety*, while expressing qualms about the propriety of the intrusion. "Obviously the placing of mikes for NBC and CBS plus WOR, WMCA, WNEW, WHN, WINS and perhaps others would tend to convert the trial into a circus without lemonade." To avoid the carnival comparisons, only WNYC, owned by the city of New York, was allowed to install microphones, but all stations would enjoy equal rights to the signal. WNEW and WMCA immediately announced plans to broadcast the trial, pending permission by the court. Even if Hauptmann's trial moved to New Jersey, radio anticipated access, with Newark-based WOR being pegged to handle technical arrangements and microphone installation, "but with all broadcasters enjoying pick-up privileges."[6]

On September 26, a Bronx County grand jury indicted Hauptmann for extorting $50,000 in ransom money from Lindbergh. The American Broadcasting System (ABS), a twenty-seven-station network along the eastern seaboard organized by broadcast pioneer George B. Storer, preempted its coverage of the *Morro Castle* inquiry for the breaking news of the Hauptmann indictment in the Bronx. For once, though, the Lindbergh case took second place. Swamped with calls from angry *Morro Castle* obsessives, the network pulled the plug on the Hauptmann feed and returned to the *Morro Castle* inquiry.[7] However, ABS continued to break into programming with Hauptmann bulletins and dramatized newsworthy developments in its popular *March of Time*–like reenactment series *Five Star Final*.

Even while New York was indicting Hauptmann for extortion, New Jersey was angling to up the ante. On September 21, 1934, Governor A. Harry Moore signed a warrant for extradition, and the two states came to the only decision that could strap Hauptmann in the electric chair. New Jersey was where the crime occurred and where the baby was killed. New York relinquished its prize catch so the suspect could be convicted of a capital crime—not for the extortion of $50,000 at a Bronx cemetery but for the commission of a burglary in a Hopewell home that resulted in a death, a capital offense.

With the Hauptmann trial set for New Jersey, radio anticipated full access for gavel-to-gavel coverage of the Trial of the Century. The networks had an enthusiastic ally in local Flemington officials who eyed commercial subvention as a way to offset the enormous costs of the trial to the city and "put the case on a cash basis by leasing the broadcasting rights."[8] The good citizens of Flemington might even turn a profit on the deal.

Not all stations, however, planned to broadcast the trial. Air space north of the border refused to join the consortium. Rupert Lucas, manager of the Canadian Radio Commission, declared that the "administration of justice would be placed in ill-repute" were the proceedings transmitted over the airwaves.[9]

American broadcasters were not so high-minded.

The News As It's Sizzling

On October 15, 1934, radio's hopes for a hit courtroom drama were dashed when New Jersey governor A. Harry Moore announced that he would not permit any broadcasting from the Flemington courtroom during the Hauptmann trial. "Every safeguard will be taken to insure an orderly, dignified trial," the governor declared. He presumed to speak for the jurist who had been assigned to preside over the case. "Knowing Justice Trenchard as I do, I know he would not permit the trial to be a burlesque. The proceedings will be dignified in conformity with judicial procedure in New Jersey. There will be no broadcasting from the courtroom."[10]

Governor Moore's haughty decree angered partisans of radio journalism. "Some sort of clear-cut policy seems imperative on the Government's part toward the question of radio eavesdropping at judicial hearings, whether in court or committee rooms," editorialized *Variety*. "Radio differs from press reports of the same proceedings in the complete candor of the medium. No friendly air reporter can make a sage philosopher of a ward heeler when listeners hear what they hear." Few American politicians were as radiogenic as FDR, whose fireside chats were already legendary, or New York mayor Fiorello LaGuardia, whose street-friendly manner and colloquial New York-erisms endeared him to listeners.[11]

Print journalists, having had their first taste of subaltern status during the radio coverage of the Lindbergh case in 1932, felt smug—and relieved. With radio exiled from the courtroom, newspaper reporters would be the privileged inside men and women. To get the texture and details of the trial, Americans would need to return to the pages of the old medium.

The relief felt by print journalists was premature. Denied live coverage, radio compensated with an intimacy and proximity that was the next best thing to being there. With news bulletins of breaking developments, reenactments of dramatic testimony, and commentary and analysis, radio placed listeners at the keyhole of the courtroom door, as close to the action as they could get without actually being inside. Looking on the bright side, *Broadcasting* pointed out that the radio ban turned out to be a blessing in disguise by saving the industry a fortune in production costs and lost advertising revenue.[12]

Newark-based WNEW was especially well positioned. The station had obtained permission to place a microphone within the courthouse and negotiated a cooperative deal with William Randolph Hearst's *New York Evening Journal* to share resources and expenses. Moderated by WNEW's popular announcer and commentator A. L. Alexander, the WNEW–*Evening Journal* broadcasts were carried over the American Broadcasting System.[13] In addition to WNEW, New York dial turners could choose among WINS, WEAF, WMCA, and WABC to hear hourly reports and special bulletins.[14]

Hearst understood that radio should be exploited, not turned off. During the Hauptmann trial, the *New York Evening Journal* ballyhooed its newspaper scoops—on radio. On January 8, after a grueling cross-examination by Edward J. Reilly, nurse Betty Gow obliged with a Hollywood moment and collapsed shortly after leaving the witness stand. "The *Journal's* flash broadcast materialized direct from the sheriff's office in the courthouse and has already stirred a city-wide reaction," boasted the *Journal*. The paper followed up the scoop with an appearance by society columnist Sheila Graham, "an Englishwoman who gave an account of her fellow countrywoman," on its regular nightly broadcast over WNEW.[15]

Radio consolidated its position by cultivating its own news operations. By 1935, two made-for-radio syndicates supplied the medium with the news it had once pilfered from the newspapers: the Press-Radio Bureau, run by the National Publishers Committee, and Transradio Press Service, an independent outfit serving 125 stations. Throughout the trial, each of the services sent out two hundred bulletins daily to member stations and about six to eight stories daily, some six thousand words. Tellingly, too, in a total reversal of the protocols of 1932, when a print source was needed for verification, radio stations that subscribed to either the Press-Radio Bureau or Transradio Press were instructed to announce news *only* when the radio services sent out the bulletin—not when the news flash came into the station by way of a newspaper syndicate.[16]

For the duration of the Hauptmann trial, radio hyped its up-to-the-minute news flashes as never before. All the major networks and independent stations were committed to breaking into programming as often, so the phrase went, "as developments warrant." Being even more committed to the profit motive, American broadcasters timed the bulletins with an eye to advertising dollars. Most station managers followed the example of WOR's Johnny Johnstone, who secured advance permission from advertisers to break into sponsored programming in order to "air any news flash that in [the] judgment of [the] news dept warrants immediate airing," as *Variety* put it, noting that the public service came with a cost-minded consideration. "Close editing and careful choice of break-in spots" prevented Hauptmann bulletins from stepping on "the commercial plug."[17] An urgent news flash was seldom urgent enough to interrupt the revenue stream.

While NBC and CBS opted to set up remote facilities in Flemington, mainly for the cachet of the "live from Flemington" dateline, George

B. Storer's eastern seaboard–only ABS network relied on Press-Radio dispatches and a single on-site reporter—positioned in the sheriff's courthouse office—who called in bulletins and provided local color. Two weeks into the trial, Storer reorganized ABS into a new network, the American Broadcasting Company (ABC), and moved quickly to establish his brand as the news channel of choice. "Vast audiences in 23 principal markets listen consistently to ABC stations which unfailingly deliver fastest first-hand reports on the Flemington trial—news story of the decade," bragged Storer's ads. "Other networks take their time, feed the public predigested doses. ABC broadcasts direct from the courthouse, serves up the news as it's sizzling." *Billboard* confirmed ABC's bluster. "First ABC had the *Morro Castle* investigation. Now it has the Hauptmann trial from the Sheriff's courthouse office. Other networks are said to be peeved."[18]

For radio, the payoff in reputation and ratings was enormous. "Radio gained considerable extra 'circulation' as a result of the comprehensive coverage offered by both Press-Radio Bureau and Transradio Press Service thruout the Bruno Hauptmann trial," affirmed *Billboard*. Moreover, "all news commentators had plenty of material and their stocks rose considerably as judged by the Crossley [ratings] reports."[19]

Though barred from the courtroom interior, radio still managed to dominate the airspace around Flemington.

The News Savants

The ascent of radio as a news medium was fueled by the on-air commentators who had emerged in 1932 during the crime phase of the Lindbergh case. In the nearly three years since, the trade press had bestowed upon them a moniker that did not stick: "news savants."

For Americans shaken by the upheavals of the New Deal and the forward march of Nazism, the news savants spoke in tones of calm reason and quiet authority. Erudite and quick-witted, they not only reported the news but filtered it with explanation, interpretation, and opinion. As radio attractions, the best of the cerebral commentators—among them, Lowell Thomas, H. V. Kaltenborn, Gabriel Heatter, and Boake Carter—ranked just below entertainment superstars like Eddie Cantor, Bing Crosby, and Jack Benny because of their appeal to "the average listener's intellectual needs," commented *Variety* in 1933, doing some needed intellectualizing itself. Unable to keep straight FDR's myriad alphabet agencies and Hitler's territorial demands, "the average listener has turned to the radio interpreters of current events for enlightenment."[20] Happy to assume the burden, CBS's resident sage H. V. Kaltenborn defined the relationship between commentator and radio listener as one of "intimacy of personal contact with the voice which brings them the word— the familiar voice they have come to know from hearing it regularly, which will tell them what lies behind the words, what it all really means."[21]

If the news savant was part mentor, part companion, his listeners had to be alert pupils else get lost in the maze of information. To track the ebb and flow of the Hauptmann trial, a court follower needed to master an advanced curriculum in forensic science, handwriting analysis, banking records, and legal maneuvers, plus the architectural blueprint of the Lindbergh home, the backroads of New Jersey, the street grids of the Bronx, and the timelines tracing the movements of the principal players.

With prestige and profits on the line, each station put its A-team of commentators behind the microphone. WOR's Gabriel Heatter made at least two daily broadcasts, the first scheduled during the noonday court recess and the second after adjournment at 6:45 P.M.[22] Heatter was on the air for the full seven weeks, six days a week, enunciating upwards of six to nine thousand words a day.[23]

NBC star and Fox Movietone narrator Lowell Thomas spoke from a pickup point in a poolroom directly across from the courtroom. He provided a solid, no-frills play-by-play:

> We all knew there'd be something of a carnival spirit here at the trial of Bruno Hauptmann. And it is a carnival—tough, noisy, pushing, jolly, laughing; a hurly burly with a touch of grimness, a frolic overshadowed by the most sensational and most pitiful crime of our time . . .

Like all the great broadcasters, Thomas understood that radio was, in its way, a picture medium and that part of his job was to paint mental images:

> Justice Trenchard is one of the most dignified men in these parts, yet he has a beaming smile, shell-rimmed glasses, and grey hair. A ruddy face that beams in competition with the red necktie he wears along with his judicial robes.[24]

CBS's resident sage H. V. Kaltenborn in 1938.

Boake Carter, who made his reputation during the kidnapping in 1932, covered the trial in his regular broadcast at 7:45 P.M. daily over the CBS network under the sponsorship of Philco, the radio manufacturer. On-site as a "commentating editorialist," Carter recapped the day's trial events and editorialized freely.[25]

NBC's even-tempered commentator Lowell Thomas in 1936.

On January 3, 1935, after attending the first day of testimony, Carter showed why, whatever the incongruity of his British accent, listeners bonded with him. He broadcast from the Union Hotel in Flemington, across the street from the courthouse, where reporters hung out in the bar and also where the jury was housed. "You could have heard the heavy footsteps of the ladies and gentlemen of the Hauptmann trial jury climbing the stairs, not ten feet away from this microphone," he confided, placing listeners at his side.

Carter had just witnessed the purgatorial anguish of Anne Lindbergh as she identified her baby's sleeping suit. He called upon all his powers of prose and intonation to evoke the pitiable moments.

"I thank providence that I did come to today's sessions for I have seen one of the most magnificent exhibitions of human courage possible to imagine," Carter began. For a full fifteen minutes, he described a scene that "made old-time reporters drip, literally, with perspiration [and] caused women to dab their eyes unashamedly."

> I have seen a young mother, robbed of her first-born son, finger the tattered remnants of the clothes he wore the night of his murder, bite furiously on her lower lip to keep back the tears, and then proudly lift her head and tell without a quiver what a mother feels when she discovers that her child has been stolen from the crib in which but a few hours before she had bidden him good night. . . . Had the case ended then and there when she stepped down from the witness stand, there would have been no need for the jury to leave the jury box to come to an opinion.

Carter told how District Attorney Wilentz had held up the baby's sleeping suit, "laundered and clean, but the story it told was enough to choke any throat to overflowing." As Carter described Anne, cradling the sleeping suit, he must have fought to keep his own throat from choking with emotion:

> There was no sound. She fingered it in her lap, her head bent over it. Then up went that little chin again—and though one could see that the breaking point was very close, she identified it as his sleeping suit and the prosecutor took it and put it on the clerk's table, offered as evidence. And it lay there, a crumpled heap—crumpled as the little body once inside it must have lain crumpled on some cold, soggy ground. Her eyes strayed constantly to that sleeping suit as she talked on—and one almost felt like crying to the attorney general: "Take it away, man, take it away."

Carter claimed that words failed him, though plainly this was not the case:

The scene cannot be described in words. Not if one had a hundred thousand in which to say it. It was an exhibition of superhuman courage—for it was not done in the heat of the moment, but the cold light of the day, before the gaze of hundreds of curious pairs of eyes. It was courage one seldom sees.

After that emotional watershed, the masculine reserve of the next witness came as almost a relief.

When Colonel Lindbergh followed his wife to the stand and described the part he played after Nursemaid Betty Gow rushed to him and asked if he had the baby, the change in atmosphere in the courtroom was amazing. It was as though one had held one's breath until almost the bursting point and then suddenly let it out with a long sigh. The sophisticated Alexander Woollcott was heard to observe cynically, "There's not enough drama."

Carter ended his report with a safe prediction. Whatever happened next in the Trial of the Century, no matter how fiery the cross-examinations or riveting the eyewitness testimony, for sheer heart-wrenching emotion nothing would equal the appearance of Anne Morrow Lindbergh on the stand.

It will not be like the picture unfolded today. It couldn't be. We have witnessed an exhibition of a woman's courage. Its magnificence has left us all there in Flemington rather limp.

And then, not forgetting his sponsor, Carter signed off:

So—Philco and I bid you merely "Goodnight."[26]

Hearing It Now

In 1935, Americans had only to reach for the dial to hear about the Hauptmann trial; the news was all over the airwaves. Alas, little of the live reporting and commentary saturating the atmosphere during the trial of the last century has survived into the present century. Only a tiny percentage of the radio heritage of the 1930s is extant and replayable; the rest has, in the evocative phrase of the day, vanished into the ether.

Until magnetic tape for recording was introduced in the post–World War II era, the only way for radio programming to be preserved was on a 78 rpm vinyl record known as a transcription disk, a cumbersome and rarely used process.[27] Unless a show was recorded on disk, and the disk was preserved, its life extended only for the duration of the live broadcast. More so than with entertainment programs, the preservation of radio news programs is hit or miss, and more miss than hit. Even printed transcripts of broadcast news shows are scarce—why save old news? Deprived of a tape or a transcript, the media historian has to rely on the ear and memory of a contemporary listener to get a sense of what was sent out over the air, before it dissipated, lost to history.

Though pervasive at the time, radio broadcasts pertaining to the Lindbergh case, both the kidnap-murder in 1932 and the trial in 1935, are maddeningly elusive now. In 1948, when broadcaster Edward R. Murrow and producers Fred W. Friendly and J. G. Gude put together a landmark archival compilation of historic radio moments entitled *I Can Hear It Now, 1933–1945*, the gaps in the record showed how little the medium cared about preserving its own heritage. Drawing on the CBS library, the five-LP set includes a representative cross section of material that would have been alive in the audio memory of the postwar generation—the iconic hysteria of NBC's Herb Sullivan watching the *Hindenburg* explode ("Oh, the humanity!"), the life-altering bolt from Pearl Harbor, and the somber narration by Arthur Godfrey of the funeral procession of FDR. Yet the excavation digs no further back than 1933. Likewise, although a subsequent three-LP collection, entitled *I Can Hear It Now 1919–1949*, issued in 1967 and billed as "thirty years of audio history," devotes one full side of its three LPs to radio moments from 1919 to 1932, almost all of the material is reenacted by soundalike vocalists and CBS technicians. "Recordings of individuals and events are either non-existent or of poor quality," explained the producers in the liner notes.[28] Neither package includes a sound, real or reenacted, from the Lindbergh case, either 1932 or 1935—an indication of the absence of material in the CBS vaults and sad confirmation that, when rewinding the radio past, you can't hear it now.[29]

Perhaps the most lamentable archival gap in the radio coverage of the Hauptmann trial is the lost legacy from the *March of Time* radio series. Every Friday at 9:00 P.M. during the trial, the show recapped the week's events.

Listening to *The March of Time* was no substitute for being in the courtroom, but the "aerial newsreel" edited out the boring parts and provided an aural highlight reel.

Ever since Hauptmann's arrest, vocal artist and foreign-accent specialist Dwight Weist had impersonated the suspect on the show. A kind of radio method actor, Weist visited the courtroom in Flemington to study the original—to hear his German accent and speech patterns, even to study his facial bone structure, which Weist believed affected the quality of the voice. He wanted not just to sound like Bruno Richard Hauptmann, but to feel what Bruno Richard Hauptmann was feeling.[30] (Weist was equally fastidious with the other German he specialized in, Adolf Hitler, whom he studied in the newsreels and listened to on radio.)[31] Neither Weist's ghosting nor the tone and content of the weekly reenactments is extant.

Another unfortunate missing radio link in the Hauptmann trial coverage is the nightly broadcasts on WNEW featuring the reporters from the *New York Evening Journal*. As ambitious with its radio as its print profile, Hearst's flagship New York broadsheet had set up a microphone in its Flemington headquarters, located a few blocks from the courthouse. From the command center, under the eye of city desk editor Ed Maher, reporters not only typed out reams of copy for the newspaper but broadcast a nightly recap of trial highlights.

Naturally, the *Journal* lauded in print the marvelousness of its radio spin-off and WNEW returned the favor. "While telegraph instruments cackled accompaniment and typewriters clicked a song of speed, a unique type of radio feature was broadcast from the 'city room' of the *Evening Journal*'s trial headquarters on Main Street," ran one of the many panegyrics in the Hearst press to itself. Via the microphones of WNEW, the nightly show evoked "a newspaper atmosphere that lacked nothing except the smell of print-er's ink."[32] The twenty-five reporters the paper had in harness ("the great-est number of reporters assigned on a single event in modern newspaper history") gave the show plenty of raw talent to draw upon: drama critic John Anderson compared the opening of the trial to a Broadway premiere, society writer Mme. Flutterbye flittered about the courtroom as if it were a salon, and photographer Clarence Albers told how the frigid winter made his job difficult. "The cameras freeze and it's difficult to make speed flashes," he complained.[33] Even the lowly copy boys were brought before the mike to share their adventures.

The *Journal* augmented the reportorial line up with regular appearances by guest speakers such as Walter Winchell, radio superstar Jack Benny, and Charles W. Lynch, a former boxing judge at Madison Square Garden, who gave a blow-by-blow of the matchup between Wilentz and Hauptmann.[34] Sheriff John H. Curtiss, "stealing a busy few minutes from his busy day," shared his Solomonic wisdom in allotting the tens of thousands of requests for seats he fielded very day. ("A resident of Fairbanks, Alaska, made a personal request for a seat. I couldn't refuse him. He sat through a morning session and was highly pleased.")[35]

Never one to shun a microphone, Edward J. Reilly was also a regular visitor. On February 2, he came by the city room to praise his client's stalwart performance on the witness stand and to tease future revelations. "In all my experience of 27 years as a lawyer, I have never seen a man so calm on the witness stand as Hauptmann; and never saw one who told the truth better than Hauptmann," Reilly declared. He urged listeners to stay tuned. "Bombshells will be dropped in the courtroom next week," he promised. "We have witnesses who will clinch the alibi of Hauptmann. We are going to save them for the concluding days of our presentation."[36]

On January 23, 1935, *Variety* editor Abel Green listened in and passed on a vivid account of the *Journal*'s radio show. "It's from this miniature newspaper office, equipped with teletypes, typewriters, phones, telegraphers, et al that WNEW also broadcasts a nightly 5:30 P.M. 15 mins of hot copy wherein the reporters are the broadcasting artists," reported Green. Conjuring the ambient noise of the on-location newsroom ("Typewriters click, keys clack, visitors and reporters chatter"), he described how "Mrs. Bruno Richard Hauptmann comes on the scene in constant charge of Jeannette Smits, one of the *Journal*'s sobbies, and feverishly the whole staff bangs out a scenario of 15 minutes of copy to accommodate WNEW's A. L. Alexander, specially engaged as announcer and conferencier of this special broadcast." Alexander was grateful to be spelled by the team from the *Journal*. After three weeks of constant commentary, "giving thousands upon thousands of audible words," he was "hoarse, cold, sick, and weary."

Green listened as a parade of *Journal* reporters came to the mike "for an action-filled lowdown" and "local color on the day's occurrences on the Flemington scene." Reporter Michael E. Claffey had just trudged through ten inches of freshly fallen snow to recount an interview with Hauptmann, conducted just after the testimony of wood expert Arthur Koehler had tied the defendant to the kidnap ladder. "Do you think what Koehler said sinks you?" Claffey asked Hauptmann. The carpenter said, "Yes." Claffey wanted to make sure Hauptmann knew what the idiom "sinks you" meant, but just then state troopers hustled the prisoner away.

Working the other side of the story, reporter Jimmy Cannon had scored an interview with Koehler and read aloud the most incriminating parts of his testimony. In a self-reflexive aside, Cannon wondered why copies of *Variety* were not on sale in Flemington, given the influx of potential readership. Like most of the journalists on the trial beat, Cannon resided in Flemington rather than drive an hour each way back and forth from Trenton in the snow. He roomed in the home of Flemington mayor John F. Schenck, who made up the reporter's bed each morning.

"These and other local colorful details go out over the air in an interesting and breezy broadcast," remarked Green. "Withal, it's great local color, blending journalism with the radio, and quite a feather for WNEW. It also explains why folks are taking their 'entertainment'—if such it can be called, although such is the case—from the periodic broadcasts on the Big Trial, and not venturing out to the cinema and theater."[37] Why go to the movies when the most compelling drama of the year was playing in the living room, free of charge?

Virtually every Hearst reporter on-site chimed in during the WNEW broadcasts, but sob sister Jeanette Smits always spoke first so she could then leave the studio with Mrs. Hauptmann in tow. Not even the hard-bitten Hearst newshounds wanted to speculate about the odds on Hauptmann's electrocution in the presence of his wife.

The Expert Advice of Samuel S. Leibowitz

In *His Girl Friday* (1940)—Howard Hawks's distaff version of Ben Hecht and Charles MacArthur's madcap newspaper yarn *The Front Page*—the unscrupulous newspaper editor Walter White, played by a motor-mouthed Cary Grant, is in desperate straits. He and his gal Hildy (Rosalind Russell), former wife and current partner in crime journalism, have been caught red-handed harboring a fugitive from justice. As the corrupt big-city mayor and his flunky sheriff prepare to haul Walter and Hildy off to the hoosegow, Walter grabs a telephone and barks an urgent directive back to his man at the city desk: "Duffy—get Leibowitz!"

The joke still works, mainly because the utterance of the ur-Jewish surname still bespeaks the desire for a clever mouthpiece, the kind of legal wizard you call when (like Walter and Hildy) you are on the wrong side of the law and caught red-handed. The original audience got the reference, though—to the most famous criminal defense attorney of the 1930s, the fast-on-his-feet, smooth-as-silk Samuel S. Leibowitz.

Born in Russia in 1893, Queens-bred, and Cornell-educated, Leibowitz was a shrewd, showboating criminal lawyer who never bothered to hide his New York attitude or Jewish roots—not that he could have. In the 1920s, his gangster clients made him rich and lent his practice an aura of shadiness that was not a professional liability. His ratio of success in death-penalty cases recommended him to well-heeled murderers of both sexes, whether the homicide was personal or professional. "Leibowitz has convinced many a jury that his client was as pure as the driven snow," remarked a reluctant admirer, who sounded unconvinced.[38]

In 1932, Leibowitz shot to fame—and south-of-the-Mason-Dixon-line infamy—by his tenacious defense of the Scottsboro Boys, the name for the nine young African American defendants who were charged with raping two white women in a boxcar in Alabama. When eight were sentenced to death and one to life imprisonment, Leibowitz swooped into the heart of the Confederacy and, at great personal risk, led the defense team. A rallying point for Popular Front progressives, the case became the most politically charged criminal case of the 1930s. In John Wexley's *They Shall Not Die* (1934), an agitprop play about the Scottsboro Boys mounted on Broadway by the Theatre Guild, Leibowitz became the first lawyer to be portrayed onstage while still alive. To prepare for the role of the Leibowitz figure, actor Claude Rains studied the original. He dialed back by half his portrayal of Leibowitz's outsize personality, but critics still complained he was overacting.[39]

For the complete run of the Hauptmann trial, radio listeners had the chance to hear Leibowitz's legal advice free of charge. A straightforward criminal proceeding with no obvious political angle or high moral stakes, the case lacked the aura of an idealistic campaign for racial justice, but few lawyers, Leibowitz least of all, could resist kibitzing from the sidelines.

Beginning on January 2 and concluding on February 12, from Monday to Saturday at 7:00 P.M., except Tuesday, when the broadcast began at 6:45 P.M.

in deference to *Major Bowes Famous and Original Amateur Hour*, Leibowitz appeared on New York station WHN to offer his expert opinion on the Trial of the Century.* For fifteen minutes each night, he conducted a master class in courtroom strategy, criminal law, and jury psychology, reminiscing about past cases, sizing up the credibility of witnesses, and handicapping the tactics of the prosecution and defense. An eloquent ad-libber, theatrical but homespun, he told jokes, gently ribbed his interviewer, and in general showed why he had charmed juries and judges for more than twenty years. WHN broadcast the shows directly from Leibowitz's law offices on the forty-second floor of the Transportation Building at 225 Broadway, placing the microphone right on his desk. To keep the setting in the minds of listeners who could never have afforded Leibowitz's billable hours, WHN announcer Brook Temple noted that the station engineer hoped that the winds whipping around lower Manhattan would not interrupt the transmission.

Temple introduced each show with a flourish. "Ladies and gentlemen, with the eyes and the interest of the world centered on a little courtroom in Flemington, New Jersey, where Bruno Hauptmann is on trial for his life, it is WHN's distinct privilege to have its microphone in the office of famed defense counsel and criminal lawyer Samuel S. Leibowitz, a very appropriate spot for a criminal lawyer's officers with a beautiful view through the south windows of the lighted Statue of Liberty." Temple lauded Leibowitz as the lawyer who has "snatched more men from the electric chair and saved their lives than any other living human being."

Leibowitz's interlocutor was Bryce Oliver, a well-known journalist and commentator in his own right, whom WHN had assigned to question "this brilliant member of the bar as to his expert and intimate opinion of the day's proceedings of the trial." Media critic Robert Landry described Oliver as an articulate liberal "forthright enough to be a bit critical but not radical," but on the WHN broadcasts Oliver was relegated to playing dimwitted Dr. Watson to Leibowitz's ingenious Sherlock Holmes.[40] In fact, Oliver's presence was superfluous: Leibowitz was quite capable of holding the floor on his own.

---

* In 2003, transcription disks of nearly the entire run of WHN shows featuring Leibowitz were discovered in the possession of Leibowitz's children Robert and Marjorie by documentarian Joseph Consentino. Virtually the only extant radio recordings from the Hauptmann trial, they can be listened to at the Paley Center for Media in New York.

"Don't be nervous," joshed Oliver at one point. "I'm not nervous," shot back Leibowitz. "You're the fellow that ought to be nervous."

In his opening remarks on the trial, Leibowitz resorted to the cliché of the courtroom as theater. "Well, to the experienced eye, all these things [are] just like stage props and a Belasco can well nigh call the turn of every shift and every change in the lighting effect as the play unfolds on the stage," he said, dating himself with a reference to the late Broadway impresario David Belasco.

Leibowitz dissected every aspect of the trial, often free-associating with little transition from point to point. He expressed incredulity that defense attorney Reilly had cross-examined Colonel Lindbergh so aggressively: not only was the witness the singular hero of the age, he was the bereaved father of the murdered child. In trying to deflect suspicion from Hauptmann, Reilly was "shooting arrows in the air," always a losing strategy for the defense. He thought that to have Anna Hauptmann in the courtroom with little Manfred would be a "calamity" for the defense, serving only to remind jurors of the missing baby murdered by the "arch fiend." Leibowitz praised Justice Trenchard's "calmness and judicial poise," qualities that made him "a byword in legal circles."

On January 9, Leibowitz devoted a session to psychoanalyzing Wilentz's star witness, "the big battleship of the prosecution's fleet," Dr. John F. Condon. "The gentleness and geniality of this old pedagogue" impressed Leibowitz. "Thus far, he has made a splendid witness for the prosecution," which meant "it may go very bad for Bruno Richard Hauptmann." Condon's emphatic callout of Hauptmann was "as positive an identification as any that I have ever heard in any courtroom." If Condon was lying, he would have to be the mastermind of the entire kidnapping, "a scoundrel and a fake," rather than what Leibowitz believed he certainly was, "a thoroughly kindly old man."

Oliver pointed out that District Attorney Wilentz addressed the witness as *Dr.* Condon, to which Leibowitz cracked that "Hey, kid!" would not be an appropriate salutation. In the trade, Leibowitz said, the show of deference is known as "salaaming the witness"—not slamming—but "salaaming," as in bowing in homage. "It is bad policy to be disrespectful to a witness who merits respect," he lectured. Young lawyers sitting by the radio were surely jotting down Leibowitz's every maxim: "Mere suspicion never proves anything in a court of justice." "Memory witnesses" must be taken with "a bit of bicarbonate of soda." "It is one thing to insinuate; it is another thing to prove." And so on.

Time and again, Oliver tried to lure Leibowitz into speculating about the outcome of the trial, but Leibowitz refused to make predictions. "Who in the name of Josaphat can tell what a jury is going to do?" But he approved of the presence of four women on the jury, a gender he valued for its intuition.

Leibowitz believed that the ransom note left in the nursery was the decisive piece of physical evidence. If Hauptmann wrote the note, his goose was cooked. In this sense, the handwriting evidence was devastating because "we can see for ourselves the similarities between Hauptmann's samples and the notes left by the kidnapper." He ventured a mild criticism of Wilentz, who in arguing that Hauptmann was the sole perpetrator was carrying more of a burden than the law required. If Hauptmann "actually participated in *any* part of the scheme to kidnap baby Lindbergh," then he was guilty under the law.

Olivier asked about what is euphemistically called "the third degree"— that is, whether Hauptmann was roughed up by New York detectives in the Greenwich Street Police Station during the initial rounds of interrogation, as Hauptmann claimed on the stand. "I can't believe that any sane member of the New York state police department would have *dared* to lay a hand on Bruno Richard Hauptmann," said Leibowitz. If the defense could prove Hauptmann was beaten, it might be his "ticket to freedom." To prove his point, Leibowitz told of a time he had a veteran police lieutenant on the witness stand. He asked the man if ever, in all of his decades of experience, he had known of a case where a suspect "got the works" while in police custody. The officer said no, never, not in all of his experience—whereupon the entire courtroom burst into laughter. The jury returned a verdict of not guilty to his client.

In his own mind, Leibowitz was a scrupulously evenhanded analyst. "Who says I am leaning toward the prosecution?" he challenged Oliver midway in the trial. "I am not here to favor either side." He pointed to a pile of letters in his office, half of which said he was too soft on the prosecution, half of which said he favored the defense. His role on WHN was "to stand behind the plate and call the balls and strikes just like the umpire, without fear of favor. "

Yet Leibowitz's clinical analysis of the trial was not devoid of passion. "I cannot conceive of a crime more dastardly and more brazen in its execution than the kidnapping of a poor defenseless child," whether it be the child of the Lindberghs or that of the humblest family. "I don't believe in capital punishment," Leibowitz confided, "but if we have it, it should include kidnapping." The thought of "that little golden-haired cherub . . . ruthlessly done to death" nearly caused his calm demeanor to crack.

Early on in the trial, Leibowitz had said he agreed with the prosecution's contention that the kidnapping was a one-man job. However, on January 15, after a dull day of handwriting testimony, perhaps to enliven the conversation, he reversed himself and revealed what he thought might have occurred on the night of the kidnapping. He based his theory on the lightness of the ladder and the windiness of the night of March 1, 1932. No rational person, Leibowitz argued, would climb into a second-floor nursery without being assured that the ladder would not blow away—else he might be trapped in the room with no way down. An accomplice would have been along to steady the ladder and keep a lookout. It was that person's footprint, he surmised, that was planted in the ground below the window, off an adjacent stone path. When the kidnapper began to descend the ladder, carrying the baby, the extra thirty pounds of weight caused the rail to break, in turn causing the person holding the ladder to step off the stone and onto the earth. The baby himself was either chloroformed or smothered to prevent him from crying out and, when the ladder broke, the baby fell, crushing its skull.

More provocatively, Leibowitz speculated that someone at Highfield must have been on the inside to signal that the coast was clear.

"Then it was a gang?" asked Oliver.

"Absolutely!" insisted Leibowitz.

By February 4, Oliver observed that we're "going in to the last lap of this long-distance Hauptmann trial, Mr. Leibowitz." The bombshells Reilly had hyped—exculpatory alibi witnesses for Hauptmann—were all duds. On February 5, even Hauptmann was showing exasperation at the dubious witnesses Reilly called to the stand, "witnesses crumbling before our eyes," said Oliver, some of whom were openly laughed at. Again, Leibowitz said he did not want to be a "grandstand manager" or "smart aleck" critic and would not impugn the tactics of the defense.

Looking back over the previous five weeks, Leibowitz pointed out that certain pieces of incriminating evidence "stand out like beacon lights," but what, Leibowitz asked Oliver, was the brightest beacon light, the single piece of evidence that more than any other proved Hauptmann's guilt? Resigned to playing Dr. Watson, Oliver gamely ventured a couple of guesses: the ransom money in the garage? the wood from the attic that matches the ladder? No, said Leibowitz sagely, none of these.

What most damned the defendant was the purchase of a costly consumer good, a lavish indulgence by an "itinerate carpenter" whose wife spent her days slaving in a hot bakery. In May 1932, Leibowitz reminded listeners, Hauptmann paid cash for a luxury item that Great Depression audiences scrimped and saved for, an item that had become an essential piece of living-room furniture and which was, in fact, necessary to tune in to Leibowitz's commentary: a radio—not just any radio but a set so luxurious that "not even Park Avenue apartments can claim so expensive a set." The price was $400! The "unusual purchase," Leibowitz points out, can only be explained by "a sudden avalanche of Lindbergh gold."

"That in my opinion is the strongest possible arrow in the sheaf of the prosecution," Leibowitz concluded triumphantly. "The radio is there."

Chapter 9

THE EYE AND EAR OF MILLIONS

U nlike radio, the newsreels had inched forward in status only incrementally since the kidnap-murder of the Lindbergh baby in 1932. Indeed, as transmission belts for journalism, they may even have stalled. The newsreel makers "are joyous in their creation, and they represent a prodigious investment," observed trade reporter Thomas Sugrue in a think piece on the medium for *Scribner's Magazine* in 1937. "[But] they are still the ill-used stepchildren of the Hollywood household, distributed as lollipops along with the supersmash productions of their owners."[1] The newsreels seemed stuck in their rut as an ephemeral diversion, tethered to cartoons and travelogues on the motion picture bill, low-nutrition appetizers served up before the high-end feature film. They may have been eyewitnesses to history, but they were also a silly sideshow.

Yet the newsreel coverage of the Hauptmann trial saw the medium at its aggressive best. During the trial, the newsreels claimed their due as motion picture journalism—and moved closer to securing a place for news on-screen under the First Amendment. "The newsreel camera, the new reporter of the new art of screen journalism, elbows its way into court, bidding Blackstone move over to make room for the movies," exulted *Motion Picture Herald*.[2] The trade magazine spoke too soon: the new art of screen journalism could also be tossed right out the courtroom door.

A Friendly Gentleman's Agreement

As in Hopewell in March 1932, the newsreel trucks rolled into Flemington in full force in January 1935. In what a Paramount News editor described as "the greatest concentration of men and equipment for newsreel coverage since the war," the five newsreel companies marshalled more than a hundred men, fifty cameras, and thirty-five sound trucks to cover the story. There were "enough motion picture cameras to film three feature pix at once," noted *Billboard*, "and movie men [vied] with news cameramen for choice locations—many on roofs across the street from the courthouses."[3]

Universal Newsreel posted a sound truck in front of the Hunterdon County Courthouse, a vehicle that also served as command headquarters for its cameramen, soundmen, and editors. "On the roof of the truck is a sound camera which makes a daily filmed record of activities outside the court-house, where throngs of curious surge each hour against the police line as celebrities enter and emerge and the twelve jurors file diagonally across the road to their hotel confinements," reported *Motion Picture Herald*. "Another cameraman with more portable sound equipment is stationed at the rear of the courthouse, which includes the jail housing Hauptmann and also is used as a means of entry by Justice Trenchard and Colonel Lindbergh, the state's ace witness."[4] Lindbergh was on the stand only one day, but he attended each day of the trial. Again and again, newsreel cameras photographed his ramrod straight figure walking into the rear entrance of the courthouse: no matter how unruly the milling crowds, a path always cleared on either side of him. Pathé News filmed man-on-the-street interviews asking about Hauptmann's guilt or innocence, but decided against screening the footage to avoid prejudicing the jury—who, being holed up by the judge in the hotel across from the courthouse, shouldn't have been going to the movies anyway.

Of course, the real story was unfolding in the courtroom. Although the newsreels had made a few inroads into the courtroom during the Scopes Trial in 1925 and Machine Gun Kelly's trial for murder in 1933, the bulky equipment, blinding lights, and noisy cameras made trial judges wary of intrusive motion picture journalism.[5] Even more than radio, the presence of newsreel cameras in the temple of justice was anathema to its robed guardians.

Still, though holding out little hope for total freedom of movement inside the courtroom, newsreel editors united to petition Justice Trenchard for permission to film the trial. They had strong arguments on their side: the case held unparalleled national interest, the working of the American legal system should be open for all to see, and the cameras could be refitted to prevent any disruption of the dignified conduct of the justice system. "The newsreels are the visualized and talking division of the American press," asserted Mike O'Toole, former secretary of the Motion Picture Theater Owners of America. "The American public can never be denied the right to see and hear any form of news presentation they may desire."[6] Besides, the main actors in the case— excepting the stone-faced suspect and the grieving parents—were only too happy to play to the cameras.

The newsreel editors assured Justice Trenchard of their deference to his authority and respect for his sanctum. They promised to be unobtrusive, nondisruptive, and quiet as mice. As proof, they had devised a special 35mm motion picture camera constructed for near-silent running. The metal gears in the machine were replaced with fiber; other moving metal parts where encased in graphite.

Lighting was a more nettlesome problem. Recognizing that their high-intensity Klieg lights were out of the question, newsreel cameramen had tested various incandescent bulbs in the courtroom's light fixtures only to find that the electrical load was too great for the antiquated wiring system. After consultation with illumination engineers, a bulb with an intensifier attached was installed in each trial room fixture.[7] The use of a higher-speed film stock also facilitated interior photography.

After the special soundproofed camera and lights had been demonstrated and deemed satisfactory, Justice Trenchard surprised everyone by granting permission for the newsreels to cover the trial. Perhaps the judge's generosity was in response to Governor Moore's high-handed edict barring radio from the courtroom—an executive-branch usurpation of judicial authority. Allowing newsreel cameras inside reminded Governor Moore—and his successor Harold G. Hoffmann, who took office on January 15, 1935—that it was Justice Trenchard who held dominion in his courtroom.

The agreement with the judge stipulated that the five newsreel outfits cooperate in a relay system of pool coverage known as "rota-coverage" in the jargon of the day. Three cameras, with personnel from each of the newsreel companies taking turns manning the equipment, were permitted inside the courthouse. A stationary sound camera—the industry workhorse, a 35mm Mitchell mounted on a tripod—was set up in a law library

Lindbergh walks past the pool 35mm newsreel camera, stationed in the law library of the Hunterdon County Courthouse, January 4, 1935. He never spoke for the cameras.

in the back of the trial room, where witnesses could repeat for the cameras the high points of their testimony on the stand. A cameraman carrying a lighter-weight silent camera roamed the courtroom floor during recesses to take shots of the featured players, the jury, the journalists, and the spectators in the gallery. Finally, the specially outfitted "quiet" camera was set up in the north end of the balcony, an area reconstructed to make room for the amplifier, sound camera, and camera operator. Equipped with a telephoto lens and enclosed in a wooden box, the camera commanded a panoramic view of the action below. It also had a clear line of sight to the witness stand.

The first week of the trial found crews for Pathé in the balcony, Hearst on the courtroom floor, and Paramount in the adjacent library. After the first week, the reels manned the three positions in rotation: Pathé, Hearst, Paramount, Universal, and Fox. Each of the newsreels got a print of any footage taken from the three pool cameras.

Justice Trenchard's permission came with a crucial caveat. Under the terms of "a friendly gentleman's agreement," the two in-court cameras—on the floor and in the balcony—were permitted to film *only* during recesses in the trial, never during the actual trial when the judge was officiating from the bench and witnesses were testifying on the stand.[8] However, as *Variety* cannily pointed out, "it is a simple matter to grind the camera in the rear of the balcony unnoticed during a session."[9]

The Outstanding Sound Pictures of a Generation

Being a motion picture medium, the newsreels put the star witnesses and lead attorneys center frame and relegated the bit players to background extras. The bereaved parents Anne and Colonel Lindbergh; the publicity hound Edward J. Reilly for the defense and the politically ambitious David T. Wilentz for the prosecution; the bombastic bagman Dr. John F. Condon; and the villain of the piece, the blank slate that was Bruno Richard Hauptmann, all got top billing and the bulk of the screen time.

However, the Lindbergh trial was about evidence as much as personalities. Though the forensic and evidentiary complexities of the trial tested the cinematic ingenuity of the medium, the newsreels painstakingly illustrated the textual evidence with maps and diagrams and allotted screen time for the experts to repeat before the camera in the courtroom library the testimony given on the stand.

New York Daily News film critic Kate Cameron shared what she saw from a seat in the Embassy Newsreel Theatre. "The Hauptmann trial still has first place on the screen bills," she observed. As per instructions, the footage from inside the courtroom was restricted to moments when the trial was not in session:

> The latest pictures of the defendant show him in a cheerful mood, as the trial nears its close, and while he is shown in conference with his attorneys just before he takes the stand in his own defense, crowds line up outside the courthouse at Flemington and stand for hours in the snow and freezing weather waiting for a chance to get into the building for a glimpse of the principal players in the world's most absorbing drama.[10]

The newspaper arm of the Hearst empire urged readers to check out what its newsreel arm was unspooling. "As dramatic developments in the trial of Bruno Richard Hauptmann pile upon each other in speedy succession, the sound movie cameras of Hearst Metrotone News record the intense and thrilling scenes," read a typical blurb. "In its current issue, Metrotone presents the State's three key witnesses who 'put the finger on' the Bronx carpenter": eighty-seven-year-old Amandus Hochmuth, who claimed he saw Hauptmann in a car near the Lindbergh home on the day of the kidnapping; Joseph Perrone, the cab driver who delivered a note to Dr. Condon; and Dr. Condon himself. In accord with the agreement with Justice Trenchard, none of the men was shown testifying on the stand. Pictures of the trio walking into the courthouse were accompanied by voiceover narration by Hearst Metrotone spieler Edwin C. Hill, a popular radio announcer.[11]

The most irresistibly cinematic scene of the trial was the confrontation between a fiery Wilentz and an alternately angry and truculent Hauptmann—the blistering cross-examination from the last thirty minutes of Friday, January 25, and the long grudge match on the following Monday and Tuesday. There was no confession from Hauptmann, no Hollywood catharsis, but the sight of the two men in the same frame was a picture-perfect face-off too good not to film. Friendly gentleman's agreement or not, the newsreel boys were not likely to pass up the chance to record the square-off between Hauptmann and Wilentz. In an act of premediated chicanery, they reneged on their solemn agreement with Justice Trenchard and filmed what they had promised not to film.

Unbeknownst to the judge and the prosecutor, the newsreel men in the balcony, their camera whirring quietly, had already filmed some of the most electric moments on the stand, probably as a test run, to see if they could get away with it. The editors had squirreled away silent footage of Anne's identification of the baby's clothing and Lindbergh's identification of Hauptmann and sound footage of Dr. Condon's emphatic *j'accuse*: "John . . . is . . . Bruno Richard Hauptmann!" and Hauptmann's snarky riposte to Reilly, "I'm a carpenter." Indeed, from the beginning of the trial, noted the *Hollywood Reporter*, there had been a "tacit, off-the-record understanding among all five of the reels that their camera crews would be instructed to 'steal' anything and everything possible during the entire course of the trial and that this 'forbidden material' would be held by the reels until the end of the trial and then simultaneously released in a Hauptmann Trial Special by each reel."[12]

In fact, the newsreel men had lied to the Judge's face about what they were up to. On January 4, when Justice Trenchard berated the still photographers for defying his orders about taking pictures of Anne and Charles Lindbergh on the stand, Walter Mullins, an electrician for the newsreel outfits, rose and indignantly assured the judge, on his honor, that no shots had been taken by any of the newsreel cameras.[13]

After a month of surreptitious filming, the newsreels had a "vault-load of this forbidden negative and each was scared to death that the others, or one of the others, would jump the gun and score a terrific beat over the other four." A. J. Richards of Paramount itched to scoop his rivals, but after conferring with Paramount's legal staff, he figured the potential liability was not worth the glory of being first out the gate. Instead, Richards called his colleagues together and proposed they meet collectively with Justice Trenchard to ask for formal permission to release the films. Of course, admitting to possession of actual trial footage also meant admitting to the violation of his order. The judge would either erupt in fury and forbid release or acquiesce to the fait accompli.

First, representatives from the newsreels tried to recruit an unlikely ally. On Thursday night, January 24, the top newsreel men—W. P. Montague of Paramount, Laurence Stallings of Fox, Mike Clophine of Hearst, C. R. Collins of Pathé, and Charlie Ford of Universal—met with Wilentz to ask him to intercede with Justice Trenchard. "They came out of that huddle with icicles down their backs a yard long," observed the Hollywood Reporter. "Wilentz froze them with contempt."

The next morning, the quintet went to see Justice Trenchard at his home in Trenton before he was to depart for Flemington. They got no further than the front door. The butler gave a cool nod. Laurence Stallings of Fox was nominated to go in and plead the case. Having lost a leg at Belleau Wood during the Great War, Stallings had a record of proven courage, but even he stammered over his request. He was, after all, trying to get permission for something the judge had expressly forbidden. "The judge misunderstood the rigmarole and thought they were asking permission to put in microphones and other equipment," continued the Hollywood Reporter. "He told them that the Court had been most lenient with them so far and would continue to be, but that under no circumstances could they put another ounce of equipment in the courtroom." Stallings decided not to disabuse the judge of his misunderstanding. "At this point, sadly cornered behind the judicial 8-ball, the reel boys retired to call it a day."

They did not however call "cut!" on the secret filming. Hauptmann's time on the stand, they knew, was the showstopper. Obtaining footage of the defendant doing battle with the prosecutor, which they filmed and recorded on late Friday afternoon, January 25, and through the following Monday and Tuesday, was the reason they had risked alienating Wilentz and tipping off the judge.

Back in Manhattan, the newsreel editors eyed each other warily and decided none of them could be trusted not to scoop the others. What happened next is perhaps too colorful to credit fully but too juicy not to repeat. According to the *Hollywood Reporter*, an emissary from the consortium was dispatched, posthaste, to Flemington "with two quarts of the very, very best stuff as a little gift for the Sheriff." That would be John H. Curtiss. The emissary was to communicate the delicate moral quandary—that the newsreels possessed footage of the cross-examination from the stand but no pictures of the judge himself officiating from the bench, that the transcripts from the trial were running in newspapers all over the country and being read out nightly on radio, and, surely, what was good for the newspapers and radio was good for the newsreels. After sufficient lubrication, Sheriff Curtiss agreed.

Upon getting the boozy green light from the sheriff, the emissary darted back to New York and told the newsreel editors that the sheriff himself had authorized release of the footage. "So, and finally," concluded the bemused account in the *Hollywood Reporter*, "the boys who could not trust one another got together and double crossed the judge!"

The newsreel editors rushed the film by motorcycle courier to New York labs for development, edited it for maximum impact, and recorded commentary tracks with their trademark announcers. The freshly printed issues were then distributed to movie houses. By Thursday night, January 31, the clips were playing in theaters in New York and, by the weekend, in metropolitan theaters around the country.[14]

As the first actual testimony from the five-week-old trial to hit the screen, the footage received the full huckster treatment. In Times Square, the Embassy Newsreel Theatre hyped the Hauptmann-Wilentz matchup like a championship bout. "Hauptmann on Stand! First Actual Sound Pictures!" shouted barkers outside the theater. "Hear him admit he lied during cross-examination with Wilentz."[15] Pathé's compilation was the featured attraction for one show and Universal's for the next, with the two issues alternating around the clock. *Variety* deemed Pathé's edit, which clocked in at eight and a half minutes, a shade better than Universal's, which ran a minute longer. Pathé was also lauded for its cleaner sound quality, "sharpening up the dialogue and removing as much of the interference from background noise as possible."[16] Fox Movietone's entry was a modest three minutes long; Paramount's and Hearst Metrotone's both ran about nine minutes. The Trans-Lux stitched together a fifteen-minute program that management considered "newsreel history." Since all five of the newsreels drew from the same raw footage taken by the pool camera, the only variations in coverage were in the editing and voiceovers.

The Hearst press spared no hyperbole in elevating its newsreel arm. "Surpassing in tense, close-packed thrills any make-believe drama of stage or screen, Hearst Metrotone News in its current issue brings to moving picture audiences the outstanding sound pictures of a generation. The actual cross-examination of Bruno Richard Hauptmann by Attorney General Wilentz undoubtedly establishes a new standard in camera reporting. Here, if ever, is a picture not to be missed: a record for posterity of the most celebrated case in the annals of American jurisprudence."[17] Distributed by MGM, the Hearst newsreels were playing in seventy high-class Loew's venues throughout New York City within twenty-four hours of release. "Sensation follows sensation," promised the print side of the Hearst empire. "Questions and answers, word for word, have been recorded in this remarkable real-life document, the first of its kind ever presented on the screen."[18]

Pathé titled its report "Bruno on the Stand" and opened with shots of Anne and Colonel Lindbergh, nurse Betty Gow, wood expert Arthur Koehler, handwriting expert Albert D. Osborn, and Dr. Condon on the stand. With the exception of a brief explanation by Koehler, shot during a recess, and a snippet of Condon identifying the defendant as Cemetery John, the bulk of the issue showcased the showdown between Hauptmann and Wilentz.

Universal limited its prefatory sequence to scenes of Anne Lindbergh, Colonel Lindbergh, and Dr. Condon, before moving quickly to Hauptmann on the stand for the synch-sound crossfire. During Reilly's direct examination, Hauptmann leaves the stand to look over the ladder more closely, as state troopers hover warily about him. When Reilly asks Hauptmann if he built the ladder found on the Lindbergh grounds, Hauptmann delivers his "I am a carpenter" wisecrack.

Paramount News editor A. J. Richards telegrammed exhibitors—who then published the telegram in prominent ads—to be on the alert for the unprecedented exploitation opportunity. "For the first time, Paramount News is devoting its entire reel to one story so big every house playing it should put [the] story in lobby [advertisements]," Richards proclaimed. "We are proud to bring you this scoop."[19]

The centerpiece of all the reports was the rapid-fire cross-examination of Hauptmann by Wilentz on January 29, the previous Tuesday, an extended, unedited sequence that in some issues lasted nearly eight minutes. Prosecutor Wilentz bores in on Hauptmann, pointing an accusing finger and shouting "Lies! Lies! Lies!" The defendant shouts back angrily, "Stop that! Stop that!" But Wilentz draws blood when he gets Hauptmann—"perspiring, white-faced, and often faltering" as the AP described him—to admit that he had lied to the police after his arrest in the Bronx in September. "I told not the truth," he sheepishly confesses.[20]

Having never seen—or heard—anything like it, moviegoers were mesmerized. "Patrons gasped, leaned forward to catch every word and the audiences buzzed for half an hour afterward," *Variety* reported. At the Embassy Newsreel Theatre, the Hauptmann-Wilentz scenes played from morning to midnight to standing-room-only crowds. "This graphic depiction of the secretive defendant hunched in the witness chair with Wilentz leaping and snapping round him like a terrier keeping a cat up a tree again demonstrates that, once in a blue moon, the newsreels can do what they set out to do," conceded Joseph C. Furnas, usually a fierce critic of the medium, in the *New York Herald Tribune*.[21]

Meanwhile, back in Flemington, court officials were furious when they learned of the release of the reels. On Friday morning, February 1, after conferring with a dismayed Justice Trenchard, Wilentz telegraphed each of the five newsreel offices in New York and demanded the pictures be pulled from circulation. "In the name of the State of New Jersey and in the name of decency, it is requested that you order the immediate withdrawal of Hauptmann trial pictures taken during actual trial sessions," he fumed. "These sound pictures were procured by trickery and in defiance of the order of the court. You owe a positive duty to cooperate with the authorities in the matter and such duty should not be avoided for money, profit, or for any other reason."[22]

That night, at a session attended by representatives of the five newsreel companies, Wilentz expressed his anger in person. "We insist so far as possible that the [newsreel] companies are not greater than the court, but are subject to it, the same as anyone else," he lectured. "'These cheap tricksters sit in their offices in New York and in Hollywood and think that nothing is superior to the movies and the dollar. They gave their word of honor through their representatives here—and it was violated. The next move is up to them."[23] If the companies refused to withdraw the reels, Wilentz threatened to appeal directly to movie czar Will Hays.[24]

Justice Trenchard issued no formal response but reportedly felt "hurt at what he considered a violation of a gentleman's agreement." Sheriff Curtiss claimed to know nothing about anything.

The newsreel editors denied signing off on any gentleman's agreement, saying the court knew full well that the camera was operating and that sound was being recorded. "Why, they had a State trooper stationed next to the camera to make sure it was not making any noticeable noise," Fox Movietone editor Truman Talley pointed out. A directional beam microphone, measuring approximately two and a half inches in diameter, had been positioned on the sill of a rear window in the courtroom, about thirty-five feet from the witness stand. Wires from the microphone, connecting it to the camera in the balcony, "were plainly visible at all times," noticed the *New York Times*.[25] Walter Winchell had a more invasive theory: "The reason the sound is so clear in those Hauptmann trial newsreel scenes is that the mike was hidden right under Justice Trenchard's bench!"[26]

Wherever the mike was, there was no denying the newsreel boys had pulled a fast one on the judge, taking a calculated risk less in the interest of the public's right to know than the newsreels' desire to scoop radio and the newspapers—and to outmaneuver a newsreel-like competitor recently arrived on the scene, the screen magazine the *March of Time*. Perhaps, too, they were bridling under the long train of restrictions and subaltern treatment that extended far back into the history of the medium. As appendages of Hollywood corporations, they were required to sidestep controversy and placate politicians. As newsmen, they knew, at times, they had to confront both head on.

No matter. The newsreel editors may have been ready for a showdown with the State of New Jersey, but the studio higher-ups wanted to avoid conflict at all cost: for them, nothing must threaten the fortunes of the real moneymaker, the feature film. The banks on Wall Street, the source of Hollywood financing, directed the studios to rein in their newsreel arms. "The bankers wanted to pussyfoot and kill the story," was the flat assertion in *Motion*

Frame enlargements from the stolen newsreel footage of the dramatic confrontation between Hauptmann and Wilentz, January 29, 1935.

Picture Herald.[27] Wilentz's outburst had also spooked exhibitors. Loew's, Inc., MGM's parent company, released a statement assuring the New Jersey attorney general that "Loew's theatres in New York and throughout the country have decided to eliminate immediately the Hauptmann trial talking pictures which were included in the current newsreels."[28] In Washington, D.C., the circuits also folded.

Following orders from above, Fox, Paramount, and Hearst Metrotone withdrew their reels. Paramount's A. J. Richard, who just a few days earlier had been so eager to release the footage, telegrammed Wilentz to say Paramount was pulling its issue. His message was a model of disingenuity. "We regret your statement that the pictures were obtained by trickery," he said. "That is not the fact. Sound camera in the courtroom was operated openly. It was our understanding that the presiding judge and other officials understood this. Prior to release, representatives of the newsreel companies interviewed Judge Trenchard. It is regrettable that we misunderstood his views and wishes." Now that the unfortunate misunderstanding had been cleared up, Richard was happy to make amends:

> We are glad to correct this misunderstanding by complying with your request to withdraw the subjects. However, we submit with all respect that our newsreel is a fair, unbiased, and authentic presentation of the facts and is in nowise calculated to interfere with or unfavorably affect the dignified administration of public justice.[29]

Yet, in a sign that at least some of the ill-used stepchildren of the Hollywood household were tired of being kicked around, not all the newsreels bowed to Wilentz's demand. Pathé and Universal held their ground. "I don't see how anyone could withdraw the subject and still have respect for their medium," declared Pathé's Courtland Smith, oozing contempt for three-fourths of his competition.[30] A defiant Robert H. Cochrane, vice president of Universal Pictures, replied that "the newsreels have been so decent and dignified that they have defaulted in their duty to the theaters they serve." He also reminded Wilentz of the sensationalism of the trial coverage by radio, which had been broadcasting updates every fifteen minutes and reenacting the trial testimony with vocalists impersonating witnesses and attorneys.

Cynics suspected Wilentz was upset for another reason. "It is the guess of the reporters that Wilentz is agitated because the shots show Bruno in a favorable light under cross-examination, with Wilentz making an unsuccessful attempt to break him," speculated *Billboard*. "It is the opinion that had Wilentz succeeded, nothing would have been said about the scenes being shown."[31]

Addressing the controversy during his nightly commentaries on WHN radio, attorney Samuel S. Leibowitz got genuinely angry over the disrespect shown to Justice Trenchard. "Now some sneak—and I use the word advisedly— some sneak or combination of them—because that is all they are—broke faith with this kindly gentleman who so honorably graces the bench of that court-room in New Jersey." Leibowitz, who seldom needed to, raised his voice:

> I am unalterably opposed to such underhanded practices as that. The public should frown down on such nefarious pieces of business and I do hope that those guilty are ferreted out and summarily dealt with. Some unscrupulous individuals are undermining the dignity of American justice for a few measly dollars. This is racketeering *ne plus ultra*!

It wasn't so much the filming ("Let us be honest about it and go the full route," conceded Leibowitz, "the motion picture and the sound box will give us a portrait of the courtroom with greater fidelity than" the newspapers) but the deception, the "bootlegging of motion pictures," that struck Leibowitz as truly "disgraceful conduct."[32]

While the lawyers condemned the tricksters and sneaks, the trade press strongly backed the assertion of journalistic prerogative by the newsreels. At *Motion Picture Herald*, Terry Ramsaye ridiculed Wilentz for his "hysteri-cal manifestations" and "frothing utterances." Like many newsreel veterans, Ramsaye was annoyed that motion pictures were singled out for criticism when "the journalistic practice of the [print] press in converting the trial into penny vaudeville" was tolerated without comment. "The newsreel camera is as definitely the representative of the people as the newspaper," he insisted. "If the courts have an obligation to stand open to the public's gaze and inspec-tion, that obligation is manifold to the sound camera which is the eye and ear of millions." Ramsaye clinched his argument with the italicized observation:

> *Any charge that the newsreel camera which recorded Hauptmann on the stand was an invasion of the peace and dignity of the courtroom is rendered obviously absurd by the fact that none there was aware that the picture was being made.*[33]

Also disgusted by the lily-livered response of three of the five newsreel companies was Phil M. Daily, the eponymous columnist for the *Film Daily*. "As usual the film biz sits back and takes it on the chin when any prominent individual outside the motion picture howls that the screen is misrepresenting, demoralizing something, or gumming up somebody's li'l game," he wrote. "Those who run newspapers and the radio realize that this Jersey trial is the biggest piece of dramatic news of the age [and] that the public can't get enough of it, so they keep feeding it to 'em and no prosecuting attorney is allowed to tell 'em how to run THEIR business."[34]

Regardless, Justice Trenchard still reigned supreme in his courtroom. When newsreel cameramen showed up for court the next Monday, he ordered them evicted and their equipment in the balcony dismantled. Sheriff Curtiss promised that his deputies would use force if necessary to keep the newsreel boys out of the courtroom. "We don't anticipate trouble," said the sheriff, now stone sober. "But we'll clear them out. They've all got to go."[35]

Perhaps it was only then that the newsreel editors realized how they had outsmarted themselves. In their zeal to deliver what the rival media of print and radio could not—actual sound recordings from the Hauptmann trial— they had blundered badly, not because they had double-crossed Justice Trenchard and infuriated District Attorney Wilentz, but because they had stepped on a bigger story. If they had been patient for just two weeks more, they could have recorded the final closing arguments of Reilly and Wilentz—maybe even the pronouncement of the verdict by the jury and sentencing by the judge. "Had the temptation to release the film not been so strong, and had they been able to wait until the end of the trial, they would have had a masterpiece," declared UP reporter Sidney Whipple, not sounding too disappointed that the newsreels had blown their chance.[36] *Billboard* agreed: "Had the newsreelers held up the shot of Hauptmann until after the verdict they could have made a feature of the entire trial that would have been a humdinger. As it is, the most important event of the trial will go unphotographed."[37]

Not totally unphotographed. Outside the courthouse, Reilly and Wilentz recapped for the newsreels what they had said inside. "The two offer an interesting contrast as they talk for the sound cameras," commented the *New York Evening Journal* about the point-counterpoint.[38] Not harboring a grudge, Wilentz repeated his closing arguments for the medium he had just censored, but in less incendiary language than he had used in court. "What type of man would kill the child of Colonel Lindbergh and Anne Morrow?" the prosecutor had demanded during his summation to the jury. "He wouldn't be an American. No American gangster and no American racketeer ever sank to the level of killing babies."

Chapter 10

THE VERDICT

On a brisk Wednesday morning at 11:51, February 13, 1935, the jury in the trial of Bruno Richard Hauptmann retired to deliberate the fate of the accused. Three verdicts were possible: guilty with no recommendation of mercy, which meant a mandatory date with the electric chair; guilty with a recommendation of mercy, which meant a life sentence; and the third, almost unimaginable option, not guilty, which meant Hauptmann would walk out of the Hunterdon County Courthouse a free man.

After sitting in the packed, overheated courtroom for six weeks, Adela Rogers St. Johns had reached a verdict of her own. The weight of the evidence convinced her beyond any reasonable doubt that Hauptmann had written the ransom note and was implicated in the kidnapping. Having watched Anne Lindbergh on the stand fondling her baby's woolen sleeping suit, St. Johns came to a bitter realization: "I'll go down to New Jersey and turn the switch on the electric chair that holds him and watch him die in it without one moment's hesitation."[1]

Hers was not a minority opinion. Though he may not have wanted to personally turn the switch, President Franklin D. Roosevelt, an avid reader of St. Johns, had become convinced by her reporting that Hauptmann had murdered the Lindbergh baby.[2] First Lady Eleanor Roosevelt agreed that Hauptmann was guilty, but she felt it unjust to sentence a man to death on purely circumstantial evidence, no matter how damning.[3] Beyond the White House, among lawyers, reporters, and people on the street, the smart money was on a guilty verdict, with Hauptmann getting the chair.

Inside the courtroom, awaiting the jury's verdict, was a captive audience: the gentlemen and women of the press. Taking no chances, Justice Trenchard had ordered the reporters sequestered inside the courtroom while the jury deliberated. He did not want any journalistic shenanigans—that is, jury tampering.

At the judge's announcement, the press corps erupted in fury. However, Damon Runyon was serene and St. Johns accepted the logic of the decision. "Being locked in was our own fault and was fully justified," she admitted. Flemington was swirling with rumors—some confirmed—that the press was tampering with the jury—not trying to sway the verdict but to learn of it before it was read. The judge "knew that there were strange schemes afoot, devilish devices deposited in an attempt to get the verdict first," recalled St. Johns, including efforts to bug the jury room.[4]

While the reporters inside the courthouse were killing time, six thousand citizens milling about on the streets of Flemington wanted blood. The day

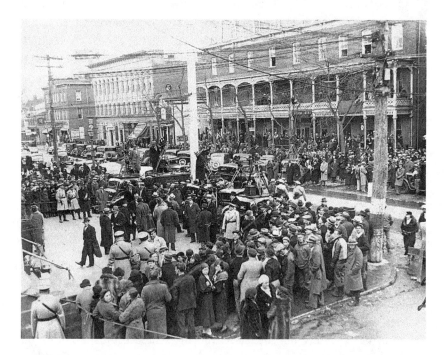

Outside the Hunterdon County Courthouse in Flemington, New Jersey, the expectant crowd and the media await the jury's verdict in the Trial of the Century, February 13, 1935.

before, a cordon of blue-uniformed state troopers had to escort the jurors to and from the courthouse through the menacing mob. Though unmolested, they were rattled by the cries for vengeance from what in less policed municipalities might have turned into a lynch mob. Throughout the day, WOR broadcast sounds from the streets outside the courthouse while reporters wandered about and ad-libbed commentary over the catcalls from the crowd. The sonic festivities on the streets of Flemington were sent out to some one hundred stations. From the Morrow estate in Englewood, Anne Lindbergh listened in, aghast at "the howling mob over the radio." "How incredibly horrible and bitter to realize that this has to do with us," she confided to her diary. "Incredible as that first night."[5]

As the jury deliberated throughout the afternoon and into the early evening hours, the hordes grew restive. By nightfall, with no verdict forthcoming, things got ugly. A stone crashed through a courthouse window. "Kill Hauptmann!" the mob howled. "Send him to the electric chair!"[6]

The False Flash

At 10:27 P.M. a deputy sheriff climbed up to the belfry of the Hunterdon County Courthouse to signal that the jury had returned a verdict. The news was heralded by an anachronistic clarion, quaint in its medieval vibrations and John Donne echoes: the tolling of the courthouse bell.

"It is an old law that the courthouse bell must be tolled whenever a murder jury is about to come in," explained Sheriff John H. Curtiss. "We have done it at every murder trial I can remember." By special arrangement with Sheriff Curtiss, who had gotten very cozy with the staff of Hearst's *New York Evening Journal*, the peal of the bell was heard live over WNEW radio.[7]

At the sound, the crowd roared. Newsreel cameramen switched on Klieg lights that illuminated the night and beamed into the courtroom. Photographers clicked off pictures and flashbulbs popped. Small boys picked up the burnt bulbs and hurled them to the pavement—more popping. To blunt the glare, and block hand signals to reporters waiting outside, Sheriff Curtiss had the shades drawn inside the courtroom.

News flashes—bolts of lightning from out of the blue—live up to their name. Yet news may also be an event that happens at a predetermined location and designated time but whose precise outcome is unknown: a ceremony, a competition, an execution. The appointed hour and certain climax (inauguration, victory, death) allow the various tributaries of the media to orchestrate resources for blanket coverage, to publicize the impending decision, and to race each other to the finish line with the results. As the jurors weighed the evidence and grappled with their consciences, the three press syndicates and individual newshounds put their battle plans into action. Each was determined to be first across the wires with the verdict.

Having been double-crossed by the newsreels, Justice Trenchard was no less determined that the pronouncement would be a solemn and dignified occasion. He ordered a series of strict protocols for press and gallery alike, defiance of which, he promised, would put the offender in handcuffs for contempt of court.

To prevent the unseemly spectacle of reporters stumbling over each other in a mad dash to the telephones in the courthouse hallway, the judge ordered the doors to the courtroom locked. Another layer of security—a burly state trooper—stood in front of the doors barring the exit. The scoop-hungry, deadline-driven journalists who had been waiting for nearly twelve hours would be forced to sit on the news until all the jurors were formally polled and the trial was officially adjourned. Only then could they bolt through the doorway and phone the city desk.

For the antsy tribunes of the Fourth Estate, the agony of waiting was intolerable. To get around the judge's closed-door policy, each of the news outlets devised a complicated series of signals and schemes by which the jury's decision might break through the back door *before* it was officially opened. Creative ingenuity vied with outright chicanery in the competition to be first off the mark.

The Associated Press went high-tech. The top dog of the news syndicates planted an experienced telegrapher in the courtroom with a small radio transmitter concealed under his coat. When the verdict was read, he was to discreetly tap out a coded signal for each of the three possible verdicts. The signal was to be received and interpreted by a telegrapher at a receiving set rigged up in a room in the courthouse attic and then transmitted to AP's clients.

United Press opted for a simpler, time-tested method. A messenger inside the courtroom would slip a note through a slit in the door to a reporter waiting outside, who would then race down the hallway to the room where a UP teleprinter was located to transmit the verdict to UP's clients. INS relied on a similar setup. Bailiffs and guards tasked with maintaining security were bribed to look the other way while the notes were passed.

Setting the scene before the jury filed in, newspaper accounts milked the tension and dwelt on the eerie portents. At one point, the lights went out in the old building. Women shrieked and reporters lit matches to see their notes. After a tense eight minutes, the lights came back on. A rolled window shade snapped up, startling the room.

In the days before digital exactitude, the timeline counting down what happened in the crucial minutes between the tolling of the bell and the reading of the verdict varies depending on the source. However, every tick-tock agrees on the sequencing of an epic journalistic screwup. The error was not quite as iconic as the "Dewey Defeats Truman" headline in the *Chicago Tribune* in 1948, but for the abashed journalists who botched the assignment, it was no less humiliating.

At 10:30 P.M. preparations were being made in the courtroom for the jurors to take their place in the jury box, but they had not yet entered the courtroom.

It was sometime around then that AP got a message from its telegrapher in the courtroom. At 10:31 P.M.—while the jurors were still in the jury room across from the courthouse—AP sent out an urgent all-caps bulletin:

FLASH VERDICT REACHED GUILTY AND LIFE

According to AP, the jury had found Hauptmann guilty, with a recommendation for mercy, an automatic sentence of life imprisonment.

AP had seemingly scored an extraordinary scoop: delivering the news *before* the jury had left the jury room and entered the courtroom. Presumably, a member of the jury or the bailiff had blabbed. But how did the telegrapher *inside* the courtroom get the word?

AP's report was dispatched, daisy-chain-like, to AP clients in city rooms and, via AP's radio partner, the Press-Radio Bureau, over the airwaves. From coast to coast, newspapers ran with the story and printed up extra editions. Radio stations broke into regular programming with the bulletin. Many of the major metropolitan dailies had taken the precaution of preparing three sets of letterpress metal plates for the front pages headlining each eventuality. As soon as the editors got the green light from the wire services, the presses would roll.

On the night of February 13, 1935, the *New York Daily News* prepares two sets of plates for the front page. (electronic image)

Editors for UP and INS, the two wire services that had apparently been scooped, screamed for updates from their reporters on scene. UP's Harry Fergusan spied his messenger—conveniently, the sheriff's daughter—through the courtroom door and slipped her a note to pass on to inside man Sid Whipple saying that the opposition—he didn't have to say it was AP—had already flashed the news that Hauptmann was guilty with a life sentence. Whipple sent back a laconic reply: "The jury is still outside the courtroom. If AP is right, it is nice to have worked with you."[8]

INS was also holding firm. Its ace reporter James L. Kilgallen sent out a short lede: "A premature verdict of life imprisonment for Bruno Richard Hauptmann for the kidnap-murder of Charles A. Lindbergh Jr., emanated from the courtroom at 10: 31 P.M. The jury had not yet entered the courtroom. . . ."

A nervous Kilgallen prayed that AP had jumped the gun. Beads of flop sweat poured out as he waited to file his story:

It came up 10:30 and no action. The judge was still at home, four blocks down the street. Then 10:31 and suddenly the red light comes up on the A.P. teletype and it starts chugging. It's a bad feeling. I felt so helpless. I couldn't just walk over there and see what the opposition was saying. I couldn't have gotten near that machine with the AP guys. But I got a break. A few days before, by mutual consent, we had agreed to let Bill Chaplin share our room. Bill worked for one of the radio networks [the Press-Radio Bureau] which subscribed to *both* our wires. He was my friend from a long way back. He took a look at AP's wire, sent a bulletin to his network, then told me. That's when I sent my short lede.[9]

For the next fourteen minutes, as AP ran with its exclusive, Kilgallen held his breath and waited.

Trusting to AP's record of accuracy, newspaper editors rushed extras onto the street. Hearst's *New York American* ignored INS, its own wire service, and ran off 55,000 copies bannering the AP scoop. "The *Washington Post* and countless other papers placed their trust in AP, caring not a whit that INS was saying 'premature' and UP was saying nothing," recalled Bob Considine, a veteran INS reporter.[10]

Radio was in the same fix as the print press. NBC's Red and the Blue Networks were on the air with a recap of the trial when, at 10:31, they interrupted the report with the false AP bulletin. Scant seconds later, CBS did likewise, breaking into a piano concert to flash the news. At 10:34 P.M., acting on the authority of the AP, the Press-Radio Bureau sent out the erroneous news that Hauptmann had gotten life imprisonment. Other subscribing networks passed along the mistake to listeners.

Meanwhile, at 10:34 P.M., unaware of the media hubbub, the jury filed in and at 10:45 P.M. jury foreman Charles Walton, a fifty-year-old machinist, announced the verdict. "We find the defendant, Bruno Richard Hauptmann, guilty of murder in the first degree." The condemned man stood erect, "as white as death and cold as ice." At defense attorney Edward J. Reilly's request, the judge polled the jury; each member solemnly repeated the whole verdict, word for word.[11] The judge then allowed reporters in the courtroom to dash to the phones to file their reports.

INS's patient James K. Kilgallen sent out his flash:

HAUPTMANN GETS ELECTRIC CHAIR

At that moment, NBC transmitted the correct verdict supplied by Transmedia Press Service. Cautious WOR, which had not fallen for the false flash, also sent out the correct bulletin at 10:45 P.M. AP, too, having detected its error and pulled its fallacious report at 10:42 P.M., sent out the correct verdict at 10:45 P.M.

On radio, the first-this/then-that confusion left on-air personalities flummoxed and stuttering. WMCA was broadcasting a discussion of the case by Max D. Steuer, a prominent trial lawyer, when the incorrect AP bulletin came in. Steuer interrupted his analysis and read the report on air. Obviously surprised, he made no criticism of the jury, but when the correct verdict came in to WMCA at 10:50 P.M., he let his true feelings be known. "The crime was brutal," he said. "It showed vicious-mindedness on the part of the perpetrator, and an utter absence of charity or soul." For the jury to have granted clemency in such a case would have been "a perversion of justice."[12]

All over the airwaves, national networks and independent stations alike, relying on the usually infallible AP, had broadcast bulletins between 10:31 and 10:42 beaming out the false verdict. Then at 10:46 or so, they reversed themselves with the announcement: "This is a correction of the previous report which said that Hauptmann had been found guilty with a recommendation of mercy."

Correcting the mistake was not as easy for the newspapers whose blunder was being hawked on the streets. Chagrined editors at the *New York American* hastily stopped distribution of the 55,000 extras with the wrong headline. The *Seattle Daily News* also paid for its trust in AP. When the false flash came in, editors rushed extra editions onto the streets before the correction came through eleven minutes later. Someone literally yelled "Stop the presses!" and the paper put out a second, revised run of extras.[13]

AP editors knew a retraction alone was not sufficient. Within an hour of the most humiliating screwup in its history, the service sent out a cover story explaining that "in transmitting the verdict from one part of the courthouse to another, the Associated Press's report of the decision was garbled" and "confusion reigned briefly."[14] The mealymouthed alibi glossed over the crucial miscalculation: that in its eagerness to scoop the competition, AP had flashed the news *before* the verdict was read, before the jury had even entered the courtroom.

The next day, AP changed its story with a more detailed statement, fessing up to the crossed signals and blaming the glitch on radio technology:

Short wave transmission, employing code, was set up to cover the verdict. The staff had been cautioned not to confuse signals and to be certain that the signals received were from the Associated Press representative.

When word came from the courtroom that the jury was ready to report, however, the Associated Press man on the receiving end picked up the wrong code signal, resulting in the erroneous and premature flash.

The courtroom being closed, minutes passed before knowledge of the error was learned. The flash and the bulletins were killed exactly eleven minutes after transmission of the erroneous report but too late to catch some editions of newspapers which had issued extras.[15]

Watching AP squirm, the competition indulged its schadenfreude. Pointing to UP's flawless coverage, the *New York World-Telegram*, a UP subscriber, noted that AP's second statement "differs somewhat from its first statement."[16]

UP had learned caution the hard way, having been badly burned a generation earlier when it flashed a false report of the Armistice in 1918.[17] Sensing the possibility of a mistake amid the frenzy to be first, UP headquarters sent out a stern directive to its editors on the night of the Hauptmann verdict: "We will not flash the verdict until it is read by the jury." To that, *Broadcasting* commented: "Newspaper editors and broadcasters reading this have made the mental addition: 'A.P. please copy.' "[18] INS also rubbed salt in the wound with a teletype bulletin calling attention "to the fact that this ticker service sent no false flashes on the Hauptmann verdict."[19]

Like UP and INS, the Transradio Press Service felt entitled to gloat for having saved its subscribers from broadcasting the false flash passed on by the AP-affiliated Press-Radio Bureau. It sent out the correct flash at 10:44 P.M., right before the verdict was returned. "Transradio Press Service, exclusive radio press association, covered itself with glory as Press-Radio Bureau, radio service of the newspapers, suffered the consequences of a colossal editorial blunder in the handling of the verdict of the celebrated Hauptmann murder case on Feb. 13," noted *Broadcasting*.[20]

The timing for NBC commentator Lowell Thomas was fortuitous. His regular broadcast that night signed off at 7:00 P.M. before a verdict, true or false, had been pronounced. "The jury is still out at Flemington," he told listeners. "No verdict yet." The next day Thomas had missed the miscues—and had the advantage of hindsight. "Today, the story turns into sheer emotion. That's to be expected after last night's verdict, with the death penalty. Hauptmann's nerve is shaken. He is even weakening, refusing food. But he told the press he was innocent—no confession to make."[21]

At least the print reporters and radio journalists were allowed in the courtroom to hear the verdict being read; the visual media were totally locked out. Of course, the newsreels had been ejected from the courtroom by Justice Trenchard after their ungentlemanly breaking of the agreement not to film live testimony. Still photographers were on the scene but forbidden from breaking out their equipment. The judge no more wanted a flashbulb-popping light show at the moment the jury foreman read the verdict than he did a melee of reporters scrambling for the doors.

Not to be deterred, Dick Sarno, the wily photojournalist for the *New York Daily Mirror*, plotted a soon-to-be legendary sneak shot to snap a picture at the moment of decision. "We [the photographers] held a war council and it was decided that I would go in and try to get a photo of the verdict being given," Sarno recalled. "We'd all share it. If I was caught, I would have been given six months on contempt." He had already taken readings on the lighting in the courtroom and figured out the optimum shutter speed for his compact 35mm Contax camera.

Sarno hid the small camera in his muffler, slipped past the bailiffs, and planted himself in the balcony next to Damon Runyon. When the jury filed in and took their seats, all eyes were on the worn faces of the eight men and four women. With Runyon providing cover, Sarno raised his camera and released the shutter. After the courtroom doors were opened, he ran across the street to a bakery where his fellow shutterbugs had set up a makeshift darkroom. The next day, the stolen photo ran in newspapers across the country.[22] To shield Sarno from the wrath of Justice Trenchard, pictured watching intently from the bench, frame left, Hearst credited the "dramatic photograph show[ing] the thrilling climax of the Hauptmann trial" only to an unnamed "*Evening Journal* staff photographer."[23]

Barred from the premises—and unable to sneak a 35mm Mitchell motion picture camera under a muffler—the newsreels could only report the verdict well after the fact. However, like the newspapers, newsreel editors had prepared for either eventuality. Pathé News and Hearst Metrotone shipped two sets of prints to exhibitors for immediate release once the verdict was read—one version proclaimed Hauptmann's conviction, the other his acquittal. When the jury reached its decision, newsreel editors telegraphed exhibitors to unseal the "guilty" reels and screen them immediately. Hearst Metrotone had spieler Edwin C. Hill record two different voiceovers. "As soon as the ver-dict was flashed to the theaters, the short was projected immediately, in most every case, beating the newspapers to the punch," reported *Motion Picture Herald*.[24] The canned releases were followed the next day by comprehensive overviews of the trial and statements from each side—prosecutor Wilentz satisfied that justice had been served, defense attorney Reilly pledging to appeal the case all the way to the Supreme Court.

So important was the story that special short subjects were issued. Par-amount News released a ten-minute review of the Hauptmann trial, which was sold and played as a "shorts special," not a regular newsreel issue. Heed-less of copyright law, Nat Saland, the operator of Mercury Film Laborato-ries, pirated, duped, and cobbled together Universal Newsreel film of the Hauptmann trial into an eighteen-minute special entitled *The Trial of the Century*.[25] Narrated by A. L. Alexander, the bootleg film reviewed Lind-bergh's 1927 flight, the mad reception in New York, his marriage to Anne Morrow, and a brief clip of the home-movie footage of the baby prior to the kidnapping. Alexander kept quiet for the last minutes of the short, letting the synch-sound face-off between Wilentz and Hauptmann speak for itself.[26] Released on February 15, two days after the verdict was read, it played as a featured attraction in Broadway theaters.[27]

Except for a red-faced AP, the coverage of the verdict in the Trial of the Century showcased all three media—the newspapers, the radio, and the newsreels—in peak form, at the top of their respective games. Competitive they were, and would remain, but each knew it had something to offer the others did not—detailed description, instantaneous bulletins, and vivid mov-ing images.

The News Behind the News with the *March of Time*

The story of AP's humiliating false flash was immortalized in the leadoff seg-ment for the second issue of the screen magazine, the *March of Time*, released on March 8, 1935. Premiering just the month before, the *March of Time* was the motion picture tentacle of the *Time* magazine empire. The series may be best known today as the inspiration for the "News on the March" obitu-ary for Charles Foster Kane that opens Orson Welles's *Citizen Kane* (1941), a note-for-note parody of the bombast and tempo that defined the house style. A widely honored template for screen journalism, it was a regular feature on some six thousand American screens until 1951, when television news ended its run.

The brainchild of Roy E. Larson, vice president of *Time* and right-hand man of *Time* kingpin Henry R. Luce, the *March of Time* was less a screen version of *Time* magazine than a film spinoff of the *March of Time* radio show. From radio it appropriated its style, structure, catchphrase ("Time—*Marches On!*"), and narrator, Westbrook Van Voorhis, whose oracular Voice of God baritone brooked no backtalk. The screen platform also inherited the conventions of the *March of Time*'s radio stagecraft, mixing voiceover exposition and dramatic reenactments to render the real-life drama of topical events.[28] Read *Time*, listen to the *March of Time*, and now watch the *March of Time*.

Disdaining the title of "newsreel," the *March of Time* billed itself as a "screen magazine" practicing a "new kind of screen journalism." The editors of the five newsreel outfits claimed to be unimpressed, but they knew the *March of Time* would be formidable competition. The *Time* imprimatur lent prestige, money, and journalistic credibility. Moreover, the screen magazine intended to do what the studio overlords forbade the newsreels from doing—shake things up by trafficking in controversy.

The first issue of the *March of Time* was slated to debut February 1, 1935, timed perfectly for coverage of the ongoing Hauptmann trial. A segment on the trial, even before the verdict was read, was a surefire way to generate excitement from moviegoers and to establish its bona fides as motion picture journalism.

Understandably, the newsreel editors were wary of the pedigreed rival yapping at their heels—and resentful of the praise, at their expense, that the critics' darling was already garnering. "Opinionated, informative, and decidedly interesting," the *March of Time* "promises to be a vast improvement upon the average stereotyped newsreel," predicted the *New York Times*.[29] The new venture in screen journalism "represents probably the best example of history that has yet to be conceived," commented the *Hollywood Reporter*. "It takes you much further than the ordinary newsreel."[30]

In fact, the aggressive stance of the newsreels during the Hauptmann trial—first in defying Justice Trenchard to film live testimony and then, in the cases of Universal and Pathé, refusing to withdraw the footage—was in part a response to the forthcoming competition from the Luce empire. The

Hauptmann-Wilentz newsreels were released on February 1, 1935, the very day the first issue of the *March of Time* was released. Not being a party to the pool arrangement among the five newsreel outfits, the *March of Time* would have had to reenact the Hauptmann-Wilentz face-off, not screen the authentic footage, had it decided to cover the trial. "The newsreels expected their Hauptmann 'scoop' would belittle *March of Time* in any position it might take as a newsreel reporter," explained a savvy article in *Motion Picture Herald*.[31]

However, in belittling the *March of Time*, the newsreels were forced to play their hand early. The newsreel companies "had planned not to release their prize film and sound track material until the trial was over," revealed the *New York Daily News*. "Their change of plan was precipitated by the backers of another movie stunt—a *March of Time* on the screen, in which the real-life actors in the Hauptmann trial were to be impersonated in the talkies. Owners of the real-life film feared the *March of Time* production—said to be ready for release also—would eat into their profits."[32] Thus, the newsreels rushed their authentic pictures into the theaters to preempt the competition—and, in the process, ruined their chance for a bigger splash by getting kicked out of the courtroom before the verdict was read.

Unable to compete with the authentic newsreel footage, the *March of Time* ignored the Hauptmann trial in its debut issue. Its less-than-timely topics included reports on New York's long-gone speakeasy culture, the Metropolitan Opera, and a man who paid a one-hundred-franc speeding ticket in France on the condition the money went toward repaying the French war debt to the United States. However, with the trial concluded and the verdict read, the second issue, slated for release on March 8, would be well positioned to offer a comprehensive overview of the trial—perhaps with Reilly, who never met a camera he didn't like, and Wilentz reciting parts of their summations in the very courtroom in which the statements were originally made.

However, the lack of authentic trial footage would have made any segment on the Hauptmann trial suffer by comparison with the historic sound footage stolen by the newsreels. To discourage the *March of Time* editors from doing what the fly-by-night short *The Trial of the Century* had done—namely, just steal the trial footage taken by the newsreels—the newsreel companies goaded Reilly and Wilentz into sending a joint telegram to the *March of Time* warning the editors not to use the Hauptmann footage. Prosecution and defense both "strenuously" objected to the footage and warned that the

March of Time would be held "strictly accountable" were it exhibited "in any state in the country."

Shut out from covering the trial with real footage, the *March of Time* devised an ingenious solution: cover the *coverage* of the trial. The decision was in line with the emergent media obsession with the internal workings and crucial importance of—the media. Entitled "New York Daily News," the segment dramatizes the editorial decision making in the city room of New York's most popular tabloid on the evening of the Hauptmann verdict.

The *March of Time* editors lifted the idea from the *New York Daily News* itself, which on February 15 published a full-page ad crowing about its scoop on the Hauptmann verdict and rubbing AP's nose in the dirt. "First and right with the Hauptmann verdict!" a headline reminded readers. The copy recounted the tension in the newsroom when, after reporter Robert Conway flashed by teletype the alert "Guilty first degree—Conway 10:24 P.M." and the presses started to roll, the contrary AP report came in seven minutes later. When AP retracted its original flash, victory was sweet: "*News* men were right, and the great AP was wrong!"[33]

The *March of Time* used the *New York Daily News* account as an outline for the first segment of its second issue—adding embellishments that ratcheted up the newsroom anxiety to allow the utterance of an immortal tabloid imperative.

"The world's fastest newspaper press is in the plant of the biggest newspaper in the United States—the *New York Daily News*," thunders Van Voorhis. "This press can print nearly two thousand copies a minute. One night two rolls of front-page plates stand ready with two different headlines." In reverse type, the huge headlines on the metal plates read: BRUNO GUILTY GETS LIFE and BRUNO GUILTY MUST DIE. The third possibility—BRUNO INNOCENT, WALKS FREE—was not typeset.

The action opens on *Daily News* assistant managing editor Harvey Duell and circulation manager Ivan Annenberg awaiting the Hauptmann verdict in a busy newsroom straight out of Hecht and MacArthur's *The Front Page*—candlestick telephones on desks, copy boys rushing in and out, and gruff ink-stained wretches smoking cigarettes. Like many personalities of the day, the newsmen turned thespian to play their parts for the *March of Time* cameras.

The *Daily News* subscribed to the teletype services of both the AP and UP, but the paper also had its own man in the courthouse, Robert Conway. It is Conway who will really scoop the world on the Hauptmann verdict.

At 10:19 P.M., fully twenty-six minutes before the verdict was read and twelve minutes before AP's false flash, Conway's teletype comes into the newsroom saying that Hauptmann is guilty, with no recommendation for mercy.* With either a bailiff or a member of the jury in his pocket, Conway had been tracking the jury deliberations all day; he even had tallies of the vote counts.

Assured by the reliable Conway, the "BRUNO MUST DIE" headline starts rolling off the presses.

A full-screen title card explains what happened next: "And now, what newsmen dread most takes place! With the presses rolling, a conflicting report comes in!" Namely: "The AP teletype types out a startling flash"—and the screen shows the all-caps alert: "FLASH VERDICT REACHED GUILTY AND LIFE."

Reading the AP report, editor Duell shouts the most delicious phrase in the lexicon of print journalism ("Stop the presses!") and barks, "Get me Conway right away!" The presses slam to a halt as the newsroom scrambles to reach the man on the scene.

Another title card underscores the dilemma: "The *News'* own reporter says DEATH! The A.P. says LIFE!"

For the *March of Time* cameras, editor Duell and circulation manager Annenberg act out a bit of dialogue that was certainly saltier in the original.

"Well, here's a mess. What do you think?" asks Duell.

"I don't know," muses Annenberg. "AP is usually right."

"But so's Conway."

At this point, a staffer bolts into the newsroom yelling that the radio is also reporting a recommendation for mercy. The radio, of course, was parroting the AP wire report passed along by the Press-Radio Bureau.

As anxiety and tension mount, the two men mull the possibilities. Eighty minutes earlier, the report was that the jury was ten to two for death. In eighty minutes did the two persuade the ten?

As the editors sweat, the teletype machine rings again. The new breaking news electrifies the newsroom.

BULLETIN KILL

KILL HAUPTMANN VERDICT—ERRONEOUS

---

* The *March of Time* dramatization puts Conway's flash five minutes *before* the *Daily News'* own account.

The *New York Daily News* gets its scoop, as chronicled in the *March of Time*, March 8, 1935.

"AP killed the flash!" exclaims Annenberg. "Conway's right!"

"Let 'em roll!" yells Duell in his best five-star-final voice.

As a montage shows tons of newspapers being stacked and trucked away for delivery throughout the city, Van Voorhis bellows: "The country's biggest newspaper roars into the streets with a clean beat of several minutes over all its competitors—and a record issue of over two million copies, the climax of the biggest news story of 1935!"

The meta-media outlook of the *March of Time*—what *Variety* editor Abel Green called "the news behind the news"—met with laudatory reviews.[34]

"The inside story of how the *New York Daily News* pulled the old newspaper stunt of re-plating plus and minus on the Hauptmann decision, how its bigwigs held their breath while the erroneous and now famous Associated Press flash was wiped out to clear the way for a three-minute beat over competitors, exciting scenes of the presses running—this is the *March of Time*'s answer to straight newsreel coverage on the trial of the century," blurbed Red Kann in *Motion Picture Daily*. "It's swell."[35] The film reviewer for the *New York Daily News* modestly noted that the second issue of the *March of Time* was "an important item" on the motion picture bill that highlighted "the scoop which the *Daily News* had on the Hauptmann verdict."[36]

The focus on the backstage machinations in the newsroom—and not the courtroom—reflected a newsworthy shift in journalistic perspective. The exposure of the operations of the media—whether print, radio, or motion picture—gave 1930s audiences privileged access to the modes of production and the protocols of editorial decision making. Every reader/listener/spectator became a canny inside-dopester wise to the ways of the newsroom, the broadcast booth, or the editing room. Never again, in covering a big story, would the media neglect to cover itself.

Chapter 11

DEATH WATCH

On February 19, 1935, against all precedent, New Jersey governor Harold G. Hoffman permitted a crew from Paramount News onto the grounds of the state prison in Trenton to film an urgent plea from the most reviled man in America. It would be the last of the many firsts in the annals of American media occasioned by the actions of Bruno Richard Hauptmann.

Speaking in tremulous, heartfelt tones from behind bars in his prison cell, reading from a prepared statement and stumbling over the words, Hauptmann looked straight into the camera lens to proclaim his innocence and beg for funds to finance his appeals.

> I want to tell the people of America that I am absolutely innocent of the crime and the murder. My conviction was a great surprise. I never saw the Lindbergh baby and I never was in Hopewell or near Hopewell and I never received any money from Dr. Condon. I want to appeal to all people everywhere to write me at this time as funds must be raised to carry my appeal to a higher court. Before God, I am absolutely innocent. I have told all I know about the crime. If my appeal to friends fails, and because of lack of money I can't have my case heard in upper court, I shall go to death as an innocent man.

Paramount played coy about where the filming had taken place "to avoid possible complications."[1] The brief clip, said *Daily Variety*, trumpeting the grim scoop, "marked the first talking picture appearance of any one under sentence to the electric chair."[2]

Between February 13, 1935, when the guilty verdict was read at Flemington, and April 3, 1936, when, to the surprise of no one and the satisfaction of most, Hauptmann was electrocuted at the state prison in Trenton, the three branches of the media monitored the ups and downs of the appeals process. Through it all, as Hauptmann's case wound its way through the courts and a formal petition for clemency to Governor Hoffman, the prisoner adamantly maintained his innocence. It was a long third act with little of the dramatic intensity of the first two.

The American public and the media alike seemed emotionally drained by the wrenching years spent monitoring the kidnapping, murder, pursuit, capture, and trial. The death watch was dutifully covered, but it played like a pro forma denouement. After all, the curtain scene was already written.

Killing Time

Though the end of Hauptmann's road was all but certain, the pathway was more circuitous and drawn out than was typical for the course of American justice in the 1930s. A full eighteen months elapsed between sentencing and execution, an unusually long period for a criminal justice system that exacted swift punishment in capital cases. Compare the Hauptmann meanderings to the streamlined efficiency with which another notorious murderer was dispatched, the assassin of Chicago mayor Anton Cermak. On February 15, 1933, while shaking hands with FDR at Bayfront Park in Miami, Cermak was shot by Giuseppe Zangara, an anticapitalist fanatic who was firing at the president-elect. The mayor died on March 6, 1933. Zangara was indicted for murder, tried, sentenced, and, on March 20, 1933, executed in the electric chair at Florida State Prison—a speedy two weeks from a charge of first-degree murder to capital punishment.

After the trial at Flemington, Hauptmann acquired an unlikely ally, Samuel S. Leibowitz, the famed criminal lawyer who had followed the trial closely as a nightly radio commentator for WHN. After the verdict, convinced that Hauptmann was guilty but had not acted alone, Leibowitz joined the appeals team, hoping to get Hauptmann to confess and name his accomplices, and thereby have his sentence commuted to life imprisonment. Leibowitz's

Criminal attorney Samuel S. Leibowitz, leaving the Trenton State Prison after trying unsuccessfully to get Hauptmann to confess and name his accomplice(s), February 13, 1936.

advocacy for the German pariah appalled his former allies in the Communist Party USA, whom he had fallen out with over the defense strategy for the Scottsboro Boys. "Samuel Leibowitz, renegade Scottsboro attorney, has joined forces with William Randolph Hearst and the Nazis in an attempt to save Bruno Richard Hauptmann, Nazi adherent indicted for the kidnapping and murder of the Lindbergh baby, from the electric chair," snarled the *Daily Worker*, mindful that Hauptmann's cause had been taken up by the German American Bund, a Nazi fifth column wired from Berlin.[3]

Leibowitz was not the only courtroom observer who wanted Hauptmann's death sentence commuted to life imprisonment. Adela Rogers St. Johns, who had said she would happily pull the switch on him herself, was willing to forgo the pleasure in the hope that in time, even years, Hauptmann might break down and name his accomplice(s). Neither Leibowitz nor St. Johns had the slightest doubt that Hauptmann was centrally involved and justly convicted. It was the thought that someone else had gotten away scot-free with the murder of the Lindbergh baby that overrode the lust for lethal vengeance.

On January 16, 1936, after months of successful delays by the defense team, Governor Hoffman inserted himself into the appeals process by granting Hauptmann a stay of execution that guaranteed the prisoner two more months of life. Heeding the call of conscience, or so he said, the governor began his own quixotic investigation into the case. Two months later, he strove to further delay the execution. "I had to do it," he explained. "The Hauptmann trial reeks with unfairness, passion, and prejudice."[4]

Hoffman's stay of execution and foray into private investigation were roundly condemned as grandstanding plays by a political poseur. Over four nights, from March 30 to April 2, CBS radio commentator Boake Carter said so on the air:

> And so crazier and crazier grows the Hauptmann affair—more and more desperate over the weekend became New Jersey's governor to justify his official blundering and save his tottering political reputation—more and more dizzy stunts are dragged across the old trails to befuddle the public and confuse the main issue. And so round and round—just as the music goes round and round—so round and round goes the Hauptmann affair—one of the most shocking exhibitions of gubernatorial meddling with the orderly process of law and order that America has displayed to the world in many a decade.

An incensed Hoffman assailed the remarks as defamatory. Demanding $100,000 in damages, he sued Carter, CBS, and WCAU, Carter's home station in Philadelphia.[5]

The case was watched closely by broadcasters as "the first broad test of alleged libel uttered over broadcasting stations and of the liability of stations along with speakers." Carter responded on air by challenging the governor to bring the suit in Pennsylvania, where the broadcasts originated, and not in New Jersey, where Hoffman heard them.[6] The governor refused, and the case was dismissed the next year on the technical grounds that the stations in question "were without license to do business in New Jersey and therefore were not subject to liability in that state."[7]

Carter's on-air defiance and the governor's decision to let the libel case drop reflected an emerging consensus that radio commentary was a species of protected speech under the First Amendment. No court ruling had yet granted the medium a constitutional right to freedom of expression, but, having assumed the mantle of responsible journalism, radio was being accorded some of the same prerogatives. Though constrained by commercial exigencies (Carter would never have dared to criticize Philco, his sponsor, the way he tore into Governor Hoffman), radio speech had gained broader freedom and flexibility in political discourse.

Despite the brickbats, the governor assumed the guise of impartial arbiter and profile in courage. In connection with Hauptmann's appearance before the New Jersey Board of Pardons, he asked to examine the newsreels of Hauptmann's testimony taken surreptitiously in January 1935. What better way to read the face and body language of the defendant at trial than to scrutinize the newsreels that the New Jersey district attorney had denounced as an unconscionable breach of judicial decorum?

The newsreel companies supplied the governor with some twenty thousand feet of footage, "promptly and without cost."[8] The editors hoped that cooperation with the governor might smooth access to Hauptmann for a pre-execution interview. Obtaining permission to film the actual execution was a newsreel first beyond even their hopes or, perhaps, desires.

In the meantime, the newsreels tracked every step of Hauptmann's slow-motion walk to the chair. "The latest clips on the Hauptmann case easily capture top dramatic interest," averred *Variety*'s man at the Embassy Newsreel Theatre on January 18, 1936, passing on his critique of the different ways Hearst Metrotone and Paramount covered the story:

> Effectively linked together for the telling of the past week's chapter in the Jersey cause célèbre are exclusive but separate interviews with Mrs. Hauptmann and Dr. Condon. Hearst contributing the first and Paramount the latter, and divers scenes in Gov. Hoffman's office and outside the Trenton prison following the issuance of the 30-day reprieve. Paramount also contributed these latter episodes. In the office interview the governor declared that great doubt existed as to certain phases of the case and that a great sense of duty had actuated the reprieve, while the quizzing of Jafsie adds nothing new to the general knowledge of the case. . . . Interview with Mrs. Hauptmann brings merely a reaffirmation of her belief in her husband's complete innocence.[9]

The newsreels were impatient to wrap up the story—though they did not, as they had done with the gangsters in the early 1930s, close out updates with a dolly shot stopping at a full-frame close-up of the electric chair.

As the newsreels scrambled to keep current with developments, the *March of Time* screen magazine withdrew from the competition. The series had planned to include a recap of the Hauptmann case in its January 1936 issue, but Governor Hoffman's reprieve issued on January 16 rendered the segment outdated. Not having enough time to give the breaking development the treatment it deserved, the editors decided to scrap the story so as not to "be accused of sensationalism merely for the sake of including leading headline copy in the issue."[10] Unlike the newsreels, the *March of Time* was building its brand on comprehensive coverage and mature reflection; too much timeliness was seen as a demerit, especially if the segment risked being overtaken by events.

Timeliness was the stock in trade of radio, however. The airwaves tracked each twist and turn with up-to-the-minute bulletins, commentary, and reenactments. WNEW did more, dramatizing the poignant chapters in the condemned man's unfortunate life in tandem with the Hearst press.

In December 1935, Hearst's *New York Daily Mirror* began serializing and syndicating Hauptmann's autobiography. Front-page teasers ("Hauptmann's Own Story! His side of the story must be heard! Read it every day in the *Daily Mirror!*") invited readers to accompany Hauptmann as, in his final hours, he saw his life pass before him. "In his death cell trooped brutal ghosts of his youth, as Bruno Richard Hauptmann, awaiting electrocution for the kidnapping and murder of the Lindbergh baby, penned this, his tragedy-laden life story." The editors included a disclaimer: "the *Mirror* assumes no responsibility for Hauptmann's assertions."[11]

In a tie-in deal, WNEW adapted the Hauptmann memoir into a nightly mini-series. Hearst had paid the Hauptmann defense team a reported $10,000 for the rights to the story, but the media mogul provided the copy to WNEW gratis, figuring to cash in on the free on-air publicity. "No sympathy for the convicted kidnapper, that being carefully eschewed from the radio dramatization, but otherwise it adheres to the day's factual occurrences," reported *Variety*.[12]

As Leibowitz pleaded and Hoffman preened, as the newsreels looked for fresh angles and radio watched the clock, the case shuffled toward its final stop. On March 30, 1936, at sunset, the pardon board announced that Hauptmann must die. The governor signed the death order.

A Morbid Recital of Events

With no microphone or cameras permitted in the execution chamber, print journalists had a clear field to set the scene, conjure the mood, and describe the last gasps of Bruno Richard Hauptmann. Sitting within feet of the chair, close enough to smell the flesh burn, the people's surrogates bore witness that justice was done. For many, it was a ghoulish but mundane job of work. Screenwriter Ben Hecht estimated that as a tabloid journalist in Chicago he had stood at the foot of the gallows and witnessed seventeen men "twisting in their white sheets on the end of the whining rope."[13] *New York World-Telegram* reporter Joseph Mitchell witnessed six men being electrocuted.[14] Drawing on long experience, the death watchers had honed a spare Hemingwayesque prose style befitting the ritual: terse, sharply observed, and emotionally restrained. The pity and terror of the ceremony packed its own jolt.

Headquarters for the media horde at the New Jersey State Prison outside Trenton was set up across the street from the death house, in a bare

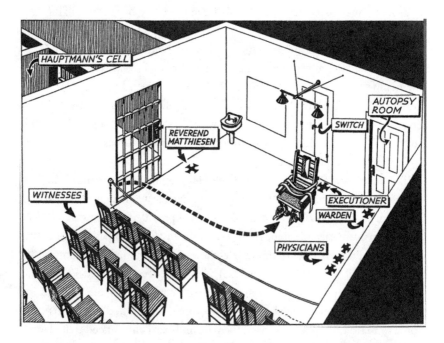

With no cameras permitted inside the execution chamber at the Trenton State Prison, print journalists and illustrators had a clear beat to conjure Hauptmann's "last mile."

garage made of cement blocks. Reporters sat before typewriters at long wooden tables, working on their copy. Wire service telegraph machines sent and received the latest bulletins. The journalists waited, biding time in the unlikely event of a stay of execution from Governor Hoffman or a last-minute confession from Hauptmann. The luckless Charles Zeid, a gangster also scheduled to die in the electric chair that night, would be relegated to the back pages.

AP reporter Samuel G. Blackman, who with colleague Francis Jamieson had been at the Lindbergh estate on the first night of the tragedy, stood watch on the last night.[15] He wrote a personal eyewitness account under his own byline and, as the designated AP witness in the death chamber, contributed to the longer unbylined report that went out over the AP wires (as usual, the AP prose was a writers' workshop–like collaboration between reporters on-site and rewrite men at the city desks).[16] Describing the dramatis personae and backstage players, Blackman singled out the most important stagehand behind the curtain, Robert H. Elliot, the official executioner for the State of New Jersey, a Grim Reaper built for the part—tall, gaunt, and sepulchral, a conscientious professional credited with more than a hundred previous executions. He came early to the death chamber to check out the chair, the straps, the electrodes, the wiring. "It's just a job as far as I'm concerned," he said. "I'm an electrician." The gloomy administration building housing Elliot's workplace was a brownstone modeled after an Egyptian tomb "with hieroglyphics and carvings of winged serpents and animals in the stone above the gate."

Having inherited a gothic set design, the AP report did not need to stretch to cast a spell:

> [Hauptmann] waits tonight in cell No. 9 half a dozen paces from the door to the death chamber, where he has been confined since February 16, 1935. He will wear the same blue-striped denim trousers he was worn for all these months, the white shirt, and bedroom slippers. The right trouser leg will be slit.
>
> He will come out into the glare of the lights, briskly for the guards waste no time. He will be put down in the chair. Electrodes will be clamped on his leg and on his head. Over his head will drop a leather mask.

AP debunked the myths: a switch was not pulled, as in the movies, nor did the prison lights dim at the moment the juice flowed. Executioner Elliot "will spin the wheel of a rheostat once, twice, a third time."[17] Elliot himself cleared up another misconception. It was not 5,000 or 10,000 volts "sizzling through the bodies of the condemned" as so many news reports said. "It's only 2,000," he pointed out. "That is plenty."[18]

In the brightly lit execution chamber "with its smudged white-washed brick walls, its high ceiling with a skylight, and its rows of wooden chairs in one-half of the room" sat fifty-five witnesses in chairs behind a three-foot-high canvas barrier that separated them from prison officials, executioner, and the condemned.[19]

Before the witnesses were led into the viewing chamber, the warden, Col. Mark O. Kimberling, ordered them to button their coats, keep their hands out of their pockets, and refrain from making any suspicious motions during the execution. The precautions were put in place to prevent a recurrence of a notorious breach of security at Sing Sing Prison in 1928, when a photographer for the *New York Daily News* with a camera concealed in his pantleg took a blurred photograph of murderess Ruth Snyder at the moment of electrocution, a ghastly image that emblazoned the front page of the tabloid the next morning under the all-caps headline: DEAD!

The mental landscape of Bruno Richard Hauptmann, whose stone face and inscrutable motives had turned courtroom reporters into amateur psychiatrists, remained an undiscovered country until the end. "Hauptmann didn't utter a syllable when he walked into the death chamber at Trenton looking like a punch-drunk fighter," wrote INS reporter James Kilgallen about the night he watched the condemned man "burn." Kilgallen thought he saw the faintest suggestion of a smile on Hauptmann's face, but Damon Runyon said no, Hauptmann was utterly expressionless.[20] Like Kilgallen, *Boston Globe* reporter Stanley Walker spied "a sort of half smile," but insisted that "Hauptmann walked to the chair almost in a trot, as if he wanted to get it over with as soon as possible."[21] Adela Rogers St. Johns did not see the rheostat turned, nor did she want to, even had women been allowed to attend.

Blackman—and AP's unnamed stylists—were cool and clinical:

There was no hysteria, no break down, no tears, inside the dirty-white four walls where Anna Hauptmann's "poor Richard" sat down to death. "I am not afraid to die," he had written Governor Harold G. Hoffman only last Tuesday. If he was, he did not show it.

Fifty-five witnesses saw him go: fifty-five, and one other, Robert Elliot, whose steady hand spun the wheel of the rheostat.

The condemned man's head was covered by a leather mask that hid his contorted face and bulging eyes. As the current surged into Hauptmann, Blackman watched the body.

> Even when Hauptmann died, there remained something of the mysterious aloofness that marked his months as a prisoner. His body stiffened, seemed to hunch when the current—21 1/2 horsepower of electricity—struck.
> But not afterward did the body slump.
> It appeared to the witnesses to hold itself erect, as though even in death the iron nerves defied the law that had plagued them so long.[22]

After the current had done its work, the formalities were observed.

> Six doctors, one at time, stepped forward, listened for the tremor of the heart of the man who could kidnap and kill a little baby, then stepped back.
> Twice they did this.
> Then, although not sure that the lightning thrusts of 2,000 volts had done their work, the doctors conferred around the chair in which he sagged, against the weight of the restraining straps.

The head physician confirmed the diagnosis: "This man is dead."

"We did not react the way human beings probably ought to react," remembered Hearst reporter James Whittaker. "When the authorities let us loose, like a lot of animals in a cage, we raced each other back through this subterranean passage by which we came to the execution chamber." They were all thinking the same thing: "You've got to get a hundred and fifty words down fast."[23] Staying behind, a correspondent for the *Philadelphia Inquirer* followed the body from the chair to the death house mortuary, "where the lax-limbed thing that was Bruno Richard Hauptmann stares unseeing the darkness."[24]

Unable to match the tightly controlled prose and detailed eyewitness accounts of the newspaper reporters in the execution chamber, radio compensated with the tick-tock suspense of a live countdown. Linked via the airwaves, announcers and listeners shared the last moments of Bruno Richard Hauptmann.

On the eve of Hauptmann's execution, broadcasting for the Tele-Flash Loudspeaker Corporation in New York, announcer Joseph O'Brien took time out from the usual business of the station—reporting the horse races—to conjure the death throes of the unrepentant killer:

> The sands of time are sinking for Bruno Richard Hauptmann. In a few hours the man who was convicted of kidnapping baby Charles Lindbergh on the night of March 1, 1932, will be strapped in the New Jersey electric chair. A few seconds later gaunt-faced Robert Elliot will throw a switch and the writhing form of the condemned man will strain and bulge at the unrelenting straps.[25]

Taking the high road, CBS declined to count down Hauptmann's final minutes. "Radio fans, who are looking forward to a morbid recital of events incidental to the electrocution of Bruno Hauptmann, are doomed to disappointment, as far as the Columbia network is concerned," *Variety* reported in schoolmarm mode. To stifle sadistic anticipation, CBS outlined the terms of its coverage:

> In the event that Bruno Hauptmann is put to death in the electric chair, CBS will, as soon thereafter as possible, make a brief news announcement that sentence has been executed upon him. In line with its conservative handling of the Hauptmann trial, Columbia has decided not to go beyond this brief bulletin. Should there *be actual news developments in connection therewith, these of course* will be covered in the Columbia broadcast.[26]

Audiences seeking a minute-by-minute recital would have to tune in elsewhere—perhaps elsewhere on CBS's own dial.

What CBS news refused to carry live was dramatized by CBS's the *March of Time*. Though the stops and starts of Hauptmann's scheduled execution kept the show's producers and vocal artists on edge, they were ready for the last episode. Weeks in advance of the actual death date, the *March of Time*'s twenty-seven-year-old wunderkind Charles Martin had completed a script depicting Hauptmann's execution. Martin both wrote and directed the script, which a reporter called "a tragic moment for the *March of Time* . . . that had to be written and rehearsed long before the switch was thrown in the death house in Trenton."[27]

After eighteen months of impersonating Hauptmann, vocal artist Dwight Weist had bonded, after a fashion, with the original. "Radio ghosts that they are, they seem to step into the shoes of those they portray with actual sympathy and pity," commented CBS publicist Hilda Cole, as she watched an episode unfold from Studio One at CBS headquarters. "Feel the full force of events they must, before they can mentally and physically impersonate the real people," she continued, adopting the backwards syntax that was the *Time* style.[28]

Weist's powers of mental and physical impersonation were put to the test as he stepped into Bruno Hauptmann's shoes for the last time. "When the night came for the re-enactment of the execution, he felt sick, frightened," reported *Radio Guide*. "He felt, he swears, as though part of him died, too." Weist confided, "It's a funny feeling, playing real people. I can't explain it. But we all have it . . . when something happens to the people we impersonate." His castmate Ted de Corsia, the longtime voice of Huey Long, had been unexpectedly grief-stricken when Long was assassinated in 1935. Weist, despite himself, felt a connection with the kidnap-murderer he had ghosted for so long.[29]

The strongest connection, of course, was felt by Anna Hauptmann, one of the few people in America who grieved unreservedly at the news that the death sentence had finally been carried out. In a small hotel room in Trenton, she awaited the inevitable "in the company of some sob sisters," no longer the exclusive property of Hearst's Jeanette Smits.[30]

The sobbies delivered the goods. When word came, Anna collapsed, hysterical. "Oh, God, why did you have to do this?" she wailed. "Oh, my poor Richard, I don't want to live!"[31]

Charles and Anne Lindbergh had no comment.

Gabriel Heatter's Golden Hour

Sometimes a story makes a journalist's career: the temperament and timing, eloquence and grace under pressure, capture the intensity of the moment and forever after associate the reporter with the news delivered. At the right time and the right place, when broadcast news was a consensual "nightly séance" not a narrowcast niche, the news bearer and the event narrated became fused together in the collective memory: Edward R. Murrow and the London blitz, Walter Cronkite and the JFK assassination, Jim McKay and the Munich Olympics. Gabriel Heatter was the name—and voice—tethered to Hauptmann's final minutes.

New York–born and Brooklyn educated, Heatter graduated from New York University Law School in 1910, attending classes while also working for the *Brooklyn Times Union* and *New York Journal*. From the local beats, he advanced to become the foreign correspondent for the *New York Tribune*. In 1933, after being invited to speak on WMCA about socialist presidential candidate Norman Thomas, he earned a permanent slot as station commentator.

Six months later, Heatter moved over to WOR, the local powerhouse. "Simplicity is Heatter's forte," an admiring profile explained. "He believes that the most dramatic form of radio presentation consists of plain, straight-from-the shoulder unadorned language."[32] Ed Bliss, the historian of CBS News, recalled that Heatter "spoke with a sense of sympathy, and restraint that stood in contrast with the insistent, dynamic voices of Boake Carter and Walter Winchell."[33] Heatter's signature salutation was "There's good news tonight!"

On the night of Hauptmann's execution, Heatter and Johnny Johnstone, WOR press public relations director, set up operations in a hotel room opposite the Trenton State Prison and in sight of the death house. To prevent another "false flash" fiasco of the kind that had befallen AP during the Hauptmann verdict, a Transmedia receiver had been installed to provide a double check against a planned signal from outside the death house confirming that the execution had taken place. Signals, as AP had learned, could get crossed.

Luck seemed to have favored Heatter. His regularly scheduled broadcast began at 8:00 P.M.; Hauptmann's execution was set for 8:05 P.M., Friday night, April 3, 1936. When Heatter went live on the air, Johnstone was at the hotel window looking for the signal from the prison. Having been assured by prison officials that Hauptmann would be electrocuted by 8:05 P.M., Heatter had prepared only five minutes of script. WOR had a comedy show scheduled for 8:15 and a musical performance at 8:30.

Heatter delivered his five minutes of prepared remarks—and no signal came from the prison. Heatter continued talking, extemporaneously. The minute hand moved further and further south and still no word. Heatter usurped the time allotted for the first show and warned listeners that he might be cut off at any moment for the second. WOR wisely stayed with Heatter's broadcast.

As the minutes ticked by, Heatter stretched—but did not sweat. Off-mike, his coworkers were not so cool. With still no high sign from Johnstone,

CBS commentator Gabriel Heatter's ad-libbed account of the execution of Bruno Richard Hauptmann on the night of April 3, 1936, helped make his career. Here he is in 1937 interviewing seven-year-old Dorothy Warner, billed as "the youngest newspaper columnist and serial writer in the world," on CBS's popular *We the People* program.

program manager Jules Seebach gestured frantically for Heatter to ad-lib and fill time. As *Broadcasting* reported:

> Fortified with a background of trial coverage, Heatter dipped deeply into Flemington as he talked and talked. Not until 8:48 did he get the Transmedia signal and his own pre-arranged outside signal. Hauptmann had died at 8:47 1/2 P.M.

Heatter waited thirty seconds to weave the news into his narrative. "There is a commotion at the prison door," he said simply. "Bruno Hauptmann has been executed—good night."

By the end of the broadcast, after more than forty minutes of seat-of-the-pants improvisation, Heatter had spoken nearly fifteen thousand words, most of them totally off the cuff.[34] Heatter's job "was as strenuous as it was an exemplary piece of radio journalism," decreed *Variety*, calling the performance "one of the most resourceful and smooth ad lib jobs ever turned in by a broadcaster."[35] Though hardly "Good news tonight!" for the featured attraction, the night of the execution was the golden hour for the broadcaster.[36] His career was made, his legend born.*

After more than four years of emotional entanglement in the Lindbergh case, Americans gathered around the medium of instant communication to hear the end of the story. Attendance at motion picture theaters plummeted. Even the few fans who ventured out had Hauptmann's fate in mind. At Radio City Music Hall, moviegoers congregated in the capacious radio-equipped lounge and asked management to tune in to a drama more compelling than the featured film that night, David O. Selznick's production of *Little Lord Fauntleroy* (1936).[37] Some of the New Yorkers listening at Radio City may have read about the execution before hearing it announced on radio. Taking a calculated risk, the city's two morning tabloids, the *Mirror* and the *News*, put extras on the street bannering Hauptmann's death twenty minutes *before* he had been officially pronounced dead at 8:47:30 that night.

---

* The fleeting nature of radio fame is measured in a punchline from Billy Wilder's black comedy *A Foreign Affair* (1948), a topical reference that now needs to be footnoted. In high dudgeon, a congresswoman (Jean Arthur) promises to go "to the War Department, and to the President, and if that doesn't do it—*I'll see Gabriel Heatter!*"

Americans on the Hauptmann death watch were especially curious about a singular human-interest detail. "How will he take it? Will his iron nerve break?" asked radio announcer Joseph O'Brien. "These are some of the questions being discussed today in hotel lobbies, in bar rooms, and at many street corners in this exciting city."[38] Hardened by the assembly-line administration of capital punishment in the eye-for-an-eye criminal justice system of the 1930s, Americans fixated on the character of the dead man walking: was he steady and stoic—or did he "die yellow"?

Thus, after the execution, when Colonel Kimberling appeared before the press and the newsreel cameras for a postmortem reckoning, the first question shouted was the one on everyone's mind.

"Was Hauptmann 'game'?" asked a reporter.

"He seemed to be very game," the warden replied.

During his summation to the jury in Flemington, District Attorney David T. Wilentz had scoffed at Hauptmann's icy front and predicted the mask would drop at the moment of truth. "He is cold," Wilentz shouted. "He will be thawed out when he hears that switch!"[39]

Wilentz misjudged his man. Hauptmann did not melt; he did not break. He went to the electric chair with the iron nerves of a convict-hero from a Hollywood gangster film.

EPILOGUE

The Legacies of the Crime of the Century

N
o criminal case in the twentieth century cast so long a shadow over American law, politics, and media as the kidnap-murder of the Lindbergh baby. All three realms were fundamentally altered by the case: new legislation was passed, new federal control was asserted over crime, and new protocols were established for electronic journalism. For the justice system, the federal government, and the media landscape, it really was the Crime of the Century.

The Lindbergh Laws

The kidnapping and murder of Charles Augustus Lindbergh Jr. persuaded most Americans that the laws of the land did not fit the crime and the lawmen were not up to the task. At both the federal and state level, politicians rushed to pass legislation to remedy the oversights. Never again would a kidnap-murderer be beyond the reach of capital punishment; never again would a heinous crime with national implications be left wholly in the hands of local constables and beat cops. Henceforth, a kidnapper risked the electric chair, and the full force of federal authority stood ready to strap him in.

An outraged Congress quickly passed the so-called Lindbergh law, which made kidnapping across state lines or to or from a foreign country a federal crime, with a penalty up to life imprisonment. Passed without a single dissenting vote, the legislation sailed through the House of Representatives. On June 22, 1932, the bill ("a direct result of the Lindbergh baby tragedy") was signed by President Herbert Hoover.[1] On May 18, 1934, FDR signed legislation amending and strengthening the Lindbergh law to treat kidnapping *ipso facto* as an interstate crime under the jurisdiction of the federal government and to provide for the death penalty if the victim was not returned unharmed.[2]

State legislatures also acted with dispatch. In California, the Lindbergh name, which had christened so many streets and babies in 1927, inspired a vengeful piece of legislature called "the Little Lindbergh Law." As home to legions of wealthy Hollywood celebrities, Los Angeles felt especially vulnerable to the threat of copycat baby snatchers. Fan magazines had long featured motion picture stars cradling infants and frolicking with kids around swimming pools in palatial homes, pictures that oozed wealth, privilege, and, to the criminal mind, opportunity. Security was tightened, bodyguards hired.[3] No star wanted a real-life reenactment of the cautionary plotline of *Miss Fane's Baby Is Stolen* (1934).

The Little Lindbergh Law made kidnapping for ransom within the state a capital crime—even if the victim was only harmed, not killed. "The day of mush-and-milk handling of such criminals in California is past," editorialized the *Los Angeles Times* in 1934 when the first capital sentence under the law was handed down to two malefactors who had kidnapped and tortured but not killed a local attorney. "Their fate could well serve to send a shiver of fear down the spines of gangsters contemplating similar crimes."[4]

The new laws demanded a new kind of lawman. The feckless New Jersey state troopers and two back-to-back headline-hungry governors displayed "some of the most noteworthy police bungling and political publicity hunting and plain everyday stupidity ever exhibited in connection with a murder case in this or any other country," editorialized the *New York Daily News.*[5] In a scathing series of syndicated articles, Arthur B. Reeve, a popular writer of detective fiction, shared his professional opinion about the real-life detectives in New Jersey. "Modern scientific criminology was apparently forgotten when the greatest crime in murder history broke," wrote Reeve. "Practically all the painstaking scientific advance of modern times was either forgotten or bungled."[6]

The condemnation of local law enforcement was in telling contrast to the lavish praise bestowed on the unflappable, relentless, and crisply efficient agents of the federal government. The accumulation of forensic evidence

Confirming the ascendency of federal law enforcement, the original caption for this INS photograph reads: "J. Edgar Hoover congratulates members of his staff who did the major share of the undercover work which led to the arrest of Bernard [*sic*] Richard Hauptmann, as the possessor of the Lindbergh ransom money." Left to right are J. E. Seyskora, T. H. Sisk, J. Edgar Hoover, and W. F. Seery, September 21, 1934.

that had convicted Hauptmann had been the work of federal employees far removed from the physical scene of the crime. Whether it was the lumber trail followed by the U.S. Forestry Service, the analysis of financial data by the Internal Revenue Service, or the tracking of gold certificates around New York by the Department of the Treasury, the expertise derived from Washington, D.C., not Trenton, New Jersey.

Firing up a publicity machine for media outlets ready to print its press releases verbatim, the FBI hogged the lion's share of the glory for cracking the case. IRS and Treasury agents, who had done the grunt work and insisted, over Lindbergh's initial objections, that the ransom money be catalogued and paid in gold certificates, seethed at the sight of J. Edgar Hoover taking credit for their work, but the T-men would have to get used to the G-men stealing the spotlight. "Every kidnapping case turned over to this division since enactment of the Federal kidnapping law in June 1932 has been solved," Hoover assured citizens at regular intervals throughout the 1930s. It was his FBI, Hoover boasted, that "put the fear of God and the law into criminals."[7] Its reputation established, its integrity unassailable, its power seemingly limitless, the FBI, with Hoover at the reins, rode the Lindbergh case to a preeminence it has never really relinquished.

Not all institutions emerged from the Hauptmann trial with an enhanced reputation. Even before the jury in the Flemington courthouse pronounced Hauptmann guilty, politicians, jurists, and editorialists rendered a harsh verdict on the conduct of the media. "Every detail of the trial is photographed for the newsreels, reported on the radio, and described in the newspapers at such length that even the President's message to Congress was relegated to second place in favor of the day's proceedings," wrote the *New Republic*, repulsed by the "sorry spectacle" that had unfolded in Flemington.[8] The novelist Edna Ferber, owning up to her part in the sorry spectacle, expressed disgust at "the jammed aisles, the crowded corridors, the noise, the buzz, the idiot laughter, the revolting faces of those of us who are watching this affront to civilization."[9]

The corrosive influence of the media on the dignified conduct of American jurisprudence was the consensus takeaway from the Hauptmann trial. "Judges should, following the early but abandoned effort of Justice Trenchard at Flemington, decline to permit cameramen to degrade the process of the law in the pursuit of their trade," advised the *New York Times*. "Those news and newsreel photographers who attempt these things hereafter should be forcibly prevented."[10]

Prevented they were—not by force but by a code of professional conduct. In 1937, as a direct result of the media sensation surrounding the Hauptmann trial, the American Bar Association adopted a resolution that condemned photography and broadcasting in the courtroom. Added as Canon 35 to the ABA's Code of Judicial Ethics, the resolution read:

> Proceedings in court should be conducted with fitting dignity and decorum. The taking of photographs in the courtroom during sessions of the court and recesses between sessions, and broadcasting of court proceedings are calculated to detract from the essential dignity of the proceedings, degrade the court, and create misconceptions with respect thereto in the minds of the public, and should not be permitted.[11]

In 1956, the ABA prohibition was updated to include television.[12] For decades, to the eternal gratitude of freelance sketch artists, Canon 35 kept cameras out of even the most headline-grabbing criminal trials. Not until 1982 would the ABA formally repeal the canon, not until the mid-1980s would state judges routinely permit television into court, and not until 1991 would enough courtrooms be wired to make Court TV a viable cable concept—gaining for television the right of coverage that the newsreels lost in Justice Trenchard's courtroom in 1935.[13]

By the mid-1990s, the march of television cameras into the courtroom seemed poised to penetrate every level of the American judiciary. Yet the intrusion halted at the federal level because of the media frenzy surrounding the only other plausible candidate for the trial of the twentieth century, the trial in 1995 of football great and Hertz pitchman O. J. Simpson for the murders of his former wife Nicole Brown Simpson and her friend Ronald Goldman. The gavel-to-gavel, wall-to-wall television coverage of every moment of the trial, supplemented by endless hours of on-air punditry from journalists and lawyers, accrued huge ratings for cable news stations and black-humor fodder for late-night comedians. Grandstanding attorneys, money-grubbing witnesses, a starstruck judge, and a shocking verdict of not guilty for a guilty-as-sin defendant, stopped cold the march of the medium into the highest courts in the land. Still invested in the majesty of the law, the federal judiciary took the sleazy reality show that was OJ-TV as a cautionary lesson. The federal courthouse remains one of the few zones in American life blocked off from the camera eye—so far.

The rules drawn up for Hollywood in the wake of the Lindbergh kidnapping also remained in place for decades. In 1934, with the establishment of the Production Code Administration, regulator-in-chief Joseph I. Breen was given full authority to enforce the Code's edicts against kidnapping. When a kidnapped-themed scenario crossed his desk, Breen curtly pointed out that the film "was filled with details of crime in connection with kidnapping, the payment of ransom, etc. It appears therefore to be in violation of the Association's regulations re 'Crime in Motion Pictures.'" Breen's advice to filmmakers was always the same: "We recommend that you withdraw your application for a Certificate of Approval."[14] Moreover, while the cinematic present was being patrolled, the cinematic past had to be erased. The troublesome kidnapped-themed films from the pre-Code era—*Three on a Match*, *Okay, America!*, *The Mad Game*, and *Miss Fane's*

Baby Is Stolen received an imperious thumbs-down when submitted for rerelease under the Code.

For the next twenty years, Hollywood not only kept kidnapping off the screen but bequeathed the prohibition to television. In 1951, the National Association of Broadcasters Code of Programming Standards, in accord with its special responsibility to children, pledged to eliminate "references to kidnapping of children or threats to children."[15] The family-friendly medium of the 1950s no more wanted to give mothers nightmares than did Hollywood in the 1930s. In 1954, the Screen Writers Guild Bulletin reminded members, "With all [television] sponsors, kidnapping of a child is an absolute 'NO!' "[16]

Actually, the kidnapping of a child on television wasn't quite an absolute "NO!" Unlike the Production Code, the Television Code lacked an ironclad enforcement mechanism: barring a violation of the Federal Communications Act, what aired on television really was a gentleman's agreement. Thus, on June 22, 1954, ABC's prestigious and risk-taking anthology series *U.S. Steel Hour* telecast a live drama entitled "Fearful Decision." Produced by the Theatre Guild and written by Cyril Hume and Richard Maibaum, the teleplay dramatized the desperate gambit by a millionaire father whose son is kidnapped: he refuses to pay $500,000 in ransom on the grounds that to accede to the demand would only encourage more kidnappings—and, the odds are, the boy is dead already anyway.[17] "You know, up to now, there's been a network taboo against kidnap stories," actor Ralph Bellamy, who played the determined father, told a reporter during a break in rehearsal, "but this one is so different and handles the subject so intelligently, we didn't have any trouble getting it okayed."[18] The critically praised teleplay was so popular it was reprised two weeks later for a second live broadcast.

Sensing a valuable property for the big screen, MGM purchased the film rights to "Fearful Decision"—and had its application for a Production Code seal turned down on the usual grounds that kidnapping was forbidden under the Code. MGM appealed the decision to the executive board of the Motion Picture Association of America in New York on the eminently reasonable grounds that denying theatrical exhibition to a motion picture that treated a theme already broadcast, twice, into the nation's living rooms was absurd. The MPAA board agreed and overturned the PCA ruling "on technical grounds."[19]

Playing up the once-forbidden theme, the film version, released in January 1956, was given an exclamation point and retitled *Ransom!* "Never before has the motion screen been permitted to portray the story of a kidnapping!" blurbed the taglines, short on pre-Code memory.[20] In the film, the eight-year-old son of a wealthy manufacturer is kidnapped. Referred to, but not depicted on screen, the method of the actual kidnapping is simplicity itself—no violence, no breaking and entering. In the safe-and-secure precincts of the Eisenhower era, a woman disguised as a nurse goes to the boy's school and says she has come to bring him to his doctor. The school principal turns him over without question.

As the boy's mother lurches from hysteria to catatonia, the father comes to a hard-nosed decision. Addressing the kidnappers over television, clutching the ransom money, he refuses to pay the $500,000 ransom demand so as not to continue the vicious cycle. "No pay off, no kidnap racket, no profit motive," as a cynical reporter explains. The police chief alludes to the pertinent background. "You've seen it yourself," he says, "the biggest men in this country openly making deals with kidnappers—and the voting public wouldn't have it any other way—even though the child were dead right straight through from the beginning." The father's fearful decision is the right one: no ransom is paid, and the boy is returned unharmed.

On December 11, 1956, the Motion Picture Association of America officially ended the ban on kidnapping scenarios. "Kidnapping of children is now okay on condition the subject is handled with restraint and discretion and the child is returned unharmed," stated the new policy.[21] "This point is a hangover from a 30-year-old outburst [over] kidnapping based on the Lindbergh case," explained Code chief Geoffrey Shurlock, Breen's more lenient successor, after the PCA granted a Code seal to *Compulsion* (1959), a thinly veiled version of the Leopold and Loeb case.[22] The kidnapping of a child, even if murdered, the nightmare of an earlier generation, would henceforth be fit subject matter for American entertainment.

The Descent of the Sky God

After the trial of Bruno Richard Hauptmann, Charles and Anne Lindbergh tried to put the pieces back together. For Anne, writing was her solace and vocation. For Charles, the work involved his first love, aviation, and a new obsession, a symbolically rich endeavor for the emotionally repressed

Midwesterner, the creation of a fully functional artificial heart. He was work-ing on the device the day Hauptmann was executed.[23]

There was also a new addition to the family. On August 16, 1932, Anne had given birth to a second son, Jon Morrow Lindbergh. He was not nicknamed Little Lindy nor dubbed the Eaglet, but he was not left alone.

Though Lindbergh pleaded—again, as ever—with the press to respect his privacy and stay clear of the baby, William Randolph Hearst had newspapers to sell. Proto-paparazzo Dick Sarno, the photographer for the *New York Daily Mirror* who snuck a camera into the Flemington courtroom for a picture of the jury foreman during the reading of the Hauptmann verdict, was deter-mined to snap a shot of baby Jon.

In December 1935, as the three-year-old boy was being driven from pre-kindergarten to his home, a large car crowded the vehicle onto the curb and forced it to stop. The newspapers described the traumatic encounter:

> Men jumped down. A teacher accompanying the child clutched him tightly. Suddenly cameras were thrust into the child's face and clicked. Then the vis-itors jumped into their machine and sped away, leaving a badly frightened teacher and little boy.[24]

Sarno got the shot and a $100 bonus.

For the Lindberghs, the ambush was the final outrage. Badgered by cranks, threated by blackmailers, and hounded by a rapacious press, they fled to England for their safety and peace of mind. The couple kept the decision secret until they were well out to sea, sailing by passenger ship on a course further south than the flight path Lindbergh had flown in 1927, and docking in Liverpool on December 31, 1935. In the sedate village greens of England, a land without a First Amendment, the Lindberghs escaped the worst of the press intrusions.

Americans understood the reasons for the defection but were shamed by the forced exile. "A national disgrace," moaned the *New York Herald Tribune*, asking when in recorded history "has a nation made life unbearable to one of its most distinguished men though a sheer inability to protect him from its criminals and lunatics and the vast vulgarity of its sensationalists, public-ity-seekers, petty politicians, and yellow newspapers?"[25] The kidnap-murder was the crime of a lone perpetrator; the harassment of the family was the work of the whole nation.

A measure of poetic justice thus informed the next phase of the media-Lindbergh relationship, which was symbiotic, not parasitic. In 1939, when the family returned to America, Lindbergh was a changed man. Suddenly, the press-averse and camera-shy flyer was everywhere and talking—making speeches at rallies, broadcasting on the radio, and posing for the newsreels. He had found a cause as close to his heart as commercial aviation: American foreign policy, in particular toward a regime that shared his value system.

In 1933, Germany had embraced an ethos of Spartan physicality, aviation-minded militarism, and racial purity—all cherished by the perfect specimen of mankind who was the Nordic, fit, and triumphant Charles Lindbergh. Courted by the Nazis, he reciprocated with the best of all celebrity endorsements. Lindbergh visited Nazi Germany six times between 1936 and 1938, bathed in its admiration, and accepted its honors.[26] The displays of comradeship during the last visit were especially warm. On October 18, 1938, at a reception at the U.S. Embassy in Berlin, he was presented with the Service Cross of Order of the German Eagle with Stars, the second highest

As Anne looks on, Reichsminister for Air Hermann Göring presents Lindbergh with a ceremonial sword at Göring's Leipziger Platz estate in Berlin, July 28, 1936, during the first of Lindbergh's six visits to Nazi Germany.

German decoration after the Iron Cross, an honor personally authorized by Adolf Hitler and bestowed by Reichsminister for Air Hermann Göring. Lindbergh thanked Göring and hung the decoration around his neck.[27] The presentation occurred less than three weeks after the Nazi invasion of Czechoslovakia.

As the American hero and the Nazi henchmen clasped hands in a mutual admiration pact, a once universal affection for Lindbergh tapered off. In 1927, the whole nation had held its breath and prayed for his safety. Five years later, it had mourned with him as the unimaginable happened and, during the Hauptmann trial, marveled at his quiet dignity. In 1938, the connective tissue that bound Lindbergh to nearly every American was torn. Lindbergh would always be a hero to many Americans for the past, and indeed to some for his words and deeds in the present, but he would never again know the unabashed, unqualified adoration of his countrymen.

To Americans whose love for Lindbergh was not unconditional, his embrace of Nazi Germany felt like a personal betrayal. "For those of us who had illusions, romantic illusions, about a young tousle-haired boy who flew over the Atlantic many years ago, it comes as a shock to read that Charles Lindbergh received and accepted the 'coveted cross of the German Eagle with stars,'" lamented *Hollywood Now*, the biweekly newspaper of the Hollywood Anti-Nazi League, the Popular Front group that was trying to do precisely what Lindbergh was trying to prevent: alert Americans to the dangers of Nazism. When the "hero of yesterday accepted the reward from the hands of the Nazi Gorilla, Herman Goering," Lindbergh broke a bond forged in triumph and tragedy.[28]

For a man used to worship, the opprobrium must have stung, but Lindbergh was deaf to the criticism. At radio microphones and before the newsreels, he hectored his fellow citizens to keep out of European affairs and to recognize that Nazi Germany was not just a geopolitical reality but the wave of the future.

After September 1, 1939, when war broke out in Europe, Lindbergh's pro-Nazi and isolationist stance intensified; he became the most prominent spokesman for the America First Committee, an eight-hundred-thousand-member cohort of isolationists and nativists who believed that European wars should be left in Europe and considered American interventionists a greater menace than Nazi Germany. He testified before the Senate Foreign Relations Committee to denounce FDR's Lend-Lease bill, a measure that gave aid to the besieged British; he spoke at huge anti-intervention rallies in Madison Square Garden in New York and Soldier Field in Chicago; and he took to radio to demand that the United States deal respectfully with the Nazis if, as he expected, they defeated England.[29] Media outlets that urged involvement in the European conflagration should be looked upon with suspicion. "We must ask who owns and who influences the newspaper, the news picture, and the radio station," he warned.[30]

Politicians and editors who had once fawned over Lindbergh now condemned him in terms that would have been unthinkable in 1935. FDR adviser Harold Ickes implied that Lindbergh was not just a naïve Nazi dupe but a conscious Nazi agent. When asked whether she thought Charles and Anne Lindbergh should just "go to Germany and stay with old Hitler," First Lady Eleanor Roosevelt tartly replied, "No, I should be sorry indeed to see poor Mr. Lindbergh and his charming wife in Germany. We ought to keep our illusions as long as we can."[31] Her husband was less diplomatic. At a press conference on April 25, 1941, FDR assailed Lindbergh's defeatism and embrace of appeasement, labeling him the moral equivalent of the Copperheads who had undermined the Union during the Civil War.[32]

Undeterred, Lindbergh stayed on course. So vital was the isolationist cause that he resolved to cooperate with the medium he most distrusted. After his radio addresses, newsreel men typically requested that Lindbergh repeat for the cameras what he had said before the microphones. "In the past, I have refused their requests," he confided to his diary on October 14, 1940, after a broadcast for Mutual radio. "First, because of the difficulty they have always caused for me; and second, and much more important, because of the Jewish interest in the newsreels and the antagonism I know exists toward me." Made media-savvy through hard experience, he knew the risks in trusting his image to un-like-minded film editors. "By speaking for the newsreels, I take the chance that they will cut my talk badly and sandwich it between scenes of homeless refugees and bombed cathedrals." Only his belief that the present precarious moment was "a critical period" made him think "it is worth the chance" to make a deal with the devil.[33]

Given the nature of the regime Lindbergh championed, his shift from the politics of isolationism to the rhetoric of antisemitism was no slip of the tongue. On the evening of September 11, 1941, in Des Moines, Iowa, in a speech delivered to cheering throngs from the America First Committee, broadcast over radio and screened in the newsreels, Lindbergh squandered

At a rally for the America First Committee in Oklahoma City, August 29, 1941, Lindbergh takes to the rostrum and radio to speak out for isolationism and nativism.

more of the residual goodwill he retained from that other night at Le Bourget Field. He warned against the warmongering partnership between the beset British, currently under Nazi bombardment, and American Jews, who looked out only for each other. He understood "why the Jewish people desire the overthrow of Nazi Germany," but Jewish and British objectives must never override American interests. "I am saying that the leaders of both the British and the Jewish races, for reasons which are as understandable from their viewpoint as they are inadvisable from ours, for reasons which are *not* American, wish to involve us in the war." Given the un-American tribal loyalties of the studio moguls and network presidents, the media required special vigilance. "Their greatest danger to this country," he said of the Jews, "lies in their large ownership and influence in our motion pictures, our radio, and our government."[34] The pronoun "our" did not include "them."

Lindbergh's Jew-baiting Des Moines speech marked a tipping point. The media—print, radio, and the newsreels—turned decisively on its once-favorite son. To be sure, the editorial policy of an influential group of isolationist-minded newspapers stood in Lindbergh's corner on foreign policy if not domestic nativism—the Hearst press, the *Chicago Daily Tribune*, the *New York Daily News*, and the *Washington Times-Herald*.[35] But almost everywhere else the once sacrosanct figure became a target of opportunity. *Daily Variety* editor Arthur Ungar enumerated a list of villains that placed Lindbergh in the worst of company: "Flynn, Lindbergh, the America First contingent, Wheeler, Nye, Bennett and Worth Clark" were doing the work of Nazism at the expense of Americanism.* The incarnation of all things American had been consigned to the lunatic fringe—or worse, the fifth column.[36]

No media figure condemned Lindbergh with more sustained venom than Walter Winchell, whose columns from 1938 to 1941 dripped derision and contempt. "When he climbed a Ratzi rostrum and let Hitler's buddies pin a medal on him," the hero of 1927 surrendered any claim he had on his countrymen's respect. Lindbergh had sacrificed universal admiration to become the "star 'Shill' for the America First Committee," a subversive outfit whose admirers "consist mainly of members of the German American Bund and various other groups which sympathize with or admire Hitler and Mussolini." To the shrinking roster of defenders who said that Lindbergh was surely sincere in his beliefs, Winchell shot back, "What of it? So is Hitler. He believes in murder and hate."[37]

Radio, whose microphones had always been open to Lindbergh, rescinded the courtesy airtime. After the Des Moines speech, New York's WOR "let it be known that unless Lindbergh drops the racial issue the station's facilities will be closed to him," *Variety* reported. The Mutual network also muffled the Lindbergh rhetoric by balancing any "Lindbergh screed with a speaker from the other side [and] leaving it up to individual stations whether to broadcast the speeches."[38] On October 31, 1941, when America Firsters demanded Lindbergh's speech at Madison Square Garden be broadcast by radio, the networks refused. CBS saw "no reason why Col. Lindbergh should have a nation-wide network every time he speaks . . . we shall not broadcast the speeches."[39]

---

* John T. Flynn was a prominent anti-FDR journalist and co-founder of the America First Committee; Burton K. Wheeler (D-MT), Gerald Nye (R-WI), Bennett Champ Clark (D-MO), and David Worth Clark (D-ID) were U.S. Senators, all fervent isolationists and nativists.

In another sign of how quickly America's uncrowned prince had become America's pariah, the *vox populi* was also registering disapproval. Motion picture audiences, who had once greeted each close-up of Lindbergh in the newsreels with spontaneous applause, now sat on their hands or yelled cat-calls. At the Embassy Newsreel Theatre, showing a clip of Lindbergh speaking to America Firsters at Madison Square Garden, hisses and boos rose up from the crowds.[40]

After Pearl Harbor rendered isolationism un-American, Lindbergh—who had resigned his commission in the reserves after FDR's blast—sought to enlist in the U.S. Army Air Force. The offer of military service by the winner of the Distinguished Flying Cross was rebuffed, a decision that came directly from FDR. Lindbergh eventually made his way to the Pacific Theater as a civilian consultant to the United Aircraft Corporation and flew fifty combat missions against the Japanese. Strictly speaking, the flights by a civilian were against regulations, but who was going to tell Charles Lindbergh he could not fly a plane?

In the postwar era, Lindbergh finally found himself to be, if not quite old news, then at least no longer automatic front-page news. In 1953, he reemerged in a new, or rather old, guise with the publication of *The Spirit of St. Louis*, a Pulitzer Prize–winning memoir that avoided mention of Lindbergh's post-1927 life and allowed amnesiacs to bask again in the glory of yore. In 1954, under a more sympathetic president, he was commissioned a brigadier general in the Air Force Reserve. He spent much of the 1950s and 1960s working quietly as a consultant to the Air Force and helping to finance the experiments of rocketry pioneer Dr. Robert Goddard.

Lindbergh spent his final years on earth trying to protect it; he became a passionate environmental activist. As with the earlier cause, the importance of educating Americans about conservation compelled him on occasion to endure the glare of a spotlight. "I have had enough publicity for fifteen lives," he said wearily, "but where I can accomplish a purpose, I will do things I otherwise abhor."[41]

In 1974, when Lindbergh died, the obituaries dwelt on the glory and the tragedy, but all noted the blindness and the bigotry. He never repented, apologized, or, so he said, had second thoughts about his prewar words and deeds. Twenty-five years after the Des Moines speech, he told journal-ist Alden Whitman, who tried to sum up Lindbergh's life for the *New York Times*, "In hindsight, I would not change my action."[42]

Anne was less closed-minded and more reflective. She acknowledged what her husband never did, that they were "both very blind, especially in the beginning, to the worst part of the Nazi system."[43]

Even before the death of her husband, Anne Morrow Lindbergh had forged an identity and a life apart from him. In time, her prodigious literary output—in prose and poetry, memoirs and musings, diaries and journalism—would surpass her accomplishments as a pioneering aviator. In 1955, she published *Gift from the Sea*, a thin volume of spiritual and philosophical mediations that sold more than five million copies. "The most important book of our times," wrote Adela Rogers St. Johns, a work of "heartfelt sentiments of faith, humor, responsibility, drama" and, most of all, hope. Never to be forgotten—St. Johns never forgot—"the giver of this gift is the same woman who, as the slim young wife of the nation's hero, found the empty crib, read the kidnap note, [and] waited minutes that were eternities."[44]

Anne bore six more children after the death of her first, four boys and two girls. She died in 2001, but not before revealing, unlike Charles, a glimpse of what was behind the brave front she had put up on the witness stand in the Flemington courtroom. "One has undergone an amputation," she wrote in her 1973 memoir *Hour of Gold, Hour of Lead*. "One still feels the lost limb down to the nerve endings."[45]

The Crackpot Aftermath of the Lindbergh Kidnap-Murder

In 1949, Hearst reporter Dorothy Kilgallen—no longer a second stringer but a heavy hitter—recalled the buzz she felt sitting behind Bruno Richard Hauptmann in an overheated courtroom in the bone-chilling winter of 1935. Like most of the press corps, she believed Hauptmann was guilty, but she was also troubled by the anomalies, the oddities, the pieces of the puzzle that never fit the picture. How could one man have taken the baby down a rickety ladder that didn't reach the window sill on a blustery night? How did the eccentric Dr. John F. Condon come out of nowhere to be a central player in the case? Why did Violet Sharpe commit suicide? And on and on. "I have never known, in any criminal trial, so much private disagreement among the members of the working press," recalled Kilgallen. "You could start a three-hour debate in the Main Street beanery just by saying, 'Yeah, what about Isidor Fisch?' "[46]

The long arguments in the Main Street beanery in Flemington would be played out forever after by scholars, journalists, and true-crime buffs. The morning after Hauptmann's execution, Damon Runyon wrote, "Bruno Richard Hauptmann is dead, but the crackpot aftermath of the Lindbergh kidnap-murder—probably destined to go on for years—already is in full swing."[47]

Runyon was prophetic. In time, the Lindbergh case would spawn a growth industry of books, films, and websites trafficking in sinister plots and frame-up scenarios. Immune to the mountains of evidence collected by the FBI, the Treasury Department, and the U.S. Forestry Service, a passionate minority felt that the New Jersey cops or J. Edgar Hoover or New York mobsters or combinations thereof had railroaded an innocent man. The conspiracy theories answered all the troubling questions and filled in all the blanks.

In 1935, however, and for decades after, generations prone to defer to official authority mainly accepted the judgment of the jury, the journalists, and the legal experts: Hauptmann was guilty and justly sentenced to die in the electric chair. Whatever questions might linger, when reporters reminisced and newspapers recapped the case, the guilt of Hauptmann was not one of them.

The verdict was sustained when a new medium, soon to be the central repository of American history, came to tell the story. In 1962–1963, a cluster of three television documentaries looked back on the Lindbergh case: "Charles A. Lindbergh: The Crowded Idol," an episode of *Perspectives on Greatness*, an hourlong monthly series, telecast on January 26, 1962, by WOR-TV in New York and hosted by H. V. Kaltenborn; "Lindbergh Kidnapping," an episode of NBC's *David Brinkley's Journal*, telecast on January 31, 1962; and "Charles Lindbergh," an episode of the syndicated series *Biography*, first telecast on March 17, 1963, and hosted by Mike Wallace. The rough synchronicity in timing was a consequence of the recent introduction of videotape editing, which facilitated the rewinding of archival newsreel footage; the chronological sequencing of representative personalities from broadcasting's past (radio commentator Kaltenborn), present (Brinkley, then one-half of the highest-rated network news team in America), and future (Wallace, not yet the bushwhacking gunslinger for CBS's *60 Minutes*) is just a coincidence.

The *Perspectives on Greatness* episode opens with direct-address exposition by a wizened H. V. Kaltenborn, eighty-four years old, a callback to the radio past of his adult televiewers. Despite appearances, Kaltenborn is emphatically not past his prime. As someone who was there, he speaks with authority and expertise and, as in the 1930s, shows no fear in uttering inconvenient truths—for example, that Lindbergh's role as an unofficial American ambassador in Europe in 1927 was an antidote to the anti-Americanism wrought by the Sacco and Vanzetti case or that the investigation of the kidnapping was inhibited by "an atmosphere of constant bickering among law enforcement agencies." The film unspools reel after reel of rarely screened Hearst Metrotone footage: Hauptmann in the police lineup at the Greenwich Street Police Station and at the first trial in the Bronx; the stolen live testimony from the Flemington courtroom; scenes of the carnivalesque atmosphere outside the courthouse. Lindbergh's strident prewar isolationism is chronicled, but its antisemitic overtones are neither seen nor heard. Bringing Lindbergh's biography up to postwar date, Kaltenborn makes a sage comment: "An idol had become simply a figure in history."

David Brinkley's Journal focused on the sensationalistic news coverage of the kidnapping and trial. On hand for eyewitness validation is James Wittaker, who covered the trial for INS, and the no-longer-ascendant Walter Winchell, whom the age of television had not been kind to. Somewhat defensively, Whittaker explains that the press was only feeding the public appetite ("people demanded that the story be kept going") but admits that under the pressure to get scoops "sober-minded reporters went hog wild." Winchell recalls the Hauptmann trial as not only "the most dramatic story I have ever covered" but, thanks to the evenhanded rulings and dignified comportment of Justice Trenchard, the fairest trial. Brinkley sums up by stating the obvious—that no criminal case since had matched the Hauptmann trial for sheer scale of coverage and media-born delirium. Fortunately, Brinkley opines, "changes in public taste and a degree of national maturity" have made a recurrence of such unseemly spectacles "impossible."[48]

Billed as "the story of the young handsome man who completed the first solo flight across the Atlantic and the terrible consequences that followed," CBS's *Biography: Charles Lindbergh* is a briskly edited biopic comprised entirely of archival footage, voiceover narration, and talking-head exposition by Mike Wallace.[49] "The Lindbergh tragedy is now a public spectacle," says Wallace over shots of the festive crowds outside the Flemington courthouse. Lindbergh's isolationism is not glossed over—he is seen behind the rostrum speaking to America Firsters, castigating FDR, and making increasingly

The CBS movie of the week, *The Lindbergh Kidnapping Case*, broadcast on February 26, 1976, with Anthony Hopkins (center) as Bruno Richard Hauptmann, Martin Balsam (left) as Edward J. Reilly, and John Fink (right) as C. Lloyd Fisher returned a guilty verdict for the defendant.

"inflammatory remarks." Like Kaltenborn and Brinkley, however, Wallace erases Lindbergh's antisemitic declamations from the archival record.[50] Also, as Kaltenborn noted, the very-much-alive Lindbergh seems frozen in the amber of an already distant past.

None of the three television documentaries expressed any doubt about Hauptmann's guilt; all accepted the justice of the verdict rendered in 1935 and the sentence carried out in 1936.

Like the documentaries, the major television dramatization of the Lindbergh case also reaffirmed the verdict at Flemington. On February 26, 1976, NBC broadcast *The Lindbergh Kidnapping Case*, a three-hour movie of the week in the days when the format was a mass-audience event watched by tens of millions. Deploying the conventional techniques of based-on-a-true-story melodrama (telescoped history, composite characters, omissions, oversimplifications, fabrications, and bonehead mistakes), the telefilm hews to the consensus wisdom: that Hauptmann was the perpetrator, likely the lone perpetrator, a pathetic loser whose motive was to bring down the supreme winner of the age. Producer and director Buzz Kulik and writer J. P. Miller convict Hauptmann beyond a shadow of doubt. When depicting the meeting between Dr. Condon and Cemetery John at St. Raymond's cemetery, the film reveals enough of the shrouded figure of Cemetery John to unmistakably identify the actor who played Hauptmann, Anthony Hopkins.

Off-screen, however, the consensus for conviction was no longer unanimous. The most persistent voice of protest belonged to the steadfast Anna Hauptmann, who throughout her life—she died in 1994 at age ninety-five—remained a tireless advocate for her husband's innocence. With equal measures of anguish and outrage, she petitioned successive New Jersey governors for a posthumous pardon, demanded the case be reopened, and assailed the Flemington trial as a gross miscarriage of justice fueled by anti-immigrant prejudice and mob hysteria. She never obtained a pardon for her long-lamented "poor Richard," but her longevity and tenacity engendered sympathy and, over time, sowed doubts.

Anna Hauptmann's cause was assisted by two revisionist works about the Lindbergh case: Anthony Scaduto's *Scapegoat: The Lonesome Death of Bruno Richard Hauptmann*, published in 1976, and Ludovic Kennedy's *The Airman and the Carpenter: The Lindbergh Kidnapping and the Framing of Bruno Richard Hauptmann*, published in 1985. Soaring on a post-Watergate zeitgeist that gave high-profile altitude to conspiracy-minded counternarratives, both books fiercely debunked the received wisdom and rendered an emphatic verdict of not guilty.[51] To generations no longer prone to defer to official authority but ready to believe the worst, an innocent man caught in a vast web of intrigue woven by operatives of a deep state seemed quite plausible.[52]

Inevitably, the conspiratorial counternarrative seeped into the bandwidth of American popular culture. On September 14, 1996, HBO telecast *Crime of the Century*, a two-hour docudrama directed by Mark Rydell and based on Ludovic Kennedy's paranoid-style book, a retelling frankly billed as "a study of the miscarriage of justice against the man convicted and executed for the kidnapping and murder of aviation hero Charles Lindbergh's infant." In the HBO version, Bruno Richard Hauptmann is no sociopathic iceman but a loving husband, a doting father, and a pitiable patsy victimized by the machinations of a police state desperate to find a hissable scapegoat.

HBO's docudrama *Crime of the Century*, telecast on September 14, 1996, depicts Bruno Richard Hauptmann (Stephen Rea) and his devoted wife Anna (Isabella Rossellini) as innocent victims of a massive frame-up.

Yet the most elegant meditations on the Lindbergh kidnap-murder have been literary, not televisual: Philip Roth's novel *The Plot Against America*, published in 2004, and the phantasmagorical *oeuvre* of the wondrous writer-illustrator Maurice Sendak. No less than law, politics, and the media, the artistic imagination has been shaped by the Lindbergh case.

A chilling experiment in counterfactual history, Roth's *The Plot Against America* conjures an alternative universe that is just a few frames out of sprocket. In the presidential election of 1940, Charles Lindbergh leverages his backstory to defeat FDR on an isolationist platform (slogan: Vote for Lindbergh or Vote for War). It can happen here and it does: the aviator is a stalking horse for an American Reich. Incited by the White House, the worst impulses of a nativist America spring to the surface. For a Jewish American family named the Roths living in Newark, New Jersey, the cloud of fascism chokes a once happy all-American life. They are cursed at in restaurants, ejected from hotels, menaced on the streets, and threatened with relocation. Newark in 1940 takes on the trappings of Berlin in 1933.

In Roth's nightmare world, only one patriot has the courage to speak out against the gangster state—Walter Winchell. Roth's imitation of the Winchell voice and his evocation of the magnetic pull of Winchell's Sunday night radio broadcasts is a virtuoso performance piece, not so much parody as ventriloquism. "It was Winchell who'd more or less originated the idea of firing into the face of the credulous masses buckshot pellets of insinuating gossip," comments Roth, before a tone-perfect mimicry of the Winchell fusillade: "Good evening, Mr. and Mrs. America and all the ships at sea. Let's go to press! Flash! To the glee of rat-faced Joe Goebbels and his boss, the Berlin Butcher, the targeting of America's Jews by Lindbergh's fascists is officially under way."[53] In due course, first network censorship and then assassination silences the gallant resistance from radio's biggest mouth. (In 2020, HBO telecast a six-part miniseries based on Roth's novel, written by David Simon and Ed Burns, a handsomely mounted production exuding as much fear of the Trump as of the Lindbergh presidency.) The plot twist in the plot against America is an inspired reversal of the blood libel promulgated to exonerate Hauptmann in 1935: the Nazis kidnapped Little Lindy, not to sacrifice in a torchlit ritual but to blackmail President Lindbergh into shredding the Constitution and befriending Nazi Germany. In the end, what saves America is what might have happened to an unluckier Lindbergh in 1927: flying back to Washington, D.C., from a campaign stop, the president-pilot vanishes into thin air. As for the fate of Little Lindy—was that really his body in the Sourland Mountains or is he living in Nazi Germany as a *Hitlerjungend*?

Even more than Philip Roth, Maurice Sendak was haunted by the specter of the Lindbergh baby. The kidnap-murder was his earliest childhood memory, and the subsequent night terrors colored the pages of much of his work, especially his masterpiece, *Where the Wild Things Are*, published in 1963, and *Outside Over There*, published in 1981, picture books that are true heirs to the Grimm fairy tales in Sendak's dark uses of enchantment.

As a frail young child in Brooklyn, Sendak remembered, he followed the news of the kidnapping closely and projected his own vulnerability onto that of the Lindbergh baby. If tragedy could befall the blond offspring of the Gentile god, then what of the sickly spawn of impoverished Jewish immigrants? The primordial fear—of abduction, of death—felt by a little boy in sympathy with another little boy created an imaginative link that found expression in Sendak's emblematic image: of a baby boy, around two years old, wearing a white sleeping suit.

In 2004, in an interview with PBS host Bill Moyers, Sendak recalled the scar left by the Lindbergh kidnapping on his childhood psyche:

> I was about three and 1/2 years old, something like that. I remember everything. I remember I couldn't read but the radio was always on.
>
> I remember Mrs. Lindbergh's tearful voice, where she was allowed to speak on radio to say that the baby had a cold. And would the man or men or women who took him rub camphor on his chest.
>
> It was a slight cold. But she didn't want it to get any worse. I remember that vividly, her voice.[54]

In Sendak's memory, the image from a photograph imprinted itself as strongly as the voice from the radio. When he was not quite four years old, while shopping with his mother, he passed a newsstand. A photograph stopped him cold. In 2011, he described the moment to critic Gary Gorth:

> I saw a picture of the [Lindbergh] baby dead in the woods with an arrow pointing down to show it had to be him, and I took my mother to see it. And apparently no one but me saw it.
>
> It's only in the past couple of years that I realized Colonel Lindbergh was enraged that the picture was used and it was taken off the afternoon edition; I saw the morning edition.
>
> I spent my whole life believing I saw that picture. But that to me is why children are so important: they see these things.[55]

Sendak would never forget any of it.

Yet Anne Lindbergh never went on radio to appeal to the kidnappers, never appeared before the press to read aloud the items for the baby's diet, and never implored the kidnappers to rub camphor on her baby's chest. The list of diet items was released to the press in a written statement, and the medicine she wanted administered was Visterol, a concentrated Vitamin D supplement, not camphor. Perhaps Sendak heard an actress read out the menu on radio or conflated a cinematic memory with a radio memory: in *Miss Fane's Baby Is Stolen*, the distraught mother goes on radio to plead for the return of her baby.

Sendak's recollection of the gruesome crime scene photo is also likely a false flashback. The scenario seems plausible enough—that the photograph appeared in a morning edition, Lindbergh objected, and the newspaper pulled the photo in later editions—but neither the newspaper nor Lindbergh's objection has left a paper trail. Perhaps Sendak misremembered the sight of a photograph taken at night on the Sourland site after the removal of the body, in which detectives and onlookers are seen clustered in a semicircle around the upturned ground, with an arrow pointing to the spot where the body was.

The media of the twenty-first century, crackpot and otherwise, have also not forgotten the crime of the twentieth century. In the age of internet blogs and chat rooms, the aftermath of the Lindbergh case thrives in the open-access portals and free-range frontiers of cyberspace. Crime buffs, forensic geeks, retired detectives, and people with way too much time on their hands collate information, post documents, and spin out scenarios of various degrees of sanity: gangsters were the culprits, Jafsie was the mastermind, Lindbergh himself orchestrated the kidnapping to euthanize a child who was born with imperfect feet. Paste an optimal keyword into a search engine and a Lindbergh obsessive can go down digital rabbit holes that never reach bottom.

The darker antechambers of the web will call up the photographs of the baby's blackened and decayed corpse, half-buried in the dirt of the Sourland Mountains and laid out on the slab in the Trenton morgue. Both photographs—the official police crime scene photographs and a photograph snapped by a cameraman who sneaked into the morgue—first emerged in public print in the 1970s. For all its sensationalism, for all the fierce competition for a scoop, the media of Lindbergh's day refused to publish the pictures. I have followed that example in this book.

THANKS AND ACKNOWLEDGMENTS

S
itting down at the keyboard to compose the end credits is happy confirmation that the book is finished, but (besides relief) an author appreciates the opportunity to express gratitude to the people who have helped along the way by giving advice, passing on information, and pretending to listen patiently even when their eyes started to wander.

A historian always depends on the kindness of archivists. Mark Falzini at the New Jersey State Police Museum and Learning Center, keeper of the local records of the Lindbergh kidnapping and Hauptmann trial, was especially generous in providing expertise, pdf-ing documents, and sharing his best sense of things. Francesca Pitaro at the Associated Press Corporate Archives in New York led me through the files of the press syndicate that beat out its rivals and made one epic gaffe. At the indispensable Library of Congress, Rosemary Hanes and Josie Walters-Johnston, of the Moving Image Section, and Karen Fishman, supervisor of the Moving Image Research Center and the Recorded Sound Research Center, helped find the requisite visual and audio texts. Jenny Romero, at the Margaret Herrick Library of the Academy of Motion Picture Arts and Sciences, smoothed access to the Production Code files. Ron Simon and Mark Ekman at the Paley Center facilitated access to the recordings of Samuel S. Leibowitz's nightly radio commentary. Katie Clements sifted through the photographs held by the Borowitz True Crime Collection at Kent State University Libraries. The staff of the microfilm room at the New York Public Library was unfailingly helpful. Laura Hibbler at the

Brandeis University Library came through with digital access to a valuable collection of entertainment trade papers. Virginia Lewick at the Franklin D. Roosevelt Presidential Library passed on an unpublished chapter from a memoir by AP reporter Lorena Hickok. John F. Ansley, head of archives and special collections at Marist College, dug out the transcripts of Lowell Thomas's broadcasts and passed them on electronically. Brian Sargent at Fox Movietone News and Benjamin Singleton and Greg Wilsbacher at the Moving Image Research Collections at the University of South Carolina shared their newsreel chops. At Columbia University Press, ace editor Jennifer Crewe, editorial assistant Sheniqua Larkin, design director Merille Poss, and publicity director Meredith Howard shepherded the book into production with their trademark kindness and professionalism. The sharp eyes of copy editor Peggy Tropp and project manager Ben Kolstad helped rid the prose of mistakes at which otherwise I would have cringed.

In the fall of 2018, I was fortunate enough to be granted a Fulbright award to work on this project. I was even more fortunate to spend the semester at the Roosevelt Institute for American Studies in Middelburg, the Netherlands, and work among a wonderful crew of bike-riding colleagues: Paul Brennan, Dario Fazzi, Cees Heere, Leontien Joosse, Nanka de Vries, Celia Nijdam, Damien Pargas, and Giles Scott-Smith. As ever, my colleagues in the American Studies Program at Brandeis University—Joyce Antler, Dan Breen, Jerry Cohen, Brian Donahue, Maura Farrelly, Richard Gaskins, Paula Musegades, and Steve Whitfield—were supportive and critical in the best ways.

For facts and corrections too numerous to enumerate, a cohort of friends and fellow media obsessives generously contributed more than their two cents' worth: Mikita Brottman, Greg Burk, Scott Feinberg, Carrie Fellows, Kathy Fuller, Andrew Hudgins, Adam Knee, Cindy Lucia, Lou Lumenick, Eve Neiger, Erin McGraw, Russell Merritt, Cynthia Meyers, Edward Monsour, Farran Smith Nehme, Geoffrey O'Brien, Steve Ross, Luke Salisbury, Josh Sheppard, Abraham Shragge, and Michael Socolow.

To my wife Sandra, I owe more than I can say.

NOTES

A Word on Sources

A good deal of library space has been taken up by works chronicling the kidnap-murder of the Lindbergh baby: scholarly studies, true-crime narratives, memoirs, forensic files, archival documentaries, graphic novels, and revisionist polemics. Although I have tried to absorb the best of the retrospective studies in the following notes, I have relied mainly on primary sources from 1932 to 1936: the newspapers, particularly the New York press and on-the-ground accounts by the wire services reporters; and the entertainment trade press, which covered the media angle on a story they knew was transforming radio and motion picture journalism even as it unfolded. Much of the newsreel record is extant and readily available for unspooling, either in original release form or culled in archival documentaries, but to get a sense of what people actually saw on the screen I've looked through the expert eyes of *Variety*, whose reporters surveyed the programs at the Embassy and Trans-Lux newsreel theaters on Broadway. Unfortunately, most of the news and commentary broadcast on radio between 1932 and 1936 has disappeared into the ether. When printed transcripts of the broadcasts were not available, I turned to the accounts by contemporary listeners. The luck of the archival draw compelled me to privilege NBC and Lowell Thomas over CBS and H. V. Kaltenborn, whose records went up in smoke in the 1980s, when CBS president Laurence Tisch, in a media version of the burning of the library at Alexandria in 48 BC, consigned much of the network's printed inventory to the dustbin of history. Finally, a minor typographical note: the spelling of the word "kidnapping" was not standardized in the 1930s; it is often rendered as "kidnaping." To avoid confusion for the reader and spellcheck, I have used "kidnapping" throughout.

Abbreviations

APCA	Associated Press Corporate Archives (New York, NY)
FDR	Franklin D. Roosevelt Presidential Library (Hyde Park, NY)
LTP	Lowell Thomas Papers (Marist University)
NJSPM	New Jersey State Police Museum (West Trenton, NJ)
PCA	Production Code Administration files (Margaret Herrick Library of the Academy of Motion Picture Arts and Sciences, Beverly Hills, CA)

Prologue: The Sky God

1. F. Scott Fitzgerald, "Echoes of the Jazz Age" [1931], reprinted in Edmund Wilson, editor, *The Crack-Up* (New York: Directions Publishing Corp., 1945), 20.
2. "Lindbergh Is Set to Fly at Daylight If Weather Conditions Remain Good," *New York Times*, May 20, 1927: 1.
3. "40,000 Join in Prayer That Lindbergh Wins," *New York Times*, May 21, 1927: 13.
4. Scott Eyman, *Hank & Jim: The Fifty-Year Friendship of Henry Fonda and Jimmy Stewart* (New York: Simon and Schuster, 2017), 38–39.
5. Charles A. Lindbergh, *The Spirit of St. Louis* (New York: Charles Scribner's Sons, 1953), 495.
6. " 'Lucky Lindy' First of Lindbergh Flood," *Variety*, May 25, 1927: 45.
7. Frederick Lewis Allen, *Only Yesterday: An Informal History of the 1920s* (New York: Harper and Brothers, 1931), 183.
8. George Buchan Fife, *Lindbergh, the Lone Eagle: His Life and Achievements* (New York: A. L. Burt Company, 1927), 35.
9. I am grateful to Luke Salisbury, who was there, for this anecdote.
10. "Collins Family of Cave Fame Disagreeing," *Variety*, September 23, 1925: 4.
11. "Lindbergh Super-Attraction from Personal Appearances," *Variety*, May 25, 1927: 1, 3.
12. "Great News Event by Radio," *Variety*, May 25, 1927: 45.
13. "Though Lindbergh Not for the Show Business, Showmen Aid Receptions," *Variety*, June 15, 1927: 3.
14. "Radio Keeps Pace with Lindbergh," *New York Times*, June 14, 1927: 14.
15. "Lindbergh and Flag Day to Share Radio Today," *Washington Post*, June 14, 1927: 10.
16. Advertisement for Fox News, *Variety*, May 25, 1927: 18; "Flight News Pictures Boost Receipts by Many Thousands," *Exhibitors Herald*, June 25, 1927: 19, 42.
17. Serge Viallet's documentary *Mysteries in the Archives: Lindbergh's Atlantic Crossing* (2009) provides a frame-by-frame breakdown of the newsreel coverage of Lindbergh in Paris.
18. "News Reels Step in Lindbergh Film Race," *Film Daily*, June 1, 1927: 1, 2; "Advertisement for Pathé News," *Film Daily*, June 1, 1927: 3; "News Reels Set New Marks on Lindbergh Paris Film," *Exhibitors Herald*, June 18, 1927: 32.
19. "Roxy (N.Y.)," *Variety*, June 22, 1927: 37.

20. Jack Alcoate, "Lindy," *Film Daily*, June 14, 1927: 1; Red Kann, "The Lindbergh Race," *Film Daily*, May 24, 1927: 1.

21. "Producers and Theatres Vie for Services of Lindbergh," *Exhibitors Herald*, May 28, 1927: 19; "Broadway," *Exhibitors Herald*, June 4, 1927: 24.

22. Roy Chartier, "Embassy (Newsreel)," *Variety*, May 28, 1930: 43.

23. Adela Rogers St. Johns, "Writer Sees All U.S. as Jurors Trying Bruno in Killing," *New York Evening Journal*, January 2, 1935: 1.

24. "Mrs. Lindbergh Wins Wings of Pilot in Secret Air Tests," *New York Times*, May 30, 1931: 1.

25. "Inside Stuff-Pictures," *Variety*, August 11, 1931: 57; "Newsreels," *Variety*, August 11, 1931: 42.

26. Will Rogers, *Daily Telegrams*, February 14, 1932; Will Rogers, *Daily Telegrams*, March 2, 1932.

1. The Crime of the Century

1. The teletype is on file at the New Jersey State Police Museum in West Trenton, NJ (hereafter NJSPM), which holds the police logs and other materials relevant to the Lindbergh case.

2. "Cops Spread Dragnet Over All New York," *New York Daily News*, March 3, 1932: 10.

3. Curt Gentry, *J. Edgar Hoover: The Man and His Secrets* (New York: W. W. Norton and Company, 1991), 150–151.

4. The Lindbergh case lives up to the title bestowed by one of the best of the raft of books published on it, Lloyd C. Gardner's *The Case That Never Dies: The Lindbergh Kidnapping* (New Brunswick, NJ: Rutgers University Press, 2004). For this chronicle of the kidnapping, in addition to contemporary newspaper accounts, I have drawn on George Waller, *Kidnap: The Story of the Lindbergh Kidnapping* (New York: The Dial Press, 1961); Jim Fisher, *The Lindbergh Case* (New Brunswick, NJ: Rutgers University Press, 1987); A. Scott Berg, *Lindbergh* (New York: G. P. Putnam's Sons, 1998), 236–275, 297–341; and Gardner. Anne Lindbergh's account is in *Hour of Lead, Hour of Gold: Diaries and Letters of Anne Morrow Lindbergh, 1929–1932* (New York: Harcourt Brace Jovanovich, 1973), 226–249.

5. Anne Morrow Lindbergh, *Locked Rooms and Open Doors: Diaries and Letters of Anne Morrow Lindbergh* (New York: Harcourt Brace Jovanovich, 1974), xv.

6. Fisher: 7–8. Dunn tried to locate Lt. Arthur Keaton, head detective, and finally reached him at his home at 10:43 P.M. via the police board in Trenton, informing him that "Col. Lindbergh had reported that his baby had been kidnapped," according to the official police logs at the NJSPM.

7. "The Lindbergh Kidnapping," *New York Daily News*, March 3, 1932: 32.

8. Edward Dean Sullivan, *The Snatch Racket* (New York: The Vanguard Press, 1932), 13.

9. Condon told his version of his role in the case in *Jafsie Tells All!: Revealing the Inside Story of the Lindbergh-Hauptmann Case*, published in 1936 (New York: Jonathan Lee Publishing Corp.) after being serialized in *Liberty* magazine.

2. A Story That Penetrated the Thickest Skin

2. A Story That Penetrated the Thickest Skin

1. Laura Vitray, *The Great Lindbergh Hullabaloo: An Unorthodox Account* (New York: William Faro, Inc., 1932). The irreverent title of Vitray's quickie book captures the madcap swirl in the weeks after the kidnapping; the introductory note is datelined April 12, 1932. Vitray dedicates the book to William Randolph Hearst, "who fired me for writing it."

2. Julia Blanshard, "Laura Vitray Becomes First City Editor of Metropolitan Newspaper," *Niagara Falls Gazette*, June 24, 1930: 20.

3. "Price Spree in Hopewell, N.J.," *Variety*, March 8, 1932: 1, 42.

4. Walter Winchell, "On Broadway," *New York Daily Mirror*, March 7, 1932: 19.

5. L. D. Hotchkiss, "Hearst Has Gone and an Era Ends," *Los Angeles Times*, August 16, 1951: A5.

6. Silas Bent, "Lindbergh and the Press," *Outlook* (April 1932): 212–213.

7. "A.P.-'News'-Lindy's Baby," *Variety*, July 16, 1930: 56.

8. Arthur Brisbane, "Brisbane Confers with Al Capone on Kidnapping," *Buffalo* (NY) *Courier Express*, March 11, 1932: 1, 3.

9. Walter Winchell, "On Broadway," *New York Daily Mirror*, March 9, 1932: 19.

10. Will Rogers, *Daily Telegrams*, March 2, 1932.

11. Walter R. Mears, "A Brief History of AP," in *Breaking News: How the Associated Press Has Covered War, Peace, and Everything Else* (New York: Princeton Architectural Press, 2007), 403–413.

12. *The Associated Press Directory*, July 15, 1933: 1.

13. A letter from Newark-based correspondent Franklin Millman to AP general manager Kent Cooper credits William A. Kinney and B. Gregory Hewitt Hewlett of the Newark bureau with writing "the great bulk of the story, all the details of which came into the Newark bureau from the various staffers and stringers by telephone." Franklin Millman to Ken Cooper, March 3, 1932. Lindbergh file, Associated Press Corporate Archives (hereafter APCA). In the New York bureau, Robert St. Johns also contributed. See Terry Fred Horowitz, *Merchant of Words: The Life of Robert St. Johns* (Lanham, MD: Rowman and Littlefield, 2014), 63.

14. Oliver Gramling, *AP: The Story of News* (New York: Farrar and Rinehart, Inc., 1940), 364–369. An unpublished manuscript history of AP, written by John Barbour and Wes Gallagher, accords with Gramling's account, varying only slightly in some of the remembered dialogue. See Barbour and Gallagher, *While the Smoke Is Still Rising*: 199–202. Lindbergh file, APCA.

15. Kent Cooper to Dr. Allan Sinclair, March 8, 1932. Lindbergh file, APCA.

16. "Lindbergh Case and the Press," *The Beacon* (NY) *News*, April 12, 1932: 4.

17. Joe Alex Morris, *Deadline Every Minute: The Story of United Press* (New York: Doubleday & Company, Inc., 1957), 186–187.

18. Bob Considine, *It's All News to Me: A Reporter's Deposition* (New York: Meredith Press, 1967), 96.

19. John Brant and Edith Renaud, *True Story of the Lindbergh Kidnapping* (New York: Kroy Wen Publishers, Inc., 1932).

20. "Bound to Happen," *Variety*, March 22, 1932: 49; "Stuck," *Variety*, March 8, 1932: 2.

21. Vitray, *The Great Lindbergh Hullabaloo*, 147.

22. James Whittaker, "Kidnappers Soon to Bargain for Release of Lindy Baby," *New York Daily Mirror*, April 2, 1932: 3, 5.

23. Lorena Hickok, "The Lindbergh Kidnapping Story." Unpublished manuscript, on file at the Franklin D. Roosevelt Presidential Library (hereafter FDR).

24. Fred Pasley, "When Gangs Rule—None Is Safe," *New York Daily News*, March 3, 1932: 3, 14.

25. "Lindy With $50,000 Cash, Ready to Ransom Baby," *New York Daily News*, March 3, 1932: 3, 4.

26. "The Challenge of the Lindbergh Kidnapping," *Literary Digest*, March 12, 1932: 7.

27. "Shall We Declare Martial Law," *New York Daily Mirror*, March 3, 1932: 15.

28. "Have We Got to Deal with Capone?," *New York Daily Mirror*, March 5, 1932: 11.

29. Hickok, "The Lindbergh Kidnapping Story."

30. Ishbel Ross, *Ladies of the Press: The Story of Women in Journalism by an Insider* (New York: Harper and Brothers, 1936), 220.

31. Quentin Reynolds, *Courtroom: The Story of Samuel Leibowitz* (Garden City, NY: Garden City Books, 1950), 321.

32. "Kidnaped Baby Needs a Special Diet," *New York Daily Mirror*, March 3, 1932: 3.

33. "Kidnappers, Read This Diet!" *New York Daily News*, March 3, 1932: 4.

34. "The Kidnapping," *New York Post*, March 7, 1932: 8.

35. John F. Condon, *Jafsie Tells All!: Revealing the Inside Story of the Lindbergh-Hauptmann Case* (New York: Jonathan Lee Publishing Corp., 1936), 115.

36. Walter Lippmann, "Let Colonel Lindbergh Alone," *New York Herald Tribune*, April 6, 1932: 19.

37. "Government Aid Asked," *New York Times*, April 10, 1932: 1.

38. "Key Used in Negotiations," *New York Times*, April 11, 1932: 11.

39. "Lindy Double Crossed; $50,000 Paid, Baby Held," *New York Daily News*, April 10, 1932: 3, 4.

40. "Press Cooperation with Lindbergh Family Unparalleled in Peace or War," *Editor & Publisher*, April 16, 1932: 1, 6–8.

41. Ibid.

42. "Cemetery Guard Tells of Kidnap Parlay," *New York Daily News*, April 15, 1932: 19.

43. Charles A. Lindbergh to the Editor of the Associated Press, April 18, 1932. APCA.

44. Edward Dean Sullivan, *The Snatch Racket* (New York: The Vanguard Press, 1932), x.

45. Vitray, *The Great Lindbergh Hullabaloo*, 11–12.

46. "City Grieves As News of Baby's Death Arrives," *Schenectady Gazette*, May 13, 1932: 12.

3. A Medium of Audible Journalism

1. "Radio Head Defends News Broadcasts," *New York Times*, April 25, 1931: 11.

2. "New York by 900,000," *New York Times*, November 5, 1924: 1; "Radio Notes and Gossip," *New York Times*, November 9, 1924: XX14.

3. I. M. Vronsky, "RCA (1925–1929) and Microsoft (1993–1997)," https://www.gold-eagle .com/article/rca-1925-1929-and-microsoft-1993-1997.

4. On the onset of sound, see Scott Eyman, *The Speed of Sound: Hollywood and the Talkie Revolution 1926–1930* (New York: Simon and Schuster, 1997). On the gestalt of early radio, see Anthony Rudel, *Hello, Everybody! The Dawn of American Radio* (Orlando, FL: Harcourt, Inc., 2008).

5. "Radio Act's Bonus," *Variety*, June 5, 1929: 39.

6. "Radio Head Defends News Broadcasts," *New York Times*, April 25, 1931: 11.

7. "Floyd Gibbons," *Variety*, August 27, 1930: 58.

8. Edward Gibbons and Floyd Gibbons, *Floyd Gibbons: Your Headline Hunter* (New York: Exposition Press, 1953), 195–196.

9. Gibbons and Gibbons, *Floyd Gibbons*, 199.

10. "Inside Stuff—Radio," *Variety*, March 13, 1932: 57.

11. "Claims 'Scoop,' " *Broadcasting*, April 1, 1932: 8; "Station Notes," *Broadcasting*, April 1, 1932: 22; "Program Notes," *Broadcasting*, April 15, 1932: 24.

12. See Michael J. Socolow, " 'Always in Friendly Competition': NBC and CBS in the First Decade of National Broadcasting," in Michele Hilmes, editor, *NBC: America's Network* (Berkeley: University of California Press, 2007), 43.

13. "Press Vs Radio Feud Rekindled by Ether's Scoop on Lindy Baby," *Variety*, March 8, 1932: 1, 34.

14. "Radio Covers Lindbergh Kidnapping," *Broadcasting*, March 15, 1932: 6, 24.

15. David Halberstam, *The Powers That Be* (New York: Alfred Knopf, 1979).

16. Police call sheet, March 1, 1932, on file at NJSPM.

17. "Radio Covers Lindbergh Kidnapping," *Broadcasting*, March 15, 1932: 6, 24.

18. Ibid.

19. "Newspapers Credit Big Extra Runs on Dillinger to Mute Radio Policy," *Variety*, July 31, 1934: 1, 54.

20. "Hauptmann's Trial Broadcast Banned," *Broadcasting*, October 15, 1934: 29.

21. "Press Vs Radio Feud Rekindled by Ether's Scoop on Lindy Baby," *Variety*, March 8, 1932: 34.

22. Ibid.: 1..

23. "Audible Journalism," *Broadcasting*, March 15, 1932: 16.

24. Lowell Thomas. *Good Evening Everybody: From Cripple Creek to Samarkand* (New York: William Morrow and Company, Inc., 1976), 313.

25. W. G. Wiles to Ralph Wheatley, May 17, 1932. Lindbergh file, APCA.

26. "Radio Probed for Wild Tales on Lindbergh," *Brooklyn Daily Eagle*, May 18, 1932: 3.

27. "Radio Hysteria Mangles News Reports," *New York Daily Mirror*, March 8, 1932: 15.

28. "See Commentators' End," *Variety*, December 19, 1933: 39, 62. For a complete account, see Gwenyth L. Jackaway, *Media at War: Radio's Challenge to the Newspapers, 1924–1939* (Westport, CT: Praeger, 1995).

29. "Press Vs Radio Feud Rekindled by Ether's Scoop on Lindy Baby," *Variety*, March 8, 1932: 34.

30. "Radio Covers Lindbergh Kidnapping," *Broadcasting*, March 15, 1932: 6, 24.

31. Cecelia Ager, "McNamee Doubts That He Could Get a Job Starting Today," *Variety*, November 21, 1933: 38. See also "Ether Slants," *Variety*, April 25, 1933: 42.

32. Thomas, *Good Evening Everybody*, 306–312. See also Mitchell Stephens, *The Voice of America: Lowell Thomas and the Invention of 20th-Century Journalism* (New York: St. Martin's Press, 2017).

33. Robert Landry, "Lowell Thomas," *Variety*, February 25, 1931: 64.

34. Lowell Thomas Broadcast, March 3, 1932. Lowell Thomas Papers, Marist College (hereafter LTP).

35. "News from the Dailies," *Variety*, January 9, 1934: 52; "Son of Kaltenborn Beaten by Nazis As He Talks with Father," *Brooklyn Daily Eagle*, September 5, 1933: 1, 2.

36. "Kaltenborn Stresses Need of Federal Kidnapping Laws," *The Daily Home News* (New Brunswick, NJ), March 3, 1932: 7.

37. Dorothy Doran, "Kaltenborn Recalls Microphone Incident Pertaining to Akron," *Akron Beacon Journal*, December 8, 1933: 19.

38. Irving E. Fang, *Those Radio Commentators!* (Ames: Iowa State University Press, 1977), 107–111.

39. A. J. Liebling, "Boake Carter," *Scribner's Magazine* (August 1938): 10.

40. "Ether Slants," *Variety*, April 25, 1933: 42.

41. Fred Smith, "Unique Psychology of 'The March of Time,'" *Broadcasting*, November 1, 1931: 13.

42. Ibid.: 13, 42.

43. Harold P. Brown, "Coming and Going," *Radio Digest* (April 1932): 6.

44. "Voices of the Listener," *Radio Digest* (May 1932): 33.

45. "Challenges Radio as Aid to Education," *New York Times*, February 27, 1932: 20.

46. "Editor's Note," *Broadcasting*, March 15, 1932: 27.

47. "The Microphone Will Present," *New York Times*, September 4, 1932: XX8.

4. Nobody Ever Walked Out on a Newsreel

1. "PathéNews Celebrates Twentieth Birthday," *Exhibitors Herald-World*, November 8, 1930: 35, 38.

2. "Pioneered as New York's Newsreel Theatre!" *Motion Picture Herald*, April 23, 1932: 74.

3. "Embassy," *Variety*, November 6, 1929: 49; "Embassy Newsreel House Celebrates First Anniversary," *Exhibitors Herald-World*, November 8, 1930: 57; "Trans-Lux," *Variety*, May 20, 1931: 118.

4. Fred S. Meyer, "Double or 'Trouble' Features—Does This Answer the Riddle?" *Motion Picture Herald*, April 23, 1932: 56.

5. H. E. Jameyson, "A Showman Discusses the Shortcomings of the Short Feature!" *Motion Picture Herald*, April 23, 1932: 49.

6. Joseph C. Furnas, "Latest in the Newsreels," *New York Herald Tribune*, February 10, 1935: D3.

7. "The Eclipse of the Newsreel," *Motion Picture Herald*, November 14, 1931: 7.

0. "Newsreels Almost 100 Percent Censor-Free," *Variety*, April 24, 1933: 4.

9. Quoted in "Importance of Newsreel Becomes Great," *Film Daily*, June 11, 1932. 10.

10. "Cutting 'Depression' From Reels," *Film Daily*, January 8, 1932: 2.

11. James Cunningham, "Asides and Interludes," *Motion Picture Herald*, August 4, 1934: 25.

12. Terry Ramsaye, "Fox and Hearst Newsreels Give Full Report on Shanghai Battle," *Motion Picture Herald*, March 5, 1932: 16.

13. "Lindy and Newsreels," *Fitchburg Sentinel*, May 26, 1932: 6.

14. Charles Peden, *Newsreel Man* (New York: Doubleday, Doran, and Company, Inc., 1932), 125.

15. "Newsreels in a Service Record in Kidnapping of Lindbergh Baby," *Motion Picture Herald*, March 12, 1932: 22–23.

16. "Mental Aberrants Throng Hopewell," *Philadelphia Inquirer*, March 7, 1932: 6.

17. Peden, *Newsreel Man*, 117.

18. "Newsreels in a Service Record in Kidnapping of Lindbergh Baby," *Motion Picture Herald*, March 12, 1932: 22–23.

19. Tom Waller, "Newsreels," *Variety*, March 8, 1932: 36.

20. Fred S. Meyer, "Double or 'Trouble' Features—Does This Answer the Riddle?" *Motion Picture Herald*, April 23, 1932: 56.

21. Tom Waller, "Newsreels," *Variety*, March 8, 1932: 36.

22. "Home Movie of Lindy Jr. Stirs Local Audience," *North Adams Evening Transcript*, March 10, 1932: 3.

23. "Paramount News Aids in Lindbergh Case," *Paramount Around the World*, March 1932: 7.

24. Jack Alicoate, "Newsreels Pull 'Em In," *Film Daily*, March 8, 1932: 1, 2.

25. Phil M. Daily, "Along the Rialto," *Film Daily*, March 16, 1932: 4.

26. J. C. M. [John C. Mosher], "The Current Cinema," *New Yorker*, March 19, 1932: 76. "Importance of Newsreel Becomes Greater than Ever," *Film Daily*, June 11, 1932: 16.

27. "Many Novel Stunts," *Motion Picture Herald*, April 16, 1932: 69.

28. "Advertisement," *Albany Times Union*, March 3, 1932: 4.

29. James Cunningham, "Asides and Interludes," *Motion Picture Herald*, March 19, 1932: 22.

30. Roy Chartier, "Newsreels," *Variety*, March 22, 1932: 34.

31. Tom Waller, "Newsreels," *Variety*, March 29, 1932: 42.

32. Tom Waller, "Newsreels," *Variety*, March 15, 1932: 37.

5. Get the Lindbergh Killers!

1. "Chaplin Confesses to Literary Pose, But Own Camera Work His Big Kick," *Variety*, July 19, 1932: 2.

2. "Negro Tells How He Found Body in Woods," *New York Times*, May 13, 1932: 3.

3. "Permit Issued for Cremation of Slain Baby," *Miami Daily*, May 13, 1932: 1. The sparse, restrained AP account was widely praised for its quiet eloquence. Again, it was a collaborative composition effort, with reporter Morris Watson on the scene in the morgue.

4.   "Associated Press Upholds Prestige," *Rome Daily Sentinel*, May 13, 1932: 2. "How He Won the Prize," *Schenectady Gazette*, May 2, 1933: 8. AP sent out a behind-the-scenes account of its epic scoop to subscribers the next day. "How World Got Word of Lindbergh Baby's Death," *Boston Globe*, May 14, 1932: 12. Oliver Gramling, *AP: The Story of News* (New York: Farrar and Rinehart, Inc., 1940), 369–373, quotes the governor as saying, "It's horrible news. The Lindbergh baby has been found dead." A letter from Walter T. Brown to Clarence T. Leighton, May 18, 1932, confirms the time of the first flash. Lindbergh file, APCA.

5.   Sidney B. Whipple, *The Lindbergh Crime* (New York: Blue Ribbon Books, 1935), 93–108.

6.   "Woodmen Find Body Hidden in Thicket," *Camden* (NJ) *Post*, May 13, 1932: 2.

7.   "Press Wires Flash Tragedy to World," *New York Times*, May 13, 1932: 3; "Inside Stuff— Radio," *Variety*, May 17, 1932: 41.

8.   "City Grieves As News of Baby's Death Arrives," *Schenectady Gazette*, May 13, 1932: 12.

9.   The *Port Huron Times Herald* editor enclosed the timeline along with the hapless UP bulletin. Box 11, Lindbergh file, APCA.

10. "First News on Street from Courier-News," *Plainfield Courier-News*, May 13, 1932: 1.

11. John F. Roches, "Unparalleled Response by Press and Public Met Lindbergh Climax," *Editor & Publisher*, May 21, 1932: 1.

12. "Entire City Shaken by Tragic News," *Lubbock Morning Avalanche*, May 13, 1932: 9.

13. "Tribune-Times Extras Carry Story of Lindbergh Tragedy," *Ames Daily Tribune*, May 13, 1932: 1.

14. "Pulitzer Awards for Journalism in 1932 Announced," *St. Louis Post-Dispatch*, May 2, 1933: 1C.

15. Frederick Lewis Allen, *Since Yesterday: The 1930s in America September 3, 1929–September 3, 1939* (New York: Harper and Row, 1939), 70–71.

16. "Press Wires Flash Tragedy to World," *New York Times*, May 13, 1932: 3.

17. "Lindbergh Bulletin Affects Show Biz," *The Billboard*, May 21, 1932: 4.

18. Marguerite Mooers Marshall, "Life to Come Makes Anne Stifle Her Sorrow," *New York Evening Journal*, May 13, 1932: 1.

19. Floyd Gibbons, "Baby's Fate Strikes at Every Mother, Says Gibbons," *New York Evening Journal*, May 13, 1932: 2.

20. "Horrified Nation Calls for Action," *New York Post*, May 13, 1932: 3.

21. "Walker, Shocked, Calls Crime Nation's Worst," *New York Evening Journal*, March 13, 1932: 14; "Roosevelt Calls State Forces to Aid in Manhunt" and "Beer Parade to Pay Tribute to Baby," *New York Daily News*, March 14, 1932: 6.

22. "Hoover Tells 28,000 Men to Hunt Kidnappers," *New York Daily News*, May 14, 1932: 2.

23. "Hoover Orders Man Hunt for Murderers of Child," *Los Angeles Times*, May 14, 1932: 1.

24. "Federal Aid Pledged in Baby Murder Hunt," *Philadelphia Inquirer*, May 15, 1932: 10.

25. "Paramount Newsreel Beat," *Film Daily*, May 16, 1932: 8.

26. "Finders of Lindbergh Baby Prosaically Return to Work," *Brooklyn Daily Eagle*, May 13, 1932: 5.

27. Tom Waller, "Newsreels," *Variety*, May 17, 1932: 29.

28. "Baby's Death Told in Dramatic Scene," *Washington Post*, May 13, 1932: 4.
29. "How the Lindbergh Baby Was Identified Is Now Revealed," *New York Sun*, September 27, 1934: 3.
30. Charles Lindbergh, *The Wartime Journals of Charles A. Lindbergh* (New York: Harcourt Brace Jovanovich, 1970), 187; "Investigation of Report That Pictures of Lindbergh's Baby's Remains Had Been Taken at Swayze's Morgue," Lieut. D. J. Dunn, May 16, 1932. NJSPM. I am grateful to Mark Falzini for pointing out this report to me.
31. Will Rogers, *Daily Telegrams*, May 14, 1932.
32. "Get the Lindbergh Killers!" *New York Daily News*, May 13, 1932: 32; "The Tragic End of the Lindbergh Search," *Literary Digest*, May 21, 1932: 10.
33. "Kidnappers Motives, Identity Unsolved by Police," *New York Evening Journal*, May 13, 1932: 5.
34. "FDR's Gold Helped Trace Ransom," *New York Daily News*, September 21, 1934: 9.
35. Tom Waller, "Newsreels," *Variety*, May 31, 1932: 35.
36. Whipple, *The Lindbergh Crime*, 174–176. The dialogue varies depending on the account.
37. Walter Winchell, "On Broadway," *New York Daily Mirror*, September 12, 1934: 19.
38. Ibid.
39. George Waller, *Kidnap: The Story of the Lindbergh Kidnapping* (New York: The Dial Press, 1961), 214.
40. Walter Winchell, "On Broadway," *New York Daily Mirror*, September 17, 1934: 21.
41. Walter Winchell, "On Broadway," *New York Daily Mirror*, October 1, 1934: 17.
42. Curtis Mitchell, "What Winchell Knows About Hauptmann," *Radio Guide*, April 4, 1936: 4-5; 16, 43.
43. "O'Ryan Reveals How Case Broke," *New York Herald Tribune*, September 21, 1934: 1, 7.
44. "Lindbergh Kidnapper Jailed," *New York Daily Mirror*, September 21, 1934: 1.
45. Warren Hall, "Lindbergh Kidnapper Jailed; Find Ransom," *New York Daily News*, September 21, 1934: 3.
46. "Lindbergh Mystery Solved with Arrest of Felon," *Newport News*, September 21, 1934: 11.
47. "Lindbergh Case Arrest Test of Newsreel Speed," *Motion Picture Daily*, September 22, 1934: 1, 3.
48. "Germany Bars Hauptmann Scenes," *Film Daily*, September 27, 1934: 10.
49. Roy Chartier, "The Newsreels," *Variety*, January 1, 1935: 12.
50. "Newsreels Give Speedy Coverage of Lindbergh Kidnapping Arrest," *Motion Picture Herald*, September 29, 1934: 10.
51. Ibid.
52. Hal Burton, "Mystery Girl Star Witness," *New York Daily News*, September 30, 1934: 4C.
53. Hally Holloway, "Time Marches On," *Radio Guide*, July 18, 1936: 20.
54. Walter Winchell, "On Broadway," *Akron Beacon Journal*, November 17, 1934: 17.
55. https://www.oldtimeradiodownloads.com/historical/march-of-time-the/-march-of-time-34-10-05-hugh-s-johnson-resigns-from-the-nra.
56. Roy Chartier, "Embassy, N.Y.," *Variety*, October 9, 1934: 22.
57. Helen Gwynne, "Not That It Matters," *Hollywood Reporter*, September 29, 1934: 3.

58. "World's Greatest Sleuths Pressed Lindbergh Hunt," *New York Daily News*, September 21, 1934: 10.

59. Ed Sullivan, "Broadway," *New York Daily News*, January 3, 1935: 38.

6. Hollywood and the Lindbergh Kidnapping

1. "War on Gangster Films," *Standard Union*, September 8, 1931: 8.

2. John S. Cohen, "Gangster Films—Their Value," *Buffalo* (NY) *Evening News*, November 28, 1931: 5.

3. "Hays Outlaws Dillinger, Studios Drop Lens Plans," *Daily Variety*, March 21, 1934: 2.

4. "Bound to Happen," *Variety*, March 22, 1932: 49; "No Kidnap Films," *Variety*, March 15, 1932: 2.

5. Jason S. Joy to Will H. Hays, June 4, 1932. *Okay, America!*, Production Code Administration (hereafter PCA) file.

6. Memorandum from Lamar Trotti, June 1, 1932; Jason S. Joy to Will H. Hays, May 31, 1932. *Okay, America!*, PCA file.

7. Harold Weight, " 'Three on a Match' Proves Another Winner for Mervyn LeRoy and Warners," *Hollywood Filmograph*, October 1, 1932: 11. The headline in no way captures the scathing tone of the review.

8. "*Three on a Match*," *Harrison's Reports*, November 5, 1932: 178.

9. Jason S. Joy to Darryl Zanuck, August 23, 1932. *Three on a Match*, PCA file.

10. Vincent G. Hart to Maurice McKenzie, July 13, 1933. *The Mad Game*, PCA file.

11. Jason S. Joy to James B. Fitzgerald, August 31, 1932. *Okay, America!*, PCA file.

12. Will H. Hays to James Wingate, July 6, 1933. *The Mad Game*, PCA file.

13. "Hollywood Inside," *Daily Variety*, September 19, 1933: 2.

14. Jeff McCarthy, "*The Mad Game*," *Motion Picture Herald*, October 28, 1933: 55.

15. J. M. Kelly to Irene Scott, September 19, 1933. *Miss Fane's Baby Is Stolen*, PCA file.

16. Maurice McKenzie to James Wingate, September 28, 1933. *Miss Fane's Baby Is Stolen*, PCA file.

17. J. M. Kelly to Irene Scott, September 19, 1933. *Miss Fane's Baby Is Stolen*, PCA file.

18. Maurice McKenzie to Joseph I. Breen and James Wingate, July 12, 1933. *The Mad Game*, PCA file.

19. "Dont's for Kidnap Yarns," *Variety*, October 3, 1933: 3.

20. Joseph I. Breen to A. M. Botsford, December 14, 1933. *Miss Fane's Baby Is Stolen*, PCA file.

21. "Hollywood Inside," *Daily Variety*, December 2, 1933: 2.

22. "*Miss Fane's Baby Is Stolen*," *Film Daily*, January 20, 1934: 5.

23. Mae Tinee, "Kidnapping Tale Makes Moving, Vivid Drama," *Chicago Tribune*, January 29, 1934: 13. "Mae Tinee" was the nom de plume of Mrs. Zack Elton.

24. Kate Cameron, "Baby LeRoy Creates Intense Excitement," *New York Daily News*, January 20, 1934: 24. For a sampling of reviews, see "New York Reviews: *Miss Fane's Baby Is Stolen*," *Hollywood Reporter*, January 29, 1934: 2.

25. "*Miss Fane's Baby Is Stolen*," *Harrison's Reports*, January 27, 1934: 14.

7. The Greatest Murder Trial the World Has Ever Known

1. "N.Y. Dailies Brother Act," *Variety*, November 6, 1934: 64.
2. Lowell Thomas Broadcast, January 7, 1935. LTP.
3. George Rosen, "Estimate $50,000 Weekly Take for Flemington; Town 'Closed Shop,' " *Variety*, January 8, 1935: 1, 39.
4. "Topics of the Times," *New York Times*, February 3, 1935: E8.
5. Ed Sullivan, "Broadway," *Washington Post*, January 12, 1935: 6.
6. Adela Rogers St. Johns, "Great Lawyers Gamble with Life at Stake," *New York Evening Journal*, February 11, 1935: 2. For the Mencken line, see "Mencken Thinks Simpson Affair Biggest News Since Resurrection," *Buffalo Evening News*, December 4, 1936: 22.
7. "Questions and Answers," *Elmira Star Gazette*, June 19, 1944: 4.
8. Phil M. Daily, "Along the Rialto," *Film Daily*, February 11, 1935: 6.
9. Joseph Mitchell, *My Ears Are Bent* (New York: Sheridan House, 1938), 29–30.
10. Dorothy Kilgallen, "Jury Just 'Main St.,' " *Syracuse Journal*, January 9, 1935: 8.
11. Sheila Graham, "Friendly Informality Marks Hauptmann Trial," *New York Evening Journal*, January 7, 1935: 13.
12. James Cannon, "Reilly, Like Owl, Claws at Eagle; But Lindbergh Soars to Safety," *New York Evening Journal*, January 5, 1935: 3.
13. Louis Sobol, "The Voice of Broadway," *New York Evening Journal*, February 8, 1935: 23.
14. "Weird Pageant at Dawn Starts Drama of Trial," *New York Herald Tribune*, January 5, 1935: 2.
15. "New York Journal Hauptmann Trial Broadcast, WNEW," *Variety*, January 29, 1935: 44.
16. Jeanette Smits, " 'Have Faith in Me!' Cries Bruno to Wife in Court," *New York Evening Journal*, January 4, 1935: 10.
17. "Lindy Case," *The New Masses*, January 15, 1935: 3.
18. "Flemington Takes on Carnival Spirit as Hauptmann Trial Opens," *Billboard*, January 12, 1935: 1, 54.
19. "Hauptmann Trial Takes Center Stage," *Literary Digest*, January 5, 1935: 8.
20. "50,000 Pleas for Bruno Trial Seats Span Half the World," *New York Evening Journal*, January 25, 1935: 5.
21. Nelson B. Bell, "Capital Managers Withdraw Films of Hauptmann," *Washington Post*, February 5, 1935: 14.
22. Lou Wedemar, "Hauptmann Winks: Thinks Jury with Him," *Times-Union* (Albany), January 5, 1935: 2.
23. Adela Rogers St. Johns, *The Honeycomb* (New York: Doubleday, 1969), 338.
24. See Bob Thomas, *Winchell* (New York: Doubleday and Company, 1971), and Neal Gabler, *Winchell: Gossip, Power, and the Culture of Celebrity* (New York: Vintage, 1995) for full-length treatments of Winchell's life and legacy.
25. "Laughter Angers Court," *New York Times*, January 22, 1935: 10.
26. Walter Winchell, "On Broadway," *New York Mirror*, January 7, 1935: 19.
27. Adela Rogers St. Johns, "Bruno Put Near Chair by Anne," *New York Evening Journal*, January 4, 1935: 1, 11.

28. Joseph F. Driscoll, "Mrs. Lindbergh Tells of Son's Kidnapping," *New York Herald Tribune*, January 4, 1935: 1.

29. Adela Rogers St. Johns, "Lindy Freezes Defense Quiz," *New York Evening Journal*, January 4, 1935: 2.

30. Adela Rogers St. Johns, "Defense Suspects Everyone but Bruno, Says Miss Johns," *Albany Times-Union*, January 5, 1935: 2.

31. Adela Rogers St. Johns, "Lindbergh Confounds Defense," *New York Evening Journal*, January 4, 1935: 1.

32. Adela Rogers St. Johns, "Lindy Freezes Defense Quiz," *New York Evening Journal*, January 4, 1935: 2.

33. Martin Sommers, "Lindbergh Armed in Court; Panic Seizes Hauptmann," January 3, 1935: 3.

34. "Margaret Bourke-White," *Pittsburgh Press*, January 30, 1935: 2.

35. Dorothy Kilgallen, "Scotch Girl Flames Menace to Bruno," *New York Evening Journal*, January 7, 1935: 3.

36. Adela Rogers St. Johns, "Betty Gow in Battle Against Suspicions of All World Today," *New York Evening Journal*, January 7, 1935: 1–2.

37. Adela Rogers St. Johns, "Novelist Sees Jafsie's Story Clinching Guilt of Hauptmann," *New York Evening Journal*, January 10, 1935: 1, 6.

38. Louis Sobol, "The Voice of Broadway," *New York Evening Journal*, January 4, 1935: 25.

39. James Cannon, "Genius of Splinter, Pegs Bruno to Ladder," *New York Evening Journal*, January 24, 1935: 2.

40. Sidney B. Whipple, *The Lindbergh Crime* (New York: Blue Ribbon Books, 1935), 287.

41. Adela Rogers St. Johns, "Rung from Ladder Fits Attic, Says Novelist," *New York Evening Journal*, January 24, 1935: 12.

42. Dorothy Kilgallen, "Jury Just 'Main St.,'" *Syracuse Journal*, January 9, 1935: 8.

43. Lou Wedemar, "Hauptman Winks: Thinks Jury with Him," *Albany Times-Union*, January 5, 1935: 2; Damon Runyon, "Several Days Required to Pick Jury," *Syracuse Journal*, January 3, 1935: 4.

44. Adela Rogers St. Johns, "Hauptmann 'Type' of Kidnapper in Lindy Crime, Says Novelist," *New York Evening Journal*, January 14, 1935: 1.

45. Adela Rogers St. Johns, "Majesty of Justice Checks Hatred As Lindy, Bruno Meet," *New York Evening Journal*, January 3, 1935: 8.

46. Joseph F. Driscoll, "Lindbergh Brands Hauptmann As Man Who Received Ransom," *New York Herald Tribune*, January 5, 1935: 1.

47. Whipple, *The Lindbergh Crime*, 271.

48. Russell B. Porter, "Expert Traces Tool Marks to Hauptmann, Part of Wood to His Attack," *New York Times*, January 24, 1935: 1, 13.

49. Adela Rogers St. Johns, "Rung from Ladder Fits Attic, Says Novelist," *New York Evening Journal*, January 24, 1935: 12.

50. Dorothy Kilgallen, "Silent Bruno Turns Wag, Jokes at Kidnap Ladder," *New York Evening Journal*, January 8, 1935: 4.

51. John Anderson, "Bruno's Calm a Triumph of Art—Or Innocence," *New York Evening Journal*, January 9, 1935: Dramatic Critic Impressed by Bruno's Granite Mask," *Syracuse Journal*, January 9, 1935: 8.

52. Bill Corum, " 'Blows' in Court Leave Hauptmann Unmarked, Says Fight Expert," *New York Evening Journal*, January 16, 1935: 3.

53. Percy Winner, "Writer Sees Hauptmann as Jekyll-Hyde Enigma," *New York Evening Journal*, January 9, 1935: 8.

54. Adela Rogers St. Johns, "Novelist Certain That Truth Told at Hauptmann Trial," *New York Evening Journal*, January 9, 1935: 9.

55. Dorothy Kilgallen, "Interest of Carpenter Now Set on Verdict," *New York Evening Journal*, February 4, 1935: 8.

56. Adela Rogers St. Johns, "Majesty of Justice Checks Hatred As Lindy, Bruno Meet," *New York Evening Journal*, January 3, 1935: 8.

57. Alexander Woollcott, "Hauptmann Trial Shed No Light on Trial Issue, Says Woollcott," *New York Times*, January 26, 1935: 9.

58. William Weer, " 'Innocent'—Hauptmann," *Brooklyn Daily Eagle*, January 25, 1935: 2.

59. Joseph Mickler, "Stand Ordeal Wilts Bruno," *New York Evening Journal*, January 26, 1935: 1, 2.

60. Adela Rogers St. Johns, "Accused Seemed Near Collapse," *New York Evening Journal*, January 26, 1935: 2.

61. Adela Rogers St. Johns, "Court Waits Own Word to Seal Hauptmann's Fate," *New York Evening Journal*, January 28, 1935: 2.

62. Bernard Postal, "1935's New Jewish Faces," *Wisconsin Jewish Chronicle*, December 29, 1935: 1.

63. "Hauptmann and the Foreigners," *The Jewish Exponent*, February 22, 1935: 4.

64. Curtis Mitchell, "Walter Winchell's Forty-Two Days at Flemington," *Radio Guide*, April 11, 1936: 43.

65. "Nazis in New York Attack Jews for Hauptmann Verdict," *Wisconsin Jewish Chronicle*, March 9, 1935: 1.

66. Phineas J. Biron, "Strictly Confidential," *Jewish Ledger*, February 18, 1936: 9.

67. "Hauptmann a Victim of Jewish Plot," *Jewish Advocate*, March 5, 1935: 1; "An Old Story," *Jewish Advocate*, March 22, 1935: 4.

8. Into the Ether

1. "21,500,000 Radio Homes," *Broadcasting*, March 15, 1936: 36. The phrase is from Cecilia Tichi, *Electronic Hearth: Creating an American Television Culture* (New York: Oxford University Press, 1992).

2. Simon Baatz, *For the Thrill of It: Leopold, Loeb, and the Murder That Shocked Jazz Age Chicago* (New York: Harper Perennial, 2008), 272–276, 400; "Today's Radio Program," *Chicago Tribune*, September 10, 1924: 10.

3. "Bar Raps Court Broadcasts," *Broadcasting*, November 1, 1932: 16.

4. Ibid.

5. "Newsreels Hop on S.S. Morro Castle," *Variety*, September 11, 1934: 3.

6. "Inside Stuff—Radio," *Variety*, October 9, 1934: 42.

7. Nellie Revell, "New York Radio Parade," *Variety*, October 2, 1934: 60.

8. "No Hauptmann Trial Pickup in Jersey," *Variety*, October 16, 1934: 37.

9. "Inside Stuff—Radio," *Variety*, October 9, 1934: 42.

10. "No Hauptmann Trial Pickup in Jersey," *Variety*, October 16, 1934: 37.

11. "Radio and Red Faces," *Variety*, October 30, 1934: 35.

12. "Lindbergh Case and Congress Covered Extensively by Radio," *Broadcasting*, January 15, 1935: 18.

13. "Journal Stars Air Trial," *New York Evening Journal*, January 16, 1935: 10.

14. "Hauptmann Trial on Air Today," *New York Evening Journal*, January 7, 1935: 15.

15. "Gow Collapse Told by WNEW," *New York Evening Journal*, January 8, 1935: 7.

16. "Hauptmann Trial Coverage Helped Radio Circulation," *Billboard*, February 23, 1935: 7.

17. Nellie Revell, "New York Radio Parade," *Variety*, October 16, 1935: 47.

18. "ABC Makes History" [advertisement], *Broadcasting*, February 1, 1935: 19; Jerry Franken, "Air Briefs," *Billboard*, January 26, 1935: 10.

19. "Hauptmann Trial Coverage Helped Radio Circulation," *Billboard*, February 23, 1935: 7.

20. "News Savants Up in Poll," *Variety*, May 16, 1933: 39.

21. H. V. Kaltenborn, *Kaltenborn Edits the News* (New York: Modern Age Books, 1937), iv.

22. Nellie Revell, "New York Radio Parade," *Variety*, February 12, 1935: 53.

23. "Heatter Starts Second Decade," *Nassau Daily Review-Star*, August 10, 1943: 7.

24. Lowell Thomas Broadcast, January 3, 1935. LTP.

25. "New Acts," *Variety*, April 10, 1935: 50.

26. Excerpt from Boake Carter's Philco Broadcast, January 3, 1935. NJSPM.

27. Paul Rigby, "Bing Crosby and the Tape Revolution," February 24, 2016, https://theaudiophileman.com/bing-crosby-tape-revolution/.

28. *I Can Hear It Now, 1919–1949, 30 Years of Audible History*. Produced by Edward R. Murrow, Fred W. Friendly, and J. G. Gude, Columbia Records, 1967.

29. Jack F. Johnson, "Murrow's *Hear It Now* Will Fascinate Generations," *The Semi-Weekly Spokesman Review*, October 29, 1967: 89.

30. Holly Pomeroy, "Time Marches On," *Radio Guide*, July 18, 1936: 21.

31. Leonard Lyons, "The Lyon's Den," *New York Post*, August 28, 1935: 11

32. "Bruno Trial's 'City Room' Broadcast," *New York Evening Journal*, January 3, 1935: 7.

33. "50,000 Pleas for Bruno Trial Seats Span Half the World," *New York Evening Journal*, January 25, 1935: 5.

34. "Bruno's Calm Discussed in Broadcast," *New York Evening Journal*, January 29, 1935: 6.

35. "50,000 Pleas for Bruno Trial Seats Span Half the World," *New York Evening Journal*, January 25, 1935: 5.

36. "WNEW Keeps Bruno Trial Alive on Air from Exclusive Courtroom Mike," *New York Evening Journal*, January 7, 1935: 12; "Reilly Boasts of New Alibi 'Bombshell,' " *New York Evening Journal*, February 2, 1935: 4.

37. Abel Green, "New York Journal–Hauptmann Trial Broadcast," *Variety*, January 29, 1935: 44; "Trial Hits Attendance," *Film Daily*, January 9, 1935: 1.

38. Phil M. Daily, "Along the Rialto," *Film Daily*, February 25, 1935: 3.

39. Leonard Lyons, "The Lyon's Den," *Post Standard* (Syracuse, NY), July 27, 1963: 13.

40. Robert Landry, "Bryce Oliver," *Variety*, May 15, 1935: 42.

9. The Eye and Ear of Millions

1. Thomas Sugrue, "The Newsreels," *Scribner's Magazine* (April 1937): 10.

2. James P. Cunningham, "There's Drama Too in Newsreel Coverage of Hauptmann Trial," *Motion Picture Herald*, January 19, 1935: 29–30.

3. "Flemington Takes on Carnival Spirit as Hauptmann Trial Opens," *Billboard*, January 12, 1935: 1, 54.

4. James P. Cunningham, "There's Drama Too in Newsreel Coverage of Hauptmann Trial," *Motion Picture Herald*, January 19, 1935: 30.

5. Raymond Fielding, *The American Newsreel, 1911–1967* (Norman: University of Oklahoma Press, 1972), 210.

6. M. J. O'Toole, "Wants Newsreel Given Same Privilege as Newspaper," *Film Daily*, October 12, 1934: 10.

7. James P. Cunningham, "There's Drama Too in Newsreel Coverage of Hauptmann Trial," *Motion Picture Herald*, January 19, 1935: 29–30.

8. "Newsreels Overplayed Hand in Hauptmann Case," *Hollywood Reporter*, February 9, 1935: 4.

9. "Pathé, U and Hearst-Metrotone Reels Continue Hauptmann Shots," *Variety*, February 5, 1935: 2.

10. Kate Cameron, "Bruno's Trial Still Featured in Newsreels," *New York Daily News*, January 28, 1935: 10.

11. "Trial Thrills in Newsreels," *New York Evening Journal*, January 11, 1935: 17.

12. "Newsreels Overplayed Hand in Hauptmann Case," *Hollywood Reporter*, February 9, 1935: 4. This unsigned piece is the most comprehensive behind-the-scenes account of the machinations of the newsreel editors during the Hauptmann trial. "Just in case you are interested—and you ought to be—here is the four-star inside on the newsreel imbroglio at the Hauptmann trial," boasted the unbylined author.

13. "Pictures Taken in Court Draw Trenchard Rebuke," *New York Herald Tribune*, January 5, 1935: 2.

14. "Court Thriller at Trans-Lux," *New York Evening Journal*, February 2, 1935: 9.

15. "Hauptmann on Stand," *New York Daily News*, February 1, 1935: 51.

16. Roy Chartier, "Hauptmann Trial," *Variety*, February 5, 1935: 14.

17. "Trial Unwinds in Newsreel," *New York Evening Journal*, February 1, 1935: 17.

18. "Trial Newsreels in 70 Theatres," *New York Evening Journal*, February 2, 1935: 8.

19. "Embassy Theatre [Advertisement]," *Reading* (PA) *Times)*, February 1, 1935: 20.

20. "Hauptmann's Phrases Same as Those Used in Ransom Letter," *Charleston Daily Mail*, January 29, 1935: 7.

21. Joseph C. Furnas, "Latest in the Newsreels," *New York Herald Tribune*, February 10, 1935: D3.

22. "Pathé, U and Hearst-Metrotone Reels Continue Hauptmann Shots," *Variety*, February 5, 1935: 2.

23. "Wilentz Demands Suppression of Newsreels Taken by 'Trickery' During Trial Sessions," *New York Times*, February 2, 1935: 1.

24. Grace Robinson, "Bruno Case Films Stir Court Ire," *New York Daily News*, February 2, 1935: 3, 13.

25. "Four Newsreel Companies Undecided," *New York Times*, February 2, 1935: 1.

26. Walter Winchell, "On Broadway," *St. Louis Post-Dispatch*, February 8, 1935: 46.

27. "Lindbergh Case Pawn in Newsreel Fight," *Motion Picture Herald*, February 9, 1935: 11–14.

28. "Two More Companies Cancel Trial Films," *New York Times*, February 3, 1935: 26.

29. "2 Theater Units to Withdraw Films of Trial," *New York Herald Tribune*, February 3, 1935: 18.

30. Courtland Smith, "To the Editor of the Herald," *Motion Picture Herald*, February 16, 1935: 28.

31. "Newsreels of Hauptmann Trial Burn Up Prosecuting Attorney," *Billboard*, February 9, 1935: 1, 16.

32. Samuel S. Leibowitz broadcast on WHN, February 6, 1935, Paley Center for Media, New York.

33. Terry Ramsaye, "Newsreel Rights and the Flemington Hysteria," *Motion Picture Herald*, February 9, 1935: 9–10.

34. Phil M. Daily, "Along the Rialto," *Film Daily*, February 11, 1935: 6.

35. "Film Cameras Barred at Trial," *Los Angeles Times*, February 5, 1935: 2.

36. Sidney B. Whipple, *The Lindbergh Crime* (New York: Blue Ribbon Books, 1935), 321.

37. "Newsreels Muffed Big Chance by Premature Hauptmann Shots," *Billboard*, March 9, 1935: 8.

38. "Trial's Close in Newsreels," *New York Evening Journal*, February 13, 1935: 9.

10. The Verdict

1. Adela Rogers St. Johns, "Anne's Story Puts Bruno Near Death," *New York Evening Journal*, January 4, 1935: 11.

2. Adela Rogers St. Johns, *The Honeycomb* (New York: Doubleday, 1969), 44.

3. Lorena Hickok, "The Lindbergh Kidnapping." Unpublished manuscript, FDR.

4. St. Johns, *The Honeycomb*, 269–274.

5. Anne Morrow Lindbergh, *Locked Rooms and Open Doors: Diaries and Letters of Anne Morrow Lindbergh, 1933–1935* (New York: Harcourt Brace Jovanovich, 1974), 249.

6. Robert Conway, " 'Kill Hauptmann,' Trial Mob Howls," *New York Daily News*, February 13, 1935: 3.

7. James Cannon, "Courthouse Bell Will Peal Hauptmann's Fate to the World," *New York Evening Journal*, February 11, 1935: 1; " 'American Sense of Justice' Hit by Elsie Robinson in Broadcast," *New York Evening Journal*, February 12, 1935: 9.

8. Joe Alex Morris, *Deadline Every Minute: The Story of United Press* (New York: Doubleday and Company, Inc. 1957), 186–190.

9. Bob Considine, *It's All News to Me: A Reporter's Deposition* (New York: Meredith Press, 1967), 87–88.

10. Ibid.

11. Martin Sommers, "Bruno Doomed to Chair As Mob Howls Approval," *New York Daily News*, February 14, 1935: 3.

12. "Wrong Verdict Sent Over Radio," *New York Times*, February 14, 1935: 11.

13. "Seattle Times Mad at Radio Again," *Variety*, February 27, 1935: 47.

14. Gilbert Cant, "How Radio Was Covered on Hauptmann Trial," *Broadcasting*, March 1, 1935: 40.

15. Teletype, Flemington, NJ, February 14, 1935. Lindbergh file, APCA.

16. Gilbert Cant, "How Radio Was Covered on Hauptmann Trial," *Broadcasting*, March 1, 1935: 40.

17. Morris, *Deadline Every Minute*, 186–190.

18. Gilbert Cant, "How Radio Was Covered on Hauptmann Trial," *Broadcasting*, March 1, 1935: 5.

19. A copy of the telegram is on file at the APCA.

20. "Transradio Scoops Hauptmann Verdict," *Broadcasting*, March 1, 1935: 43.

21. Lowell Thomas, *History As You Heard It* (New York: Doubleday, 1957), 63.

22. Louise Steneck, "He Pictured History in the Making," *The Yonkers Herald Statesman*, January 27, 1973: 6; John Farber, *Great News Photos and the Stories Behind Them* (New York: Dover Publications, Inc., 1978), 64. When Sarno told the story decades later, he remembered James Kilgallen with Runyon shielding him in the balcony during the reading of the verdict—but Kilgallen was outside the courtroom manning the INS desk in a room down the hallway.

23. " 'We Find the Defendant Guilty of Murder in the First Degree,' " *New York Evening Journal*, February 14, 1935: 1.

24. "Newsreels First with Hauptmann Verdict," *Motion Picture Herald*, February 23, 1935: 28; "Oscar, Take a Bow," *Motion Picture Herald*, February 23, 1935: 87.

25. "Newsreels Studying Use of Trial Shorts," *Motion Picture Daily*, February 19, 1935: 1, 6; "The Trial of the Century," *Box Office*, March 2, 1935: 18.

26. "Hauptmann Gets Special Par Newsreel—," *Daily Variety*, February 1, 1935: 3.

27. "Hauptmann Trial Showing as Feature," *Hollywood Reporter*, February 16, 1935: 3.

28. Raymond Fielding, *The March of Time, 1935–1951* (New York: Oxford University Press, 1978).

29. Andre Sennwald, "Hollywood Vs. 'The Good Fairy,' " *New York Times*, February 10, 1935: X5.

30. "Fine Example of Celluloid History," *Hollywood Reporter*, February 1, 1935: 3.

31. "Lindbergh Case Pawn in Newsreel Private Fight," *Motion Picture Herald*, February 9, 1935: 11–14.

32. Grace Robinson, "Trial Talkies Stir Court Ire," *New York Daily News*, February 3, 1935: 3, 4.

33. "First and Right," *New York Daily News*, February 15, 1935: 27.

34. Abel Green, "March of Time," *Variety*, March 13, 1935: 15.

35. Maurice Kann, "Number Two Release Clicks," *Motion Picture Daily*, March 6, 1935: 2.

36. Kate Cameron, "Murder and Comedy Blended at Capitol," *New York Daily News*, March 9, 1935: 26.

11. Death Watch

1. "Newsreel First with Hauptmann Verdict," *Motion Picture Herald*, February 23, 1935: 28.

2. "Par Shows Bruno in Death Cell News Clip," *Daily Variety*, February 20, 1935: 1.

3. Allen Johnson, "Leibowitz Supports Hearst in Defense of Nazi Suspect," *Daily Worker*, January 18, 1935: 1, 2.

4. Robert Conway, "Hoffman to Spare Hauptmann Again—If He Has the Power," *New York Daily News*, March 28, 1936: 2, 9.

5. "Hoffman Goes Through with Carter Suit," *Billboard*, July 18, 1936: 7.

6. "Boake Carter Case Offers Libel Test," *Broadcasting*, August 1, 1936: 62.

7. "Slander Suit Dismissed Against Carter Withheld," *Broadcasting*, July 15, 1937: 52. The defendant, however, agreed to pay litigation costs.

8. "Inside Stuff—Pictures," *Variety*, January 15, 1936: 6.

9. Odec., "Embassy, N.Y. (Newsreels)," *Variety*, January 22, 1936: 16.

10. "Inside Stuff—Pictures, *Variety*, January 22, 1936: 6.

11. "Hauptmann's Own Story," *New York Daily Mirror*, December 4, 1935: 1.

12. "More About Hauptmann," *Variety*, December 11, 1935: 49. Again, no episodes of the *March of Time*'s dramatizations seem to have survived.

13. Ben Hecht, *A Child of the Century* (New York: David I. Fine, Inc., 1954), 152.

14. Joseph Mitchell, *My Ears Are Bent* (New York: Pantheon Books, 1938), 33.

15. Samuel G. Blackman, "Retired AP News Editor Tells Story of Lindbergh Kidnap Case," *Standard-Speaker* (Hazelton, PA), August 28, 1974: 12.

16. Samuel G. Blackman, "Witness Tells of Hauptmann Death," *Boston Globe*, April 4, 1936: 3.

17. "Death Order Stirs Trenton Only Slightly," *Buffalo* (NY) *Courier Express*, March 31, 1936: 4.

18. Joseph Harrington, "Killing Bruno 'Just a Job,' He Says," *New York Evening Journal*, February 15, 1935: 2.

19. Russell B. Porter, "Hauptman Put to Death for Killing of Lindbergh Baby; Remains Silent to the End," *New York Times*, April 4, 1936: 1, 2.

20. James L. Kilgallen, "On Broadway," *Indianapolis Star*, July 27, 1937: 4.

21. Stanley Walker, "Hauptmann Goes Almost Eagerly," *Boston Globe*, April 4, 1936: 1.

22. "Hauptmann, 'Not Afraid to Die,' Walks Calmly to Electric Chair, Silent and Unshaken to the End," *Ossining Citizen Daily Register*, April 4, 1936: 1.

23. "Lindbergh Kidnapping," *David Brinkley's Journal*, January 31, 1961 in the Transcript on file at the Motion Picture Division, Library of Congress.

24. "Hauptmann's Death Fails to End Doubt," *Philadelphia Inquirer*, April 4, 1936: 13.

25. Geoffrey O'Brien, *Sonata for Jukebox: An Autobiography of My Ears* (Berkeley, CA: Counterpoint, 2004), 85.

26. "Hollywood Insider," *Daily Variety*, January 13, 1936: 2. Italics in original.

27. Jack Stinnett, "New Yorker's Viewpoint," *Rochester Democrat and Chronicle*, August 4, 1937: 14.

28. Hilda Cole, "Screen and Radio Weekly: Time Marches On!" *Detroit Free Press*, November 18, 1934: 12–13.

29. Hally Holloway, "Time Marches On," *Radio Guide*, July 18, 1936: 21, 42.

30. Stanley Walker, "Hauptmann Goes Almost Eagerly," *Boston Globe*, April 4, 1936: 7.

31. "Dear Wife May Take Own Life," *Boston Globe*, April 4, 1936: 7.

32. "Heatter Starts Second Decade," *Nassau Daily Review-Star*, August 10, 1943: 7.

33. Edward Bliss Jr., *Now the News: The Story of Broadcast Journalism* (New York: Columbia University Press, 1991), 34.

34. "Heatter's 15,000 Words," *Broadcasting*, April 15, 1936: 63; "Gabriel Heatter, Radio Newsman Dies," *New York Times*, March 31, 1972: 32.

35. "Gab Heatter's 35-Min. Ad Lib Draws Praise," *Variety*, April 8, 1936: 37.

36. "Gabriel Heatter," *Variety*, April 5, 1972: 111.

37. "Bruno-Vera Decisions Keep 'Em Near Radios," *Variety*, April 1, 1935: 1.

38. O'Brien, *Sonata for Jukebox*, 85.

39. "Wilentz's Shout, 'He'll Thaw Out' in Chair, Recalled," *New York Post*, March 31, 1936: 3.

Epilogue: The Legacies of the Crime of the Century

1. "House Is Unanimous for Kidnap Measure," *New York Times*, June 18, 1932: 18; "President Signs Bill on Kidnaping Penalty," *Washington Post*, June 23, 1932: 1.

2. "Roosevelt Opens Attack on Crime, Signing Six Bills as Challenge, " *New York Times*, May 19, 1934: 1, 3.

3. "Kidnap Scare Hits Film Parents," *Variety*, March 8, 1932: 3.

4. "Death for Kidnappers," *Los Angeles Times*, March 2, 1934: A4.

5. "Jersey Justice Speeds Up," *New York Daily News*, January 4, 1935: 31.

6. Arthur B. Reeve, "Science Left Blind in Failure to Guard Clues, Reeve Finds," *Morning Post* (Camden, NJ), January 5, 1935: 11.

7. "Liquor Racket to Be Tougher," *Los Angeles Times*, September 13, 1933: 9.

8. *New Republic*, January 23, 1935: 288.

9. Edna Ferber, "Miss Ferber Views 'Vultures' at Trial," *New York Times*, January 28, 1935: 4.

10. "News Photographers," *New York Times*, December 7, 1935: 18.

11. Lloyd Acuff, "Bar Will Continue Fight Over Black," *New York Times*, October 1, 1937: 10.

12. "Bar Assn. Stands Pat on TV-AM Courtroom Nix," *Variety*, February 22, 1956: 24. See also Anthony Lewis, "U.S. Bar Group Again Supports Ban on Cameras," *New York Times*, February 6, 1963: 1, 8.

13. "At Last," *Broadcasting*, August 14, 1982: 90.

14. Joseph I. Breen to Harry Zehner, December 7, 1937. *Okay America!*, PCA file.

15. "Highlights of Television B'casters Code of Programming," *Variety*, October 24, 1951: 36, 42.

16. "Writers TV Taboos on Upbeat," *Daily Variety*, June 11, 1954: 1, 4.

17. Chan., "Tele Follow-Up Comment," *Variety*, June 30, 1954: 28.

18. Steven H. Scheuer, "Bellamy Goes 'Live'; Really Enjoys It," *The Tribune* (Scranton, PA), July 1, 1954: 6.

19. "Film Code Lowers Bar to Permit Pix Utilize Same Material As TV," *Daily Variety*, April 27, 1955: 1, 8; "Has Code Opened Door?" *Variety*, November 2, 1955: 2.

20. "Selling Approach," *Motion Picture Herald*, February 4, 1956: 39.

21. "Dope, Kidnapping, and Other Tabu Plots OK Under Revised Film Code," *Variety*, December 12, 1956: 1, 20.

22. "No Code Pix Taboos on Stories," *Daily Variety*, September 16, 1963: 22.

23. "Col. Lindbergh Works on Mechanical Heart," *Boston Globe*, March 31, 1936: 13.

24. Lauren D. Lyman, "Lindbergh Family Sails for England to Seek a Safe, Secluded Residence," *New York Times*, December 23, 1935: 1, 3; Louise Steneck, "Down Memory Lane with Dick Sarno," *Journal News* (White Plains, NY), January 21, 1973: 6E–7E. The photograph was published in the *New York Daily Mirror*, December 24, 1935.

25. "Press Sees Nation 'Shamed' in Lindbergh Exile," *New York Times*, December 24, 1935: 2.

26. A. Scott Berg, *Lindbergh* (New York: G. P. Putnam's Sons, 1998), 355–383.

27. The INS account of the presentation of the medal portrays Lindbergh as flustered when Göring, in a receiving line of greeters, suddenly handed him the award. The AP report describes the presentation as "unceremonious," but with Lindbergh saying "thank you" and then hanging the medal around his neck. See "Col. Lindbergh Flustered As Goering Gives Him Nazi Next-Best Decoration," *The Courier* (Waterloo, IA), October 19, 1938: 1; "Nazis Honor Lindy," *The Birmingham News*, October 19, 1938: 1.

28. "Lindbergh Falls," *Hollywood Now*, October 21, 1938: 4.

29. "Chi Bund's Order That All Hear Lindbergh Leads to Radio Blackout," *Variety*, August 7, 1940: 1, 44.

30. "Lindbergh's Appeal for Isolation," *New York Times*, September 15, 1939: 9.

31. Walter Winchell, "The Man on Broadway," *Syracuse Herald Journal*, July 21, 1941: 15.

32. "Lindbergh Quits Air Corps; Sees His Loyalty Questioned," *New York Times*, April 29, 1941: 1.

33. Charles Lindbergh, *The Wartime Journals of Charles A. Lindbergh* (New York: Harcourt Brace Jovanovich, 1970), 404–405.

34. "Lindbergh Sees a Plot for 'War,' " *New York Times*, September 12, 1941: 2.

35. Lynne Olson, *Those Angry Days: Roosevelt, Lindbergh, and America's Fight Over World War II, 1939–1941* (New York: Random House, 2013), 231 and *passim*.

36. Arthur Ungar, "Flynn's Puppet Show," *Daily Variety*, September 12, 1941: 1, 9. See also "Unwitting Pro-Pix Shill," *Variety*, September 17, 1941: 5.

37. Walter Winchell, "On Broadway," *Morning Post* (Camden, NJ), April 29, 1941: 17; Walter Winchell, "On Broadway," *Cincinnati Enquirer*, April 25, 1941: 2; Walter Winchell, "On

Broadway," *Tampa Bay Times* (St. Petersburg, FL), May 4, 1941. 10. Winchell's blasts at Lindbergh were sometimes softened or eliminated in syndication, depending on the locale. "Ratzis" was often edited to "Nazis."

38. "WOR Wants Assurances Lindbergh Won't Repeat Anti-Semitic Cracks," *Variety*, September 17, 1941: 1, 29.

39. "America Firsters Charge Radio Gag," *Daily Variety*, October 27, 1941: 1, 3.

40. Walter Winchell, On Broadway," *Jamestown Evening Journal*, May 3, 1941: 4. See also Odec., "Embassy, N.Y.," *Variety*, May 7, 1941: 25.

41. Alden Whitman, "Daring Lindbergh Attained the Unattainable with Historic Flight Across Atlantic," *New York Times*, August 27, 1974: 18–19.

42. Ibid.

43. Eric Pace, "Anne Morrow Lindbergh, 94, Dies; Champion of Flight and Women's Concerns," *New York Times*, February 8, 2001: A29.

44. Adela Rogers St. Johns, *The Honeycomb* (New York: Doubleday, 1969), 569.

45. Anne Morrow Lindbergh, *Hour of Lead, Hour of Gold: Diaries and Letters of Anne Morrow Lindbergh, 1929–1932* (New York: Harcourt Brace Jovanovich, 1973), 214.

46. Dorothy Kilgallen, "I Sat in Seat 13," *Post-Standard* (Syracuse, NY), July 10, 1949: 15–16.

47. Damon Runyon, "Jersey Political Upheaval and Perjury Indictments Loom After Bruno's Death," *Albany Times Union*, April 4, 1936: 1.

48. "Lindbergh Kidnapping," *David Brinkley's Journal*, January 31, 1962. Transcript on file at the Motion Picture Division, Library of Congress.

49. "TV Programs and Personalities," *Philadelphia Inquirer*, May 19, 1963: 7.

50. Both the *Perspectives on Greatness* and *Biography* episodes on Lindbergh are available commercially from EarthStation1.com. For the discussion of *David Brinkley's Journal*, I have relied on a transcript from the Motion Picture Division of the Library of Congress.

51. Anthony Scaduto, *Scapegoat: The Lonesome Death of Bruno Richard Hauptmann* (New York: G. P. Putnam's Sons, 1976); Ludovic Kennedy, *The Airman and the Carpenter: The Lindbergh Kidnapping and the Framing of Bruno Richard Hauptmann* (New York: Viking Press, 1985).

52. See, for example, Jay Maeder, "The Bread Thief, Richard Hauptmann, 1934," *New York Daily News*, May 14, 1998: 41. Recent evidence "has made it abundantly clear that much of the trial evidence against [Hauptmann] was fabricated and satisfied many investigators that he almost certainly had nothing to do with the crime."

53. Philip Roth, *The Plot Against America* (New York: Vintage Books, 2005), 20, 228.

54. Bill Moyers, "A Conversation with Maurice Sendak," March 12, 2004, https://billmoyers.com/content/bill-moyers-talks-maurice-sendak/.

55. Gary Groth, "Maurice Sendak Interview," *The Comics Journal* (Seattle: Fantagraphic Books, 2013), 79.

INDEX